1.80

THE ARCHAEOLOGY OF THE
TRANSPORT
REVOLUTION
1750–1850

In the 1820s fast travel meant, as it always had, the speed of a galloping horse; and when in 1829 the directors of the Liverpool & Manchester Railway held a prize competition, the Rainhill trials, for a steam locomotive which would be a 'decided improvement' on any previously constructed, they were still thinking in terms of 10 mph or so. But Rocket, *built for the trials, proved able to run at over 30 mph—and a revolution in land transport followed. In the illustration overleaf J. U. Rastrick, one of the Rainhill judges, records details of* Rocket *in his notebook and sketches her multi-tubular boiler which was to make it all possible.*

5 Oct.r 1829. Mr. Robt. Stephenson's Rocket Black & Yellow.

Boiler 3..4 D.r 6 feet long ¼ In thick full, Ends the same

Fire Place 2 feet long 3 feet wide and 2 feet deep.

25 Copper Tubes run thro' the Boiler each 3 In D.r 6 ft long and 3/32 thick

Chimney 14 In d.r at Top and 15 High from the Rails.

2 Cylinders each 8 Inches D.r 16½ In Stroke

2. Engine Wheels 4..8½ D.r 3¾ wide on Sool 1/8 thick ... inside Tire ½ thick

2. Small Wheels 2..8½ D.r Cast Iron case hardened.

Axis for Engine Wheels 3¼ D.r — Axis for small Wheels 3 In D.r —

Forcing Pump 1½ Inch diam.r 16½ Inch Stroke

Lock ups and Safety Valves each 2.55 Inches diam.r.

weight of Valve 1⅛ lbs   Weight of Leaver 4½ lbs.

The Weight of the Leaver will operate in press upon the Valve, according to the Ratio of the distance of the Fulcrum is to the full length at the end of the Leaver: it would require 2¼ lbs to hold it up & consequently it pushes down with a force of 2¼ lbs. $\frac{225 \times 2.25 \text{lb}}{3} = 16.875$ Pounds. pressure which the leaver produces upon the Valve.

Area of Valve 2.55 D.r   5.1 Area

$\begin{array}{r} 50 \\ \overline{2.55} \end{array}$ total pressure on Valve

Valve 1.125

Leaver 16.875

18

237. Pressure to be produced by Valve

$\frac{237 \times 3}{32.5} = 21.56$ Inches distance the weight must be from the fulcrum to produce a pressure of 237 lbs. on the Valve.

10 Miles is 52.800 Feet — and $\frac{52.800}{60}$ = 880 feet per Minute equal to 60 ten Miles per Hour.

A Wheel 4..8½ D.r or 56.5 Inches diam.r is equal to 177.5 Inches Circumference equal 14.8 feet — Circumference.

$\frac{880}{14.8}$ = 59.459 say 59½ Strokes per will be ten Miles per Hour.

"I believe 60 Strokes per Minute were ment for 10 per Hour

$\frac{16.5 \text{ Inch Stroke}}{12}$ = 1.375 feet Stroke = 2.75 double Stroke

2.75 × 59.5 = 163.625 feet Velocity of Piston per Minute

6.225 × 2 = 12.45 Horse Power at 10 Miles per Hour supposing the Steam kept constantly up to 50 Pounds per square Inch on the safety valve (will be 10 Horse Power) Or at 20 lb effective Pressure per Square Inch on the Piston

8 In D.r 50.25 Area

25 lb effective Pressure

Cylinder 1256.25

163625

205,554 Pounds raised one foot high per Mt equal to

$\frac{205,554}{33,000}$ = 6.225 Horse Power from one Cylinder

THE ARCHAEOLOGY OF THE
TRANSPORT
REVOLUTION
1750–1850

P. J. G. Ransom

'. . . a steam engine is greatly to be preferred . . .'
John Blenkinsop's patent, 1811

WORLD'S WORK LTD

by the same author

Holiday Cruising in Ireland
Railways Revived
Waterways Restored
Your Book of Canals
The Archaeology of Canals
The Archaeology of Railways
Your Book of Steam Railway Preservation

N.B. Mention in this book of any
transport route, structure or artefact
does not imply any right of access

Designed by Victor Shreeve
Maps by Reginald and Marjorie Piggott
Index by Indexing Specialists of Hove
Copyright © 1984 by P. J. G. Ransom

Published by World's Work Limited
The Windmill Press, Kingswood, Tadworth, Surrey

Printed in Great Britain by BAS Printers Limited,
Over Wallop, Stockbridge, Hampshire

CONTENTS

ACKNOWLEDGEMENTS OF ILLUSTRATIONS

Illustrations are by the author except maps and those are listed below

COLOUR ILLUSTRATIONS

Pontcysyllte aqueduct *Waterways Museum, Stoke Bruerne*, 65
Painting, Regent's Canal and fly boats *Waterways Museum, Stoke Bruerne*, 66
Sirhowy Tramroad viaduct, *Ironbridge Gorge Museum Trust, Elton Collection*, 70
Lithograph, Dalswinton Loch steamboat trial *Trustees of the National Library of Scotland*, 70
Arrival of stage coach *Mary Evans Picture Library*, 72
Quicksilver Devonport Royal Mail Coach *The Post Office*, 72
Mail guard with snowbound coach, *The Post Office*, 145
Holyhead Mail recreated for TV *John Richards/Horse & Driving*, 145
Mail coaches in Chaplin's yard *The Post Office*, 145
'A Trip up Loch Lomond' *Mary Evans Picture Library*, 146
Steam boats off Gravesend *Trustees of the National Library of Scotland*, 146
PS **London Engineer** *Mary Evans Picture Library*, 146
Aquatint, 'Entrance of the Railway at Edge Hill', L & M Rly *Photo. Science Museum, London*, 147
Aquatint, 'Taking water at Parkside (The station where Mr Huskisson fell)' L & M Rly *Photo. Science Museum, London*, 147
Constructing the L & B Rly *Mary Evans Picture Library*, 147
Hexham, from 'Views on the Newcastle & Carlisle Railway' *Crown copyright, National Railway Museum, York*, 148
Railway travel in 1850 *Mary Evans Picture Library*, 149
Coaches and locomotive of the 1830s and 1840s, *Crown copyright, National Railway Museum*, 149
London-Louth mail coach on rail *Author's collection*, 149
'Fores's contrasts: drivers and guards of 1832 and 1852' *Ironbridge Gorge Museum Trust, Elton Collection*, 150/1
Watercolour, 'Carting Ice on the Surrey Canal' *Waterways Museum, Stoke Bruerne*, 152
SL **Dolly** *Windermere Nautical Trust/Charles E Jackson*, 152

BLACK AND WHITE ILLUSTRATIONS

Rastrick's notes on **Rocket** *Crown copyright, Science Museum, London*, frontispiece
Paddle tug **Charlotte Dundas** *Trustees of the National Library of Scotland*, 9
Trevithick high-pressure steam engine *Trustees of the National Library of Scotland*, 10
Trevithick engine powers dredger *Trustees of the National Library of Scotland*, 11
Trevithick steam engine adapted as locomotive *Crown copyright, Science Museum, London*, 11
Newcomen atmospheric steam pump *Trustees of the National Library of Scotland*, 13
Watt's rotative engine *Trustees of the National Library of Scotland*, 18
Ironbridge, 1892 *Photo. Science Museum, London*, 26
1780 engraving of stage coach *Mary Evans Picture Library*, 28
1765 engraving of waggonway *Photo. Science Museum, London*, 30
Drawing of C19th narrow boat *Trustees of the National Library of Scotland*, 38
Fulton's plans for inclined plane *Trustees of the National Library of Scotland*, 45
Fulton's advanced plans *Trustees of the National Library of Scotland*, 45
GJ Canal carriers invoice, *Waterways Museum, Stoke Bruerne*, 48
Passenger boat **Duchess-Countess** *Waterways Museum, Stoke Bruerne*, 49
Plateway-waggon designs *Trustees of the National Library of Scotland*, 56
Waggon, Derby Canal tramway *George Batey*, 58
Plateway coal tub *George Batey*, 58
Extant edge railway *Photo. Science Museum, London*, 58
Ribble bridge and inclined plane of Lancaster Canal Tramroad *Harris Museum & Art Gallery, Preston*, 60
Incline top and engine house, Lancaster Canal Tramroad *Harris Museum & Art Gallery, Preston*, 61
Surrey Iron Railway notice, *Photo. Science Museum, London*, 62
'The teams and trams of coal' 1821 *Welsh Industrial & Maritime Museum*, 62
Murdock's model steam carriage *Birmingham Museum and Art Gallery*, 74
Symington's steam boat engine *Crown copyright, Science Museum, London*, 76
William Symington, portrait *Photo. Science Museum, London*, 81
Charlotte Dundas, diagram by William Symington, jnr *Trustees of the National Library of Scotland*, 81
Original drawing, Trevithick's locomotive *Crown copyright, Science Museum, London*, 86
Trevithick high-pressure stationary engine *Crown copyright, Science Museum, London*, 87
Robert Fulton, portrait *Photo. Science Museum, London*, 89
Richard Trevithick, portrait *Photo. Science Museum, London*, 89
Fulton's steam-boat engine layout, *Photo. Science Museum, London*, 91
PS **Clermont** *Trustees of the National Library of Scotland*, 94
Telford road-making designs *Trustees of the National Library of Scotland*, 98
Menai Bridge *Trustees of the National Library of Scotland*, 104
Stamford Hill tollgate *The Post Office*, 109
Specimen mail-coach timebill *The Post Office*, 111
Mail-coach timepiece *The Post Office*, 111
Standard mail coach *Crown copyright, Science Museum, London*, 111
Mail coach using skid brake *The Post Office*, 113

One Transport Revolution or Two?

Lock 20

In Scotland, in March, it is still winter. Westerly gales sweep across the country with a ferocity unimagined in the South. On 28 March 1803, westbound traffic on the Forth & Clyde Canal was brought to a standstill by a head wind so strong that no vessel of any description could move to windward – neither under sail, or course, nor yet under tow by horses which was the usual method of moving boats along the canal.

There was an exception. Let us imagine ourselves on that day as spectators, people of the period, at lock 20. Vessels entering the canal from the sea at Grangemouth and heading west had to climb 20 locks in 10 miles; then, when they were through lock 20, there lay ahead of them the canal's long level summit pound – no more locks before Glasgow, $19\frac{1}{2}$ miles away. On that blustery day we find above the lock two sloops, *Euphemia* and *Active*, heading west and making ready to move. But there are no horses. Instead, there is a third vessel, a strange craft with, in place of a mast, a tall funnel from which black smoke is pouring, torn away and scattered by the wind. This is the boat which, like many other people, we have come to see: Mr William Symington's newest steam boat, the *Charlotte Dundas*. Many inventors have previously attempted to build boats driven by steam, including Mr Symington himself on this very canal, but no one in Great Britain has made one able to do any useful work. Now, with his latest vessel, the product of three years of experiments, Mr Symington proposes to demonstrate that she can indeed do just that. *Charlotte Dundas* will take the two sloops in tow and, in the face of the wind, haul them to Glasgow.

She is a curious vessel, this steam boat, low and wide at the bows with, set back a little from them, a steering wheel mounted horizontally on a pedestal on the deck. From the stern she appears to have not one hull but a pair,

each narrow, and with a rudder: set between them is the paddle wheel which propels her. Forward of this they merge into one and there the boiler and steam engine are mounted. The boiler does not appear unfamiliar, if we assume some knowledge of the stationary steam engines and pumps which are already, in 1803, common in factories and mines. It is of the type called 'waggon-top': with a semi-cylindrical top set on a rectangular base, its shape resembles that of the waggons common on every turnpike road. It is mounted in brickwork which contains flues to distribute the fire's hot gases about the boiler's surface.

The engine, however, is like nothing we have ever seen before. The cylinder we recognise but, unlike the cylinder of every other engine we know of, it is mounted not vertically but, to our amazement, horizontally. The great overhead rocking beam of the usual steam engine is absent – instead, the piston rod is connected directly by another rod to a crank which, through a pair of gears, drives the paddle wheel. We are not to know that Mr Symington has hit on a layout which will in years to come be – apart from the gears – one of the most familiar layouts for the steam engine.

What we can see however is that the cylinder, unlike that of many steam engines, including those which Mr Symington himself has built previously, is not open at one end but closed in at both ends. And since we have assumed enough engineering knowledge to ask a sensible question of the designer, it is not too fanciful to imagine Mr Symington straightening himself up from last-minute adjustments to the paddle shaft drive, wiping his hands on an oily rag and taking a minute or two off to reply. He reminds us that he had considered using a horizontal cylinder in a steam carriage years ago; but it has only been during the last couple of years that he has been able to develop the idea, since the expiry of the all-embracing patent held by that wretched man Watt, who was so obstructive to other

William Symington's paddle tug Charlotte Dundas *(above). By towing two sloops along the Forth & Clyde Canal for the 19½ miles from lock 20 to Glasgow against a headwind so strong that no other vessel could move to windward, she convincingly demonstrated in 1803 the practicability of steam as a source of power for boats.*

Lock 20, Forth & Clyde Canal, looking west (below) : it was from this point that the Charlotte Dundas *set out on her historic voyage on 28 March 1803. The photograph was taken in the spring of 1978 – the canal had been closed to navigation since 1963 but at this point remained largely intact.*

inventors such as himself. At last he has been able to condense the exhaust steam in a chamber separate from the cylinder – the nub of Watt's patent – and this has meant that he can use the pressure of steam to drive the piston to and fro in a horizontal cylinder, instead of relying as hitherto on the pressure of the atmosphere to push the piston downwards in a vertical cylinder, against the partial vacuum produced by condensing steam beneath it.

At this point we realise tactfully that we had better withdraw and let Mr Symington get on with it, for much depends on the result of this demonstration. We know, to be sure, that he was approached three years ago by Lord Dundas, Governor of the canal company, to build a steam tug for it, and still has his support (isn't that Dundas arriving now, his carriage rumbling over the wooden drawbridge that spans the lock?); but we know too that Dundas has failed to carry the local management committee of the canal with him; that rumour has it that since last summer the canal company has even been refusing to pay the bills for building the steam engine, and Mr Symington is desperate for whatever funds he can lay his hands on. But he has a trump card – and how we know that I am not quite sure, unless we assume Mr Symington taking a few more minutes off proudly to tell us – for Dundas has introduced him in London to the great Duke of Bridgewater, the canal duke himself, and Bridgewater was so impressed by a model of the proposed vessel that he has ordered Mr Symington to build as many as eight steam tugs for his canal in Lancashire.

Let us return to the present before getting carried away. That Symington's steam tug *Charlotte Dundas* did that day successfully tow the *Euphemia* and the *Active* over the $19\frac{1}{2}$ miles to Glasgow in 6 hours, on a day when no other boats could move in that direction against the wind, is history. In Symington's words, every person who witnessed it was satisfied of the utility of steam navigation. It is also, sadly, history that the *Charlotte Dundas* did not go into regular service and that Symington did not receive the reward of success. Just how that came about will be described later, however, in chapter four.

The Pre-Steam Transport Revolution

The point here is that with the *Charlotte Dundas* Symington demonstrated for the first time the ability of steam to propel a ship or boat that could do useful work. Indeed he did more than that: this was the first time that a steam

engine – or indeed any form of mechanical power – had been used as a mobile power unit in a vessel or vehicle with the potential for successful operation (although there had already been many earlier experimental vehicles and vessels, and stationary steam engines were already providing the power to haul canal boats on wheeled cradles up inclined planes between one level of canal and another). Though Symington himself benefited little from his achievement, many others benefited from his example, and others again, working independently, soon achieved similar results. The effect was that, although in 1790 transport in the British Isles had been dependent on the power of animals, men, gravity and the wind, by 1850 steam had become its prime mover. Steam boats and steamships plied the seas, the steam railway system was established on land. Sailing vessels at sea, and roads, rivers and canals inland, all seemed at best old-fashioned and at worst obsolete. It is mainly with this transport revolution, and its physical traces, that this book is concerned.

Yet not entirely, for although steam as a motive power brought a revolution, it was not introduced to transport against a background of stagnation. Quite the opposite: during the second half of the eighteenth century there were already the makings of a transport revolution, even though it was dependent on traditional forms of power. Roads were

improved, fast reliable coach services introduced, a nation-wide network of canals was constructed, and iron-railed tramroads began to supersede old-established wooden waggonways. At sea, sailing-ship design had been evolving steadily over three centuries. All of these, on land and sea, continued to develop during the early years of the nineteenth century, so this book is about them too, so that the introduction of steam transport may be seen in true context. As one who was there remarked*: 'One of the most novel and useful applications of steam-engines has been to propel navigable vessels. It enables us to traverse the waters with nearly as much certainty as mail coaches travel the land'. Sailing ships could never attempt a regular schedule: they were at the mercy of wind and tide.

So those who were there at the time viewed the introduction of steam transport, in its various forms, against the background of other recent and contemporary developments. It would not be necessary to make this seemingly obvious point, were it not that in looking back at those events from today we almost invariably consider them in the light of subsequent history. To us, George and Robert Stephenson's *Rocket* appears primitive compared with later locomotives. To contemporaries in 1829, she was an outstanding advance on anything then known. Furthermore, today, we tend to consider the developments which took place in each form of transport in isolation from

each other. Most of those who study the history and archaeology of railways at the period in question know little of the history and archaeology of canals, and vice versa; but they both have in common that they know little of shipping, and marine historians and archaeologists pay no great heed to land transport. (One of the perils of attempting a book which incorporates diverse fields is that there are certain to be some readers whose specialised knowledge of one or other of them is greater than the author's: if they find any inadequacies in the treatment of their specialities, they will I hope bear with me.)

When steam transport was new, ideas were freely exchanged between transport in its various forms, and many of the individuals concerned knew no rigid distinctions between them. Richard Trevithick, for instance, did not – as those who study only railways might be forgiven for assuming – design the first railway locomotive out of the blue in 1803. He conceived the idea, about 1798, of using high pressure steam as a means to evade Watt's patent; he himself patented a high pressure steam engine in 1802 and many stationary engines were built under this patent for use in mines and factories. At the same time Trevithick, and others, experimented with engines of his type adapted to power road carriages (1801 and 1803), railway locomotives (1802, 1803, 1805 and 1808), a boat (1804) and dredgers (1806).

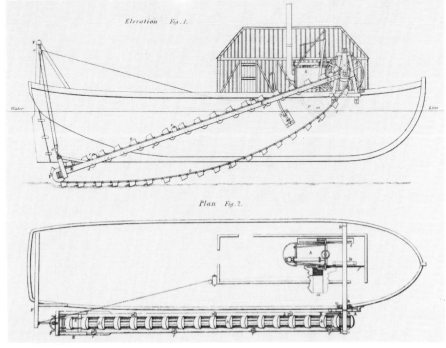

Many high pressure steam engines to Richard Trevithick's design were built in the 1800s to provide power for mines, factories and mills. The example shown (left) was installed in a dredger (right) used on the River Thames. Both these illustrations appeared originally in Ree's Cyclopedia of 1819. When such an engine was adapted as a locomotive in 1803 (above) its cylinder was positioned horizontally instead of vertically but it was otherwise basically similar.

*George Dodd, *An Historical and Explanatory Dissertation on Steam Engines and Steam Packets*, 1818.

There are many comparable instances. William Jessop, the greatest canal engineer of his day, was also an enthusiastic proponent of iron tramroads, and in due course laid out the first public railway. John Ericsson, to those who know their railways, is familiar as the designer of the *Novelty* locomotive, *Rocket*'s rival at the Rainhill Trials of 1829. To marine historians, though, he is famous instead as one of the two successful inventors of the screw propeller in the late 1830s. Even where individuals tended to restrict the scope of their activities, there were frequently close personal links between them. The Duke of Bridgewater, for instance, had much of the engineering work on his canal supervised by his agent John Gilbert. Gilbert had grown up with Matthew Boulton; Boulton eventually entered into a partnership with James Watt; Watt's patented ideas on steam engines were pirated by Bateman & Sherratt; Bateman & Sherratt in the 1790s built a steam engine for the duke to have installed in an experimental tug boat on his canal. And so it goes on. The engineering world in those days must indeed have been a small one.

Nevertheless, once steam power for transport had been shown to be feasible, the most experienced of existing engineers were in no hurry to help bring it into general use. While George Stephenson was struggling to build the Liverpool & Manchester Railway in the late 1820s, Thomas Telford, who had just completed the greatest engineering work of the turnpike road era, the Menai Bridge, was working on the most advanced of canals – the Birmingham & Liverpool Junction. All the same the early railways were built using existing civil engineering techniques derived from road and canal engineering as much as from tramroads and waggonways: even Stephenson, when he built the Liverpool & Manchester Railway across quaking Chat Moss on a foundation of heather and hurdles was not – despite the adulation of later railway historians – introducing a great innovation. He was using the standard technique of the period for building a road across a bog. Only later, in the 1840s, when steam railways seemed set to supersede all other forms of long-distance inland transport did the best of engineering talent flock to their construction and desert roads and canals.

Before starting to look at the period and its surviving traces in detail, there are two other things to be considered. The first, very briefly, is the policy I have followed in including as illustrations portraits of engineers and other notables of the period. Of the best known and most famous, you will find no portraits here – no picture of George Stephenson or Isambard Brunel, nor yet of James Brindley or the Duke of Bridgewater. Their appearances are too well known, and indeed familiar to excess, for the supply of authentic portraits is limited and they have been much reproduced elsewhere. There are portraits of others, though – of individuals who are important to the story, whose features are not so familiar, and who deserve to be better known.

The second is to consider the early history of the stationary steam engine, from which the engines which powered early steam vessels and vehicles evolved; and this must be done at much greater length.

Stationary Steam Pumps

Until the early eighteenth century industries were local affairs: they were dependent for power on wind and water, animals and men. The heights of technology were represented by water mills, windmills and sailing ships and, on a smaller scale, locks, clocks and other instruments. It was into such a world that the steam engine came to provide the first mechanical power.

So familiar is the later concept of the steam engine which uses steam under pressure in a cylinder to push a piston to and fro, that it is always a surprise to be reminded that the first engines to use steam were a consequence of experiments made by seventeenth century savants into the properties of the atmosphere. Steam was involved only because to condense it in a cylinder was a convenient way to create a vacuum. By the mid-seventeenth century it had been realised that the atmosphere had weight and exerted pressure. Otto von Guericke demonstrated the power of atmospheric pressure dramatically with his experiment of the Magdeburg hemispheres: when two small hollow hemispheres were sealed together and exhausted of air, sixteen horses could not pull them apart. Denis Papin in 1690 first and experimentally condensed steam in a cylinder to create a vacuum beneath a piston, so that atmospheric pressure might propel the piston downwards. He proposed to the Royal Society that the principle might be used to pump water out of mines.

The Newcomen atmospheric steam pump, as depicted in Rees's Cyclopedia. *The near wall of the engine house is shown cut away; the boiler, on the right, delivers steam to the large vertical cylinder, and the 'arch-heads, I,I, at the ends of the beam are for giving a perpendicular direction to the chains of the piston and pump rods'.*

Atmospheric Steam Engine.

Fig. 1.

Regulator

Fig. 2.

Section

Mine drainage was an increasing problem at this period, as surface scratchings after minerals gave way to ever deeper shafts. The problem was particularly acute in Cornwall, where tin mining proper had started to replace the working of alluvial deposits two hundred years earlier, and deeper and deeper mines were encountering volumes of water too great to be extracted by pumps powered by horse gins or waterwheels. Thomas Savery of Exeter attempted to provide a solution with a 'fire engine': steam in a cylinder was condensed to draw water up a pipe past a non-return valve; more steam under pressure then expelled the water past another non-return valve up a further pipe. That was the theory; in practice problems were that the lower pipe could be no more than twenty-eight feet long, which meant that the whole apparatus had to be installed part way down the mine shaft; and that contemporary technology could not produce boilers able to withstand the steam pressures needed. Savery's pump was protected in 1698, by a patent covering a steam chamber device for raising water by the impellant force of fire, but it saw little use.

Enter Thomas Newcomen, inventor of the first satisfactory steam – or, to be precise, atmospheric – pump. Newcomen, of Dartmouth, Devon, was described as an ironmonger (a term which had a much broader connotation than it has today) and from travelling among the Cornish mines he was aware of their drainage problems. His pump followed the principles proposed by Papin, although he may not have been aware of this. He was certainly aware of the work of Savery, whom he knew; he had to work under Savery's patent and after the latter's death in 1715 became part-owner of it.

Newcomen experimented for many years. He had business contacts in the Midlands, and it was not in Cornwall but to drain the Earl of Dudley's Conygree Coal Works at Tipton that his first engine was set up in 1712. In principle it worked thus: from one end of an immense wooden rocking beam, pivoted at its mid-point, was suspended the pump rod, and from the other was suspended the piston, free to move up and down a large, open-topped cylinder. When steam at no more than 1 lb per sq. in. pressure was admitted beneath the piston, the weight of the pump rod made the far end of the beam descend and so caused the near end, and with it the piston, to rise. When the piston reached the top of its stroke, water was injected into the cylinder; the steam rapidly condensed and atmospheric pressure then drove the piston downwards, making the pump rod rise on its working stroke. The piston was kept steam and air tight by a stuffing of oakum, and a layer of water on top of it. Most of the machine was built into the engine house; the beam was pivoted upon one of the walls and extended outside over the pump shaft. The Conygree engine had a brass cylinder, of dimensions 1 ft 9 in. bore by 7 ft 10 in., fed with steam from a boiler made of copper and lead; it operated at 12 strokes a minute to lift 120 gallons of water during that time.

Newcomen's engines worked well, and their construction was within the technical capabilities of the era. By 1733, the year Savery's patent expired, at least seventy-five had been installed throughout Britain (many of them in Cornwall) and eight abroad, and possibly more; and subsequently installations continued to increase in number. Iron boiler plates were in use by 1717, and iron cylinders by 1718. The engines were built on site: parts such as cylinders and pump barrels were bought in, but many other parts were made on the spot. As the number of Newcomen engines increased, so did a body of engineers skilled in their erection and maintenance.

The oldest surviving Newcomen engine was re-erected in Royal Avenue Gardens, Dartmouth, in 1964 to mark the 300th anniversary of the inventor's birth. It was originally built in the 1720s for Griff colliery near Nuneaton, and much later was re-installed beside the Coventry Canal at Hawkesbury, near Coventry. Canal companies made much use of Newcomen and later types of beam engine to supply their canals with water. The National Coal Board preserves a Newcomen-type pumping engine at Elsecar, South Yorkshire.

John Smeaton carried out trials and experiments from 1769 onwards on Newcomen engines to investigate their efficiency. Smeaton (1724–1792) was the first professional civil engineer: the term 'civil', at this period, was used to make a distinction between civil engineering and military engineering, and civil engineering embraced what we now call mechanical engineering, so far as it then existed. Smeaton was the son of a Leeds lawyer and had been intended for the same profession, but he showed great mechanical talent and so was allowed to take up employment under a London instrument maker. Having set up in due course his own instrument business, he turned in the 1750s to engineering. In this he became successful and indeed famous, notably from construction of his Eddystone Lighthouse off Plymouth – the third lighthouse on the site, but the first to be entirely successful. The earlier two had been destroyed by gale and fire respectively.

Smeaton's work on the atmospheric engine, however, was not among his greatest successes. He increased its efficiency, certainly, by better proportioning and construction of its parts; but he made no great step forward in engine design. That was left to his near contemporary and in due course friend, James Watt.

Watt and the Separate Condenser

James Watt (1736–1819) was twelve years younger than Smeaton. His father, also James Watt, was a merchant and shipowner in Greenock; Watt junior, like Smeaton, trained as an instrument maker in London. Then, returning north, he became in 1757 'mathematical instrument maker' to Glasgow university: a highly skilled man, with good friends among the professors and access to the store of knowledge that they represented. In 1763, in his capacity as instrument maker, he was asked to repair a working model of a Newcomen engine, the property of the university's Natural Philosophy class; but he found that the engine, even when in good order, would make only a few strokes before stopping for lack of steam. The boiler, although it appeared large enough in proportion to the cylinder, was evidently not so in fact.

There was at that time only a limited understanding of the properties of heat and steam, and Watt had to establish by experiment the volume of steam produced from a given volume of water, and also that, in this instance, the volume of steam provided for each stroke was much greater than the volume of the cylinder. An excessive amount of steam, he reasoned, was being lost by condensation, because with each stroke the cylinder and piston had to be heated to the temperature of boiling water and were then cooled again; and the same would apply to any engine on Newcomen's principle.

He pondered the problem over a couple of years. It was in 1765 that the solution occurred to him: if at the end of the piston's upward stroke a connection were opened between the cylinder and a separate vessel in which there was a vacuum, the steam would rush into it and could be condensed there while cylinder and piston were kept hot. This vessel was the 'separate condenser'. To test this theory experimentally he built a small model with an inverted cylinder, in which steam was admitted above the piston and the initial condenser vacuum produced by a pump. He was delighted to find that, in his own words,

'on turning the exhausting cock [to admit steam to the condenser] the piston ... ascended as quick as the blow of a hammer'.

A model of this apparatus – certainly Watt's, and probably the original – is preserved in the Science Museum.

It was a brilliant discovery: but it was one thing to make it and another for an instrument maker without engineering experience to adapt it to the monstrous proportions of Newcomen's pumps. One might draw a parallel with a skilled model engineer, accustomed to building 5 in. gauge locomotives, who makes a discovery of fundamental importance to locomotive efficiency and so sets out to prove it in practice by building a full-size express locomotive. Moreover, this was not all: Watt's most fertile brain did not stop short at this point, but went on to consider complete redesign of the engine – as a beam-less direct-acting steam pump, or even as a 'steam wheel' to produce rotary motion.

In converting these ideas into practice he was hampered, firstly, by lack of finance. A solution appeared in the form of a partnership with Dr John Roebuck, to whom he was introduced through university connections. Roebuck had been in 1759 the principal founder of the Carron Ironworks near Falkirk, the first ironworks to be set up in the Scottish lowlands. The works had prospered and acquired coal mines to supply the coal they needed: but in these Roebuck had the familiar problem of flooding, flooding too severe for drainage by an atmospheric engine.

Roebuck asked Watt to build an engine to drain his mine at Kinneil near Borrowstounness. Parts were to be provided by Carron Ironworks, and here another difficulty arose: the engineering methods and skills available were unable to produce work accurate enough to meet Watt's needs. This applied particularly to boring cylinders. The work went forward, but intermittently.

Sometime in the middle of 1766 Watt set himself up in business as a land surveyor and engineer. As an engineer he was responsible for construction of several atmospheric engines and gradually gained experience in construction of large machines. As a surveyor he was employed to lay out several proposed canals. As will be related in chapter three, this was the time of the first great upsurge of interest in canals: the Duke of Bridgewater's canal, the first canal independent of natural waterways to be built in Britain, had been completed from Worsley into Manchester in 1765 and was being extended; and in May 1766 Parliament passed Acts authorising construction of two much more ambitious canals, the Trent & Mersey to link the rivers of its name, and the Staffordshire & Worcestershire to link the T & M to the Severn. By the end of the year Watt was surveying routes for a canal to link the Firths of Forth and Clyde. This was one of several rival surveys being made at this period – the first had been made by Smeaton in 1763–4. Watt's survey was the first of many canal surveys he undertook.

Early in 1768 Watt returned to experimenting with his ideas for improving the steam engine. The performance of models impressed Roebuck to the extent that he entered into a partnership with Watt, who then set off for London to apply for a patent. During his return journey he met, at Birmingham, Matthew Boulton. This was the first meeting between two men whose names were to become closely linked: they already had many mutual friends, including Roebuck himself. Matthew Boulton (1728–1809) had moved his family business out from Birmingham to what was then a green field site at Soho in 1765, and his Soho Manufactory was already famous. It produced steel, silver and plated goods – buttons, buckles, toys, watch chains, sword hilts and so on. Watt not only formed a firm friendship with Boulton but found at Soho standards of workmanship far superior to those at Carron: here, perhaps, it might be possible to build his engine. He suggested to Roebuck that Boulton should be taken into partnership, but terms could not be agreed.

In January 1769 James Watt's patent was granted for 'a new method of lessening the consumption of steam and fuel in fire engines'. It was the principle of the separate condenser that was patented, not a particular application of it. Meanwhile Watt had agreed with Roebuck to erect a small full-size engine at Kinneil for trials. In its construction he reverted to the beam engine layout of Newcomen's pumps: but the open-topped cylinder of the latter was replaced by one that was closed in (the piston rod passed through a stuffing box) and steam was admitted both above and below the piston. When the piston was at the top of its stroke, steam supply to the lower part of the cylinder was cut off, and access to the condenser opened: so the pressure of the steam above the piston – between 1 and 5 lb per sq. in. – was added to that of the atmosphere to drive the piston downwards. The cylinder was made of tin, with a stroke of 5 ft and a diameter of 1 ft 6 in.: but this diameter varied by as much as $\frac{3}{8}$ in., a good example of the manufacturing problems with which Watt was faced.

This engine was built during 1769 and the early part of 1770: some trials were carried out, but not to the point of wholly satisfactory operation. Meanwhile, Watt's canal engineering business was on the increase – he had surveyed the Monkland Canal near Glasgow and in June 1770 started to supervise construction – but Roebuck was falling into financial difficulties.

Boulton & Watt

The years 1772 and 1773 were a period of severe commercial depression, and one of the casualties was Roebuck, who became insolvent in 1772; work on the part-complete Monkland Canal ceased the following year. Out of these misfortunes came Watt's – and Boulton's – opportunity: Watt discharged Roebuck's debt to him and in the process became the owner of the Kinneil engine, which he promptly dismantled and shipped down to Soho. Thither, after completing a survey for a canal from Fort William to Inverness, he followed it, in 1774.

Boulton had purchased Roebuck's share in the engine partnership and the little engine was set up at Soho to pump back water used by the waterwheel which powered the manufactory, for the supply was inadequate. By the end of 1774 Watt had the engine working satisfactorily, and during the following year it was still further improved when the tin cylinder was replaced by one of cast iron, accurately bored: this was supplied by John Wilkinson who had fortuitously, also in 1774, patented a boring mill, intended initially for gun barrels, which could not only bore a cylinder circular but also cylindrical throughout its length.

Unfortunately Watt's condenser patent had been granted only for a term of fourteen years, and six of these had already slipped by. In 1775 Watt applied to Parliament for an Act to extend it and this, despite fears of monopoly, was passed: it extended the life of the patent until 1800. Then, with the prospect of a long enough period ahead of them to produce a return on investment, Boulton entered into a partnership with Watt for the extended term of the patent.

With the news getting about that Matthew Boulton, highly respected man of business, was becoming a partner in a new fire engine, enquiries were already coming in. Among the first Boulton & Watt patent engines built was one for that same John Wilkinson who had supplied the iron cylinder, and another for a colliery at Tipton. Other engines were set up in Fife and in London, but the market that Boulton & Watt took by storm was the tin-mining district of Cornwall. Here coal was expensive, and the economies derived from Watt's design correspondingly advantageous. The first Boulton & Watt engine in Cornwall was set up in 1777: by 1783 there was twenty-one at work, and only one Newcomen engine left there.

The methods by which these early Boulton & Watt engines were built followed the long-established practice with Newcomen engines. That is to say, they were built on site with parts from various suppliers. Boulton & Watt at first supplied small parts only, such as valves. But they did the vital design work, and supervised erection of the engines – initially Watt personally attended to both and rapidly became overworked. The main source of income for the partnership was royalties, continuing payment of royalties by users of Boulton & Watt engines: the rate of royalty was estimated as one third of the saving in fuel costs resulting from use of a Watt engine rather than a Newcomen engine.

Watt engines from this period survive in the Science Museum and in the Birmingham Museum of Science & Industry. The first of these engines, known as *Old Bess*, was set up at Soho Manufactory in 1777, and on it Watt experimented with expansive use of steam: that is, the valve gear was arranged so that steam would be cut off from entering the top of the cylinder before the piston reached the end of its downward stroke. After the point of cut-off, the steam already in the cylinder continued to press on the piston as it expanded. In consequence, fuel economy was improved. This engine worked at Soho until 1848 (no doubt with some replacement parts) when it was sold by auction and after passing through other hands was presented to the Patent Office Museum, the forerunner of the Science Museum where it is now displayed.

The engine in the Birmingham museum was built during 1777–8 to pump water back up the flight of six locks that then existed at Smethwick on the Birmingham Canal, opened in 1769. It continued in operation for over a century, probably receiving two new cylinders during this period, but in 1891 was found to be beyond economic repair. It was dismantled about 1897 but the canal company's engineer, G. R. Jebb, unusually enlightened for the period, arranged for it to be re-erected – preserved, in effect – at the canal workshops at Ocker Hill. These works in turn closed in 1960 and the engine was presented to the Birmingham Museum of Science & Industry where, after some years in store, it is again being re-erected, as I write, in a purpose-built canalside extension. It is this museum's

pleasant and instructive custom to operate its steam engines from time to time with steam drawn from its central heating system, so that in due course the public will again be able to see this very early engine operating under steam.

Rotary Motion

With the partnership fairly launched and engines built and building, Watt was at last able gradually to introduce further improvements in engine design. Many of these had been in his mind for some time. The introduction of expansive working has just been mentioned. The idea of the double-acting engine, in which steam would drive the piston up as well as down, and would be condensed alternately from the top as well as the bottom of the cylinder, was clear to Watt by 1775 or earlier, for he described and illustrated it in his application to Parliament to extend the separate condenser patent. The double-acting engine was eventually patented in 1782 and the first such engine built in 1783.

By the late 1770s there was a strong demand for a steam engine which would produce rotary motion and power machinery, replacing waterwheels and horse gins. Watt's 'steam wheel' proved impracticable and he started work on schemes to produce rotary motion by means of a connecting rod from the beam end to a crank on a revolving shaft – an arrangement long familiar on treadle lathes. But design and construction of pumps for Cornwall was more pressing, and in the meantime another engineer, Matthew Wasbrough, had arranged an atmospheric engine to drive machinery in the Birmingham mill of James Pickard. At first a pawl-and-ratchet arrangement converted the beam's reciprocating motion into rotary; when this did not work satisfactorily, it was replaced, in 1780, by a connecting rod and crank, which did work, and its application to the steam engine was then patented. Watt's reaction was to design five other devices for the same purpose and patent them, in 1781.

Although Watt was pessimistic about the likely financial return for the trouble involved in developing rotative engines, his first was set up at Soho in 1782, and the first for an outside customer the following year, to be followed by many more. Cranks, however, were not used in Boulton & Watt engines for many years. Watt's fertility of invention in engine detail was remarkable: notably, it produced the 'sun-and-planet' gearing he substituted for the crank, the parallel link motion to join piston rod to beam, and the

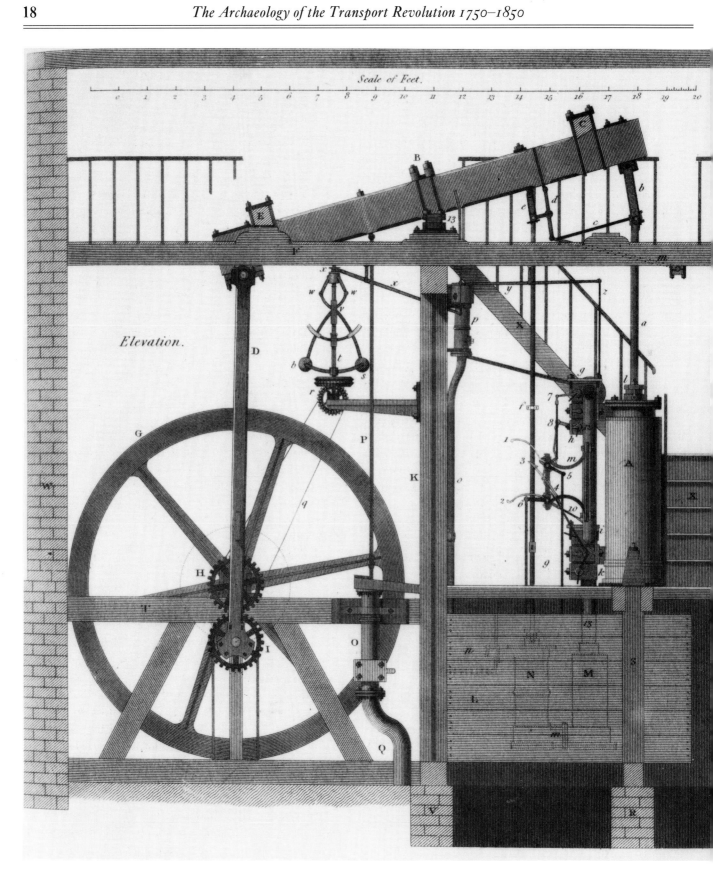

centrifugal governor (already used in windmills) to control engine speed. Even an excess of paperwork stimulated the invention, in 1780, of the copying press, which became a standard piece of office equipment until the coming of the typewriter and carbon paper.

Unlike coal owners, proprietors of mills and factories who ordered rotative engines seldom had staff skilled in their erection. So more and more of the engine parts were manufactured in Soho and supplied made up. The name of Boulton & Watt had become famous, but by 1795 the separate condenser patent had only five years to run. A new establishment for making engine parts was set up on a new site: The Soho Foundry operated by Boulton, Watt & Co. The partners in this were Boulton, his son, and James Watt's two sons. Their father was growing old and gradually withdrawing from business, though he joined Matthew Boulton on the committee of the Birmingham Canal in 1804 and remained on it for the rest of his life.

By 1800, the date of expiry of Watt's patent and the termination of the original Boulton & Watt partnership, it is probable that Boulton & Watt had produced about 450 engines for British customers. Throughout the period of the patent, Newcomen engines were still being built: by the same date there were probably in total 1,000 steam engines in use in Britain. Eighteen years later there were said to be ten times as many. Canal companies made much use of them to pump water into their canals: notable examples are preserved in operation including those at Crofton, Kennet & Avon Canal (OS grid ref. SU 262623) where the older of two engines was supplied by Boulton, Watt & Co. in 1812 and is run under steam from time to time, and at Lea Wood, Cromford Canal (OS grid ref. SK 315559).

James Watt and Steam Transport

Throughout the term of their patent Boulton & Watt consistently refused to allow others to manufacture Watt engines under licence, and on only two occasions allowed existing engines to be converted to Watt principles. This attitude had two main effects.

James Watt developed the atmospheric pump into an elegant producer of power for mills and factories. This is how it was illustrated in Rees's Cyclopedia. *The condenser is at M and the air pump, to remove air and condensate from it, at N. Parallel link motion connects piston rod and beam end, ensuring that the former reciprocates up and down while the latter is describing an arc of a circle, and sun-and-planet gearing joins the connecting rod to the flywheel shaft.*

One was the growth of engine 'pirates': manufacturers and engineers who either clandestinely copied Watt's engines, or invented engine designs which attempted, almost invariably unsuccessfully, to circumvent Watt's patent. Despite litigation, the 'pirates' probably built some seventy-five engines for British customers. It was from the second group of pirates, the inventive engineers, that there came several men such as Symington who were to be important in the application of steam power to transport and who will be mentioned in chapter four.

The other effect of Watt's reluctance to grant licences was that, to all intents and purposes, the only developments in steam engine design could be those he made himself: and Watt, particularly in his later years, was resolutely opposed to adapting the steam engine to power vehicles or vessels. Although he included the application of the double-acting engine to road carriages, with or without the condenser, in a patent of 1784, he did not pursue the subject himself. He also discouraged the attempts of others.

Why this should have been so has been a minor mystery ever since. It does not appear to me to have been simple pig-headedness. Watt was brilliant in ingenuity, and in scientific and technical innovation and reasoning; he was given to acute headaches and bouts of extreme depression; and he was painstakingly thorough, almost to a fault. He could have brought the separate condenser into use much more quickly than he did (manufacturing difficulties apart) had he not first attempted to follow many other possible avenues of development, and then, perhaps in reaction, realised that for a time at least he must follow some more immediately rewarding pursuit such as surveying canals.

Just so, I think, when the Boulton & Watt steam pumping engine had become solid and rewarding fact, he realised that he must devote himself to its further improvement, and not be tempted into wider fields of experiment. He was extremely reluctant to get involved with the rotative engine. Besides, he knew from experience, as other inventors did not, just how much continuing effort and financial backing was needed to convert a bright idea from model form to massive reality. He had become the expert who knew what could not, or should not, be done. His attitude was perhaps akin to that of those stalwarts of the present-day railway preservation movement who, having by dint of years of fund raising and hard work recovered their branch lines from dereliction or their locomotives from the scrap yard, quite naturally do all they can to dissuade later innocents from attempting to follow a similar course.

CHAPTER TWO

Road, River and Sea down to 1800

Roads and Coaches

When the young James Watt set out from Greenock for London in 1755 he travelled on horseback: the journey took twelve days, by way of Coldstream, Newcastle and the Great North Road. Meanwhile his heavy luggage, a chest, had been sent from Greenock by road to Leith, whence it was sent to London by sea.

Since time immemorial people and their belongings had travelled thus. People themselves went on horseback or on foot, and animals on the hoof often in huge herds or flocks; pack horses carried light goods but heavy goods went, so far as possible, by river barge or coastwise sailing ship. Letters, both government and private, were carried by post-boys on horseback. The Post Office arranged for relays of horses to be made available for them along the principal roads, by postmasters (who were often also innkeepers). Travellers used the same system: the postmasters provided relays of horses for them to ride.

But things were changing, and were soon to change much more. Had Watt travelled only three years later, in 1758, he would have had another option: in that year for the first time a stage coach started to run between Glasgow and London. Throughout most of Britain, wheeled vehicles were on the increase. Originally, of course, the Romans had used them and throughout the Dark and Middle Ages their use never entirely died out. In the mid-sixteenth century came the gradual introduction of stage waggons – great lumbering vehicles, drawn by teams of six or eight horses, which carried the goods and passengers from stage to stage of their journeys, at 2 mph or thereabouts. Carriages were introduced into Britain from Europe at about the same period, initially as playthings – or perhaps status symbols – of royalty and nobility. Queen Elizabeth I had one of the earliest. By 1694, however, there were said to have been over 700 in use in London alone.

By then, in the middle of that century, stage coaches to carry passengers had been introduced. At first they ran only in summer, and their routes increased slowly, but by the end of the seventeenth century London was connected by stage coaches with Coventry, Preston, Chester, Oxford, Exeter and York, among other places. Journey times were quoted in days. These coaches were primitive – they comprised a wood-and-leather body slung by leather braces from upright posts attached to the 'carriage'. That term was then applied only to what we would now call the undercarriage or chassis; its principal component was a longitudinal timber beam of great strength, called the perch, to which the swivelling fore-carriage was pivoted, and the rear axle bed rigidly fixed. Originally they were hauled by the same team of horses throughout each journey, but in 1734 relays of horses were provided to re-horse the Newcastle–London 'Flying Coach' at intervals: this enabled a journey of twelve days to be reduced to one of nine. The principle of re-horsing stage coaches at intervals later became general. For the wealthiest of travellers, a similar system developed: at posting inns along main roads they could hire relays of horses not to ride but to draw their own coaches forward from one inn to the next. Alternatively they could hire a post-chaise, a light carriage, to be re-horsed at intervals in the same way. Though Watt in 1758 rode from Greenock to London in twelve days, James Boswell, travelling from Edinburgh to London in 1762, went by post-chaise in five.

Maintenance of Roads and Bridges

The development of wheeled vehicles and the increase (or sometimes decrease) in their average speeds was closely linked with the condition of roads and their improvement – or deterioration. Originally the term *road* meant no more than a right of passage across country. To a network of ancient trackways the Romans had added military roads, paved and straight, but these had deteriorated after the Romans left. Most roads in England in the Middle Ages were tracks of earth – or, in wet weather, mud. Responsibility for upkeep of these, the King's Highways, lay with the lords of the manors, with the monasteries, and with the king.

With bridges, the situation was similar. They were built and maintained by religious orders, by guilds, by landowners and by individuals. For some of them, endowments by benefactors paid for repairs; for others, tolls, called pontage, were levied on goods which crossed.

Dissolution of the monasteries, which had had a strong interest in maintaining good communications between their scattered possessions, left a conspicuous gap in the arrangements for maintenance of both bridges and roads. For bridges, it was filled by the Statute of Bridges in 1531. It was no longer known who was responsible for maintenance of many bridges: if such a bridge lay within a city or town it was, said the statute, to be kept in repair by the inhabitants; if outside, by the county in which it lay. Local rates could be levied to pay for repairs.

For roads, an Act of Parliament in 1555 codified existing practice by making road maintenance in England the responsibility of the parishes. It obliged parishioners to spend, each year, four consecutive days (later increased to six) working on the roads; they had to bring their own picks and shovels, and those who were fortunate enough to own a team of horses had to provide that, with cart and driver. To supervise the work – carting gravel and stones, repairing road surfaces, cleaning ditches and cutting back hedges – each parish had each year to appoint two Surveyors of Highways. The post was no sinecure: it was unpaid and unpopular. This system of 'statute labour' worked, though none too well. Parishioners were too inclined to loiter over their tasks, surveyors to direct their limited attention to the by-roads which led to their own fields rather than the main roads from market town to market town. Road rates, introduced in 1654, enabled surveyors to pay for labour and teams of horses; and for many parishioners money payments gradually came to replace physical labour. The statute labour system was introduced in Scotland in 1669.

The improvement in English road conditions that resulted from statute labour was offset during the seventeenth century by the increasing number of wheeled vehicles. In clay areas particularly, wheel ruts were now added to a multitude of hoof prints, to render roads in winter almost unusable. One reaction was that Parliament passed, during the seventeenth and eighteenth centuries, a great many Acts to limit the use of wheeled vehicles and regulate their construction. This applied particularly to wheels – broad wheels with rims of nine, thirteen, or even sixteen inches width were encouraged in the late eighteenth century with the intent that instead of making ruts they would roll the roads. But wheels of too great a width proved to be as damaging as those that were too narrow, for they ground the road surface to dust and mud.

Turnpikes are Set Up

More constructive was the establishment of the turnpike system by which travellers paid tolls, for road maintenance, at gates set across main roads at intervals. The name 'turnpike' referred originally to the type of gate – a horizontally-swinging barrier upon which pikes were mounted, similar to a form of defence against cavalry which was then familiar. Perhaps the first turnpike gates were really built like this, but it seems more likely that it was a term that arose in jest.

Where a busy main road ran through part of a small and poor parish, statute labour had proved both an excessive imposition on the parishioners and an ineffective means of maintaining the road. So it was on the Great North Road that the first three toll gates were authorised by Parliament in 1663. Of these, one was not put up and another was easy to avoid: so the first effective turnpike gate was the one put up at Wadesmill, near Ware, and administered by the County Justices of Hertford. (This was long before the days of county councils.) Further turnpike acts between 1695 and 1705 gave similar powers to justices elsewhere, but in 1706 Parliament for the first time set up a turnpike trust. The road from Fornhill, Beds., to Stony Stratford, Northants. (which formed part of the main route from London to Coventry and Chester), was placed under control of a group of trustees. This was the prototype of the turnpike trust, the form of main-road administration which, superimposed on statute labour, became familiar to travellers throughout the period covered by this book.

Typically, turnpike trustees had powers to erect gates, collect tolls at levels authorised, appoint surveyors and collectors, demand statute labour or its equivalent in money, mortgage tolls, elect new trustees and repair roads. The

This stretch of former turnpike road at Braunston, Northants, was last used as a main road in the early part of the nineteenth century, when Telford built a diversion as part of his improvements to the Holyhead Road which are described in chapter five. It is still used as a farm track and its condition at the end of the hard winter of 1981–2 perhaps provides a glimpse of what usual eighteenth-century road conditions were really like. OS grid ref. SP 543653.

original intention was that a trust would borrow the money it needed, to pay for putting its road into repair, against the security of future tolls: and that when income from tolls had paid off the debt, the road would revert to the parishes. So trusts were set up for limited periods, usually twenty-one years. In practice, they seldom if ever did succeed in paying off their debts, and were renewed by Parliament as a matter of course.

Turnpike acts were sought from Parliament by residents of the areas concerned, against the opposition, sometimes, of road users, and of river navigation authorities. By 1750, turnpiking of the thirteen principal routes radiating from London was almost complete; then, in the years 1751–1772 came what William Albert (*The Turnpike Road System in England 1663–1840*) calls the 'Turnpike Mania'. During those twenty-one years 389 new trusts were set up.

The extent of the roads administered by a trust was, on average, quite small – a consequence in part of the piecemeal way in which roads were turnpiked, and in part of a natural reluctance by trustees to attend meetings so far away that they could not ride to them and return home the same evening. There might be a great many trustees named in a turnpike trust act – as many as 200 perhaps, though a quorum might be as low as seven. The list commenced with the nobility of the district and continued with gentry, prominent townsmen, professional people and clergy. The list of trustees named in the Act for the Hitchin, Shefford and Bedford trust (1757), for instance, commences with the Marquis of Tavistock and the Earl of Upper Ossory; somewhere in the middle comes farmer Joseph Ransom, the present author's great-great-great-great grandfather.

The trustees acted through a clerk – who was usually a lawyer, a treasurer – often a banker – and a surveyor or surveyors, whose qualifications, throughout the eighteenth century, were in most cases minimal, for there was as yet only limited knowledge of how to build a road suitable for wheeled vehicles. In South-East England, ditches were dug either side of the road, the earth from them piled on it, and covered with gravel; in the North of England a deep trench was dug throughout the width of the road, filled with large stones and topped off with small ones. Both types of road tended to become waterlogged. Despite these inadequacies, however, turnpike roads were an improvement on what had gone before. Coach journey times were reduced – London to Edinburgh, for instance, came down from 10 days in 1754 to 4 days in 1776; and freight rates could be reduced because the cost of tolls was more than offset by the reduction in the number of horses needed to pull heavy loads. By 1777, Matthew Pickford was advertising 'flying waggons' which took only $4\frac{1}{2}$ days to go from Manchester to London.

One surveyor, John Metcalf (or 'Blind Jack': he had lost his sight as a child) did produce an improved road by using a firm foundation covered with road stone which formed an arched surface to throw off rainwater into the ditches. He first used this technique in Yorkshire in 1765 and eventually extended it to 180 miles of turnpike road in that county. Metcalf's work was a forerunner of the more extensive road improvements carried out early in the next century by Telford and McAdam, which are described in chapter five.

The network provided by turnpike roads remained the basis of the main-road system until construction of motorways and other new roads within the last twenty-five years or so; and even today many main roads follow former turnpike road routes. The surfaces of the latter, however, have disappeared under tarmac, and tollgates went in Victorian times with abolition of the trusts. However many tollhouses, provided by trusts for their gatekeepers, remain and are a familiar sight, recognisable by being set exceptionally close to the road edge, and often provided with a bow front or a porch with side windows, so that the gatekeeper might observe traffic approaching from both directions. Even more frequent survivors – though less conspicuous – are the mileposts which turnpike trusts provided as one of their statutory duties. Cheshire and West Yorkshire seem particularly rich in them.

All through this period, throughout the turnpike era, local roads remained the responsibilities of the parishes, or were perhaps left to their mercy. Their condition during a wet season was ruefully epitomised in 1782 by William Cowper in his poem *The Distressed Travellers*. He describes an attempt to walk from Olney, Buckinghamshire, to the neighbouring village of Clifton Reynes:

'I sing of a journey to Clifton
　　We would have performed if we could,
Without cart or barrow to lift on
　　Poor Mary and me thro' the mud.
　　　Sle sla slud
　　　Stuck in the mud
Oh it is pretty to wade through a flood

So away we went, slipping and sliding
　　Hop, hop, *à la mode de deux* frogs. . . .'

and so on through nine verses. I have lived in that district, and can testify to the continuing adhesive qualities of its mud.

The Military Roads of General Wade

During the period when eighteenth-century turnpike trustees and parish surveyors were doing their limited best with the roads in their charge in England, a quite remarkable road system was being built by the government in another part of Britain. This was the network of military roads originated by General George Wade, and to a large extent built under his direction, in the Highlands of Scotland.

At the beginning of the century there were roads, of a sort, in parts of the Highlands, and the county authorities had power to raise funds and use statute labour for their maintenance; and where there were no roads for wheeled vehicles, there were footpaths, and green drove roads along which cattle in enormous quantity were driven south for sale. But these were inadequate for the military presence demanded by governmental fears of a Jacobite uprising: troops in quantity could not move freely enough to be effective.

General Wade, appointed Commander-in-Chief, North Britain, late in 1724, made various proposals to the government the following year: among them was one for mending the roads between garrisons and barracks. By the summer of 1725 his troops were at work making the military road up the Great Glen between Fort William and Killichuimen, later called Fort Augustus. In 1726 this was continued towards Inverness, reached the following year.

Wade travelled along it in a coach and six, through country in places previously impassable on horseback. What was probably more important was its suitability for artillery. Over the next few years Wade built further roads, notably one from Lowland Dunkeld through the central Highlands to Inverness, one from Crieff, also on the edge of the Lowlands, northwards to join the former road at Dalnacardoch just south of its summit at Drumochter; and one from Dalwhinnie beyond the summit north-westwards to Fort Augustus. By 1740 when Wade, following well-deserved promotion, was posted elsewhere, he had built about 250 miles of military roads.

Wade had appointed Major William Caulfield in 1732 to be his Inspector of Roads and, after he left, Caulfield became solely responsible for building the military roads. Any tendency for further construction to lapse was promptly dispelled by the rising of 1745, during which the existing military roads were used by both sides, and subsequently the network was much expanded. Caulfield, by the time of his death in 1767, had constructed more than 800 miles. Most of these roads lay in the Highlands south of the Great Glen. Beyond it, a military road was built from Fort Augustus to Bernera on the coast opposite the Isle of Skye, and outside the Highlands a military road was built from Gretna (north of Carlisle) to Portpatrick in the interest of troop movements to Ireland.

Some of the military roads were existing roads rebuilt, but many were entirely new. They were constructed to suit military needs; although they avoided the highest hills, in many places they climbed over lesser ridges rather than going round. They included long straight stretches where practicable, but when the going became too steep maintained their general alignment by ascending by zigzags to right and left; and they incorporated innumerable bridges. The actual work was done by a labour force of soldiers, assisted by civilian masons and craftsmen, and by civilian labour provided by the counties. The roads were 16 ft wide; to build them, the topsoil was removed, and a layer of boulders provided as foundation. Above this was a layer of broken stone, and above this again a surface of gravel. The roads were properly drained by ditches either side, but nevertheless the surface needed constant maintenance.

By the 1780s the Jacobite menace, in the eyes of the government, had passed. Where the military roads traversed areas populous enough to support their maintenance, they were gradually handed over to the counties; elsewhere roads were still maintained by the government, although

troops were last employed directly on military road maintenance in 1789. Many of the military roads eventually passed to the Commissioners for Highland Roads and Bridges, whom we shall encounter in chapter five.

The most important single relic of the military road era is Wade's bridge over the River Tay at Aberfeldy, Perthshire (OS grid ref. NN 851493), which is still in use by the present-day traffic of the B846. Most of Wade's bridges are plain and functional but this one, 400 ft long and with five arches, was the greatest engineering work on his road system and William Adam, considered the best architect in Scotland, was employed to design a suitably handsome structure.

Originally this bridge carried the Crieff to Dalnacardoch road. The B846 generally follows this northwards, and by following it more of Wade's works can be seen. At Tummel Bridge the military road crossed the River Tummel by a more typical structure, a single high-arched masonry bridge (OS grid ref. NN 762592); present-day traffic uses a modern bridge alongside. Beyond Tummel Bridge a minor road follows the course of the military road and runs, typically, straight and purposeful over high moorland before descending into the next glen at Trinafour. To climb out of the northern side of this glen, Wade was obliged to resort to a series of zigzags (OS grid ref. NN 725653) which are far from devoid of problems for the twentieth-century car driver.

For a military road incorporated into the present-day road system, this one is, apart from its tarmac surface, unusually close to its original line and condition. It debouches on to the modern A9 at Dalnacardoch and that is in some ways more typical: its line originates from that of Wade's road northwards from Dunkeld, but it is today a modern dual carriageway, with little trace of the original. At the other extreme come those military roads which still exist as tracks but no longer form part of the modern road system; of these, the most evocative that I have visited is the one which leads from Dalwhinnie over the Corrieyairack Pass to Fort Augustus. From the south, it climbs steadily up the northern flank of the Spey Valley: the tarmac ceases at OS grid reference NN 468959, and shortly beyond this the road becomes a very rough track indeed, so badly eroded in places that the immense foundation boulders are exposed to view. The road climbs so steadily and gradually – it is a grand road to march along, swinging one's arms – that it comes as a surprise to look round and find hills with patches of snow on them, not far above one's

Wade's military road of the 1730s from Dalwhinnie to Fort Augustus climbs steadily up the north flank of the Spey Valley towards Corrieyairack pass. No present-day motor road reaches the area. OS grid ref. NN 449965.

own altitude – and this in July. The road bears to the right into the corrie that gives the pass its name, then climbs out of it by an impressive and remarkable series of zigzags (OS grid ref. NN 428984). These, however well suited to marching soldiers, were scarcely practicable for horse-drawn carriages, and after completion of an alternative but much longer route about 1827 the surface of the Corrieyairack road was no longer maintained. Beyond the zigzags it reaches a summit some 2,500 ft above sea level.

Those who seek extended details of the military roads and their present-day condition will find them in William Taylor's *The Military Roads in Scotland*.

Bridges and their Builders

Wade's task of building new roads through an almost road-less country included construction of culverts and bridges as a matter of course: but elsewhere the position was much less clear cut. At this period in England some ancient bridges remained the responsibility of those who had always maintained them – townships, landowners, chari-table foundations. But many bridges had become the responsibility of the counties, and as time went by the tendency was for more and more to do so – even bridges built privately became a county responsibility, if they were of general usefulness.

Medieval bridge builders, when they built in stone rather than wood, had usually built massive ponderous structures which crossed wide rivers by a succession of small arches. In the eighteenth century the expansion of road traffic on wheels led to developments not only in road maintenance but also in bridge construction. Early civil engineers such as John Smeaton (1724–1792) started to build masonry bridges with wider spans, narrow piers and lighter appearance.

Bridges provided Thomas Telford (1757–1834) with his introduction to transport engineering: it was later that he became famous as a builder of canals and roads. Telford was the son of a Dumfriesshire shepherd. He served his apprenticeship as a stonemason at Langholm, then set out to build his career farther afield – successively in Edinburgh, London, Portsmouth and Shrewsbury. At this stage his ambition was to become an architect, but about 1787 he was appointed Surveyor of Public Works for the county of Salop. This appointment brought with it responsibility for bridges, and forty were built under his

direction during the years 1790–6. Montford Bridge, the first to his design, was built of sandstone between 1790 and 1792: the road it carried over the River Severn was later to become part of the London-to-Holyhead Road, for improvements to which throughout its length he was to become responsible some twenty-five years later. The bridge still stands (OS grid ref. SJ 432153), widened in recent years, and the road is now designated the A5.

At Montford Bridge Telford used well-established tech-niques, but when he started work the Severn had already been spanned for some ten years in the south of Shropshire by a structure which must have greatly excited his lively mind: the bridge of cast iron which gave its name to the adjoining town of Ironbridge. It was completed in 1779 and is generally considered the first metal bridge, although D. Nortcliffe (*Industrial Past*, spring 1980) has found con-vincing records of an ornamental iron footbridge built in

Ever since it was built in 1779 the iron bridge over the River Severn has been a feature of Ironbridge, the locality which took its name from the bridge itself. There is clearance beneath it for the masts of Severn trows, one of which is seen in the foreground. The photograph was taken in 1892, shortly before commercial traffic ceased to use this part of the river.

Paying tolls at toll gates (left) was a familiar experience to our ancestors, however rare it is today. This is the tollgate and house (which dates from 1769) at Swinford bridge, which is still privately owned and crosses the Thames near Eynsham. OS grid ref. SP 443087.

1769 in the grounds of Kirklees Hall, West Yorkshire, and regrettably dismantled in the 1840s. The iron bridge at Ironbridge was built by Shropshire ironmasters (principally Abraham Darby) for road traffic, replacing an earlier ferry, and it is with us yet (OS grid ref. SJ 673034): a striking structure, its arch reaching high above the river, with components dovetailed together and secured by wedges, a method reminiscent of timber bridges.

As Telford records in his *Life*, 'an uncommonly high flood in 1795 having destroyed the old Buildwas bridge, led me to consider a new mode of bridge building'. His new bridge over the Severn at Buildwas, designed the same year, was of cast iron: and although its span of 130 ft was 30 ft more than the Iron Bridge, its weight was less than half. This first iron bridge of Telford was replaced early in the present century, unfortunately from our point of view, for he was soon after to make much more use of iron both for road bridges, and for canal aqueducts, mentioned in the next chapter.

Coach Design Improves

Along with the gradual improvement in roads and bridges there came a gradual improvement in the vehicles that used them. Leaf springs were first used in the middle of the seventeenth century, but not as part of any modern form of suspension. Rather they were used in combination with the leather braces which slung a coach body from its carriage; gradually they came to replace solid upright posts and evolved in the nineteenth century into upright C springs conspicuous fore and aft. By the 1780s coach travel had become so smooth – compared with formerly – that it was actually possible to read a book while travel-ling, and driving coaches became so enjoyable an occupation that light open coaches were introduced for sporting owners to drive themselves. The type was given the name 'phaeton'.

The driver of a stage coach originally sat on a box seat mounted over the fore boot (for luggage) which was fixed rigidly above the front axle. The possibility of attaching seat and boot instead to the body of the coach was for a time resisted by coach proprietors, lest too soft a ride make drivers inattentive; but by the end of the eighteenth century both these and a hind boot had been incorporated with the body into a single structure. This enlarged body was carried on 'telegraph springs', so named after the coach in which they were first used. At each end of the vehicle, four semi-elliptic springs formed a horizontal square: the two crosswise ones were inverted, supporting the coach body at their centres, and were linked at their ends to the ends of the lengthwise springs, which were positioned over the axle-trees (although not, at the front, attached to the axle but to part of the carriage, for otherwise the axle would have been unable to swivel). The arrangement can be seen in the illustration of a mail coach on page 111. Telegraph springs were a highly ingenious arrangement, but they still left the vehicle with, in today's terms, a wholly un-sprung chassis, on which the body was mounted. The rigid

Use of six horses rather than four was unusual, and there is something peculiar about the relative proportions of the rear horses and the front of the coach: but this spirited engraving of 1780 gives a useful impression of the point to which stage-coach design had developed at that date. The perch, the single strong horizontal wooden beam linking front and rear pairs of wheels, is still prominent, and the large basket at the back for parcels and low-fare passengers has yet to develop into an enclosed rear boot.

enlarged body enabled several seats to be provided on the roof in comparative safety, and with it stage and mail coaches reached the form familiar to all during the remainder of the era of long-distance travel by horse-drawn coach, and to us today both from the many prints and engravings surviving from that period, and from the attentions of more recent designers of Christmas cards.

The Mail Coach System

The mail coach has just been mentioned. In the last decade of the eighteenth century, and the first three of the nineteenth, the requirements of the Post Office had immense influence on both coaching and roads. But as late as the early 1780s there was no sign of this. On the contrary, a conservative Post Office still clung to the ancient system of carrying mails by post-boys on horseback, or, very rarely, by mail cart. The letter post was not only slow and unpunctual, but also insecure: post-boys were often robbed.

Reform came not from within the Post Office but from without, in the person of John Palmer, theatrical manager of Bath. At this period a stage coach was already running between Bristol, Bath and London in seventeen hours – less than half the time taken by the post-boys – and although it and others like it were not allowed to carry letters, for this was a monopoly of the Post Office, they could and did carry parcels, some of which were no more than urgent letters in disguise.

To Palmer it appeared that the mails would be better carried by a fast coach guarded by an armed man. Through contacts he was able to put this scheme in 1782 to William Pitt, then aged twenty-three and already Chancellor of the Exchequer. Over the next two years the Post Office raised copious objections but Pitt became Prime Minister and Palmer was authorised to arrange a trial at his own expense between London and Bristol.

So the first mail coach left Bristol for London on 2 August 1784: travelling via Bath it made the journey overnight in one hour less than the stage-coach time. The service was successful and the following year was extended to fourteen other routes. The coaches were horsed by contractors: innkeepers along the route who were paid 3d a mile by the Post Office, the same rate that it paid for post-boys. It was later for coaches reduced to 1d a mile. Revenue from passengers and parcels – outside London there was no parcel post until the 1880s – provided contractors with their profit. At first four passengers were allowed, later more when passengers outside on the roof were permitted. In 1786 Palmer received Post Office recognition by appointment to the new post of Surveyor and Comptroller General of the Post Office.

Inevitably, perhaps, such an appointment provoked extreme animosity among existing Post Office officials; and since Palmer still had not got what he considered Pitt had promised, a totally free hand, he seems to have spent an excessive amount of time attempting to extend his own influence at the expense of his superiors, those two noblemen known in the usage of the time as Their Lordships the Postmaster General. So equally inevitably, perhaps, he was dismissed, in 1792 – or rather, his post was abolished and he retired on a pension.

Palmer's former subordinate, Thomas Hasker, became Surveyor and Superintendent of the Mail Coaches, and it was under Hasker that the mail coach system was developed and perfected. Within a few years it covered most main roads in Britain and the principal routes in Ireland. In 1797 at least twenty-two mail coach services radiated from London, and there were a further fourteen or more 'cross-post mails' between provincial centres. According to their schedules, Bristol was reached from London in 15 hours, Holyhead in 44 hours 50 minutes, Edinburgh in 57 hours 50 minutes. In fact, because the time in each locality still depended on its longitude (Greenwich Mean Time was still a thing of the future) the actual journey times must have been a few minutes longer: but the point here is that minutes now counted, where not long before schedules had been estimated in days.

The original mail coaches were little more than stage coaches with the addition of a locked boot over the rear axle for the mail and a guard who sat alongside the driver. Such vehicles proved insufficiently robust for their arduous new work, and coaches of a type patented by coach builder John Besant were adopted. In addition to various innovations which proved unworkable, the patent coach included two of lasting importance: the rear boot, with guard's seat above, was made as part of the coach body, and the wheels were securely fastened on by what became known as the mail axle. During assembly, a loose fitting flange was placed on the axle shaft, and a collar of lesser diameter was then welded to the shaft. The wheel was bolted to the flange which bore against the collar. Carriage wheels had traditionally been fastened by a linch pin through a slot in the end, which was prone to jump out

The wooden waggonway and waggon of 1765.

Causey Arch (OS grid ref. NZ 201559) was built in the 1720s to carry a branch of the Tanfield Waggonway across a narrow but deep ravine. By the standards of its time it was gigantic.

or break with consequent loss of the wheel.

Even these patent coaches were far from perfect. After travelling in one, Matthew Boulton described it as being 'loaded with iron trappings and unmechanical devices', and within a few years they had been replaced by coaches of the type fitted with telegraph springs described earlier. Soon after the adoption of the patent coach, however, Besant had entered into a partnership with another coach builder, John Vidler, but had then died suddenly: so it was Vidler and his successor who built, owned and maintained the mail coaches until expiry of their contract in 1836. Throughout, that is, the golden age of coaching: but that is described in chapter five.

Waggonways

During the seventeenth and eighteenth centuries, roads of another sort were coming into use. They were of limited length and local importance, little known outside their own immediate districts: and to those who did know them, the notion that they contained the germ of an idea which would eventually render orthodox roads obsolete for long distance transport, for the best part of a century, would have seemed fanciful. These were the waggonways, the Newcastle roads: on their wooden rails waggons were for the first time guided by flanged wheels. That is the essence of the railway.

Wooden railways originated in the mines of central Europe; in Britain, on the surface, the first was built about 1604 in Nottinghamshire, quickly followed by others in

Shropshire and North-East England. They were built by mine owners to carry coal. It was during the sixteenth century that coal had started to become an important fuel, as reserves of wood became depleted. 'Sea-coal' was shipped down the East Coast to London from Northumberland and Durham. To carry coal from pit to staithe or quay, waggonways were built – a few in the seventeenth century, far more in the eighteenth. Their use spread to other parts of Britain where there was a similar need – such as Cumberland, South Wales, Central Scotland – but always they were commonest in North-East England. To give an indication of their extent is not easy, but Dr M. J. T. Lewis (*Early Wooden Railways*) estimates that by 1800 there were some 290 miles of waggonway in use, half of this on Tyneside. Lengths of individual lines were quite short, usually only a few miles.

Where a coal owner wished to build a waggonway across the land of others, he obtained way leaves. In 1758 Charles Brandling (of a Tyneside family) obtained an Act of Parliament to confirm way-leave agreements that enabled him to make a waggonway to carry coal into Leeds from his colliery at Middleton south of the town. Much later, the Middleton line was to be the scene of Blenkinsop's and Murray's pioneer work with steam locomotives, described in chapter six.

This was the first time a railway was authorised by Parliament. The actual construction methods of waggonway builders were well established by the end of the eighteenth century and were described thus in a guide *The Picture of Newcastle upon Tyne . . .* published in 1807:

way waggons were far ahead of contemporary vehicles on ordinary roads: stage coaches were braked by the horses, which held them back when going downhill; this method was supplemented on the steepest hills by slipping the skid, a metal shoe attached to the coach by a chain, beneath one of the rear wheels, so that the coach ran on three wheels and the skid and was slowed down accordingly. Brakes as we understand them were first fitted to coaches only in the mid-1830s.

Where the lie of the land was such that a waggonway had to descend a slope too steep for laden waggons to run down by gravity alone in safety, self-acting inclined planes were built. Laden waggons about to go down an incline were attached to a rope which led, round a braked winding drum at its head, to the incline foot where empty waggons were attached to it. So the descending laden waggons were able to draw up the ascending empties, passing them en route.

The chaldron waggon (chaldron was a measure of coal: 53 cwt) of Tyneside waggonways was built with sides sloping outwards from the floor, in which was a trapdoor: when a loaded waggon arrived at a staithe it was positioned on an elevated track and the trapdoor opened to discharge the coal down a chute into a waiting vessel.

Wooden waggonways were in many cases rebuilt into later railways, or obliterated by later industrial developments, so traces of them are rare. The National Railway Museum has a length of track – two rails, two sleepers – and Greater Manchester Museum of Science and Industry has a single rail and sleeper. Both were recovered from mines. The most notable waggonway relic by far is Causey Arch (OS grid ref. NZ 201559) built for the Tanfield Waggonway in the 1720s. This waggonway ran southwards from the Tyne across a watershed, so since its loaded waggons had to be hauled uphill its engineering works were ambitious in order to keep the uphill grade as easy as possible. It crossed a valley at OS grid reference NZ 204561 by an embankment said to be 100 ft high, which was used by rail vehicles until 1962 – for that part of the Tanfield Waggonway was rebuilt as a steam railway which closed in that year – and it may see them again, for a preservation society is active. Causey Arch itself lacks that particular distinction, for it was disused by the early 1800s, but is otherwise even more remarkable: a single masonry arch of 105 ft span which crosses a deep ravine. The works of the Tanfield Waggonway were the wonder of the age in which they were built.

'The first thing to be done in making a railway is to level the ground in such a manner as to take off all sudden ascents and descents, to effect which, it is sometimes necessary to cut through hills and to raise an embankment to carry the road through vales. The road is formed of pieces of timber about six feet long, and six inches in diameter, which are laid across it, being eighteen or twenty four inches distant from each other.

'Upon these sleepers [*sic*] other pieces of timber, called rails, of four or five inches square, are laid in a lateral direction, four feet distant from each other. . . .'

That gauge between the rails of 4 ft was not invariable, but gauges of 4 ft to 5 ft were usual on Tyneside: they were appropriate for a large waggon pulled by a single horse. In Shropshire and some other parts of Britain, narrower gauges were used and small waggons coupled together. Where possible waggonways were built with a gentle downward slope in the direction taken by laden waggons: they ran down by gravity and the horse trotted behind. Speed was controlled by a brake block bearing on one of the wheels, applied by the driver (who sat on the projecting end of the brake lever). In this feature waggon-

The course of a waggonway built orginally in 1766 is now a footpath through the centre of Alloa, Clackmannanshire, at OS grid ref. NT 886928. The tunnel takes it beneath a street.

Other waggonway traces can be found: I mentioned the courses of the Tranent-Cockenzie Waggonway of 1722 and the Alloa Waggonway of 1766 in *The Archaeology of Railways*. Lewis's *Early Wooden Railways*, Morgan's *Railway Relics* and Warn's *Waggonways and Early Railways of Northumberland* give many other locations (and about complete the literature of the subject). In West Yorkshire, traces of the Flockton Waggonway can be seen: the mouth of a tunnel at OS grid reference SE 255158 (the road at this point passes above it), a viaduct at SE 253153 visible from the same point and an overbridge at SE 256162. These date probably from the early 1800s.

By that date, changes were coming into the waggonway world. Wheels of cast iron had probably been used as early as the 1730s, and iron rails were first cast at Coalbrookdale, Shropshire, in 1767, for use on local waggonways. They were no more than bars of rectangular cross-section which were fastened to the tops of existing wooden rails to reduce friction and wear – a rail of this type may be seen in Glasgow Museum of Transport. Then, as the guide quoted earlier put it in 1807, 'An improved method of making a railway, intirely of cast metal, has been lately introduced'. Rails wholly of cast iron were coming into service. But before considering this development – and there is more about it towards the end of chapter three – I want to say

something about transport by water: for although a few waggonways led from pit to point-of-sale at a nearby town, most led to a shipping point – on the coast, on a tidal river such as the Tyne or Wear, or a non-tidal river such as the Severn. The horse which could haul half a ton in a cart on a road could haul three tons on a waggonway, but, for bulk commodities such as coal, water transport was even more economical. It was also used by passengers.

Travellers used coastwise shipping as an alternative to land transport (between places such as London and Margate, and London and Leith) even though dependence on wind and weather made journey duration variable and times, or even dates, of arrival uncertain.

How Sailing Ships Evolved

As Laird Clowes pointed out in *Sailing Ships – their History and Development*, until the advent of the steam engine an ocean-going sailing ship was incomparably the most elaborate structure and the most complicated mechanism evolved by man. One may add that the ship continued to be so during the early development of the steam engine, until its successful application to vehicles and vessels early in the nineteenth century. But unlike land transport, which had then been developing rapidly over the previous half-century, sailing ship design had been evolving gradually for three centuries.

In medieval Europe, there had been two distinct lines of development. North European ships were descended from those of the Vikings: their bows and sterns were similar to each other, they were clinker-built and they gradually became less and less dependent on oars and more on their square sails. By the thirteenth century, the steering oar was being replaced by the rudder. In the Mediterranean, ships were descended from the galleys of classical times: carvel-built, with bow and stern of different shapes, and with triangular lateen sails adopted, about the ninth century, from the Arabs.

Then, early in the fifteenth century, these two traditions fused, to produce within a few years the three-masted ship, carvel-built, transom-sterned and square-rigged but for a lateen sail on the mizen mast. Manoeuvrable in adverse winds, such vessels could make ocean voyages: they enabled Columbus to discover America, Vasco da Gama to set up the trade route to India round the Cape of Good Hope. With the introduction of cannon (first recorded in an English ship late in the fifteenth century) design of war-

Sailing ships at the end of the eighteenth century would have seemed to our eyes short in relation to their beam. These proportions are perpetuated in the shape of the locks of the Caledonian Canal, which were set at 170 ft by 40 ft so that they could take a 32-gun frigate.

ships diverged from that of merchant ships; but both settled down to a long period of gradual detailed improvement. Top masts, which carried additional sails but could be lowered to the deck in bad weather, were introduced in the sixteenth century. Jib sails appeared at the same period. Gaff sails evolved from lateen sails and the fore-and-aft rigged schooner came into use. Wheel steering replaced the tiller. By the end of the eighteenth century a full-rigged ship bore some thirty-seven sails, about six times as many as the ships of the time of Columbus. The size of ships, though they were still small by modern standards, continued to increase – the usual size of an East Indiaman, 400 tons burden (with a carrying capacity of 400 tons, that is) at the beginning of the eighteenth century, had increased to 1,200 tons at the end. But most sailing vessels were much smaller than this – of 200 tons burden or less – and their variety, in name, type and purpose, was great.

The proportions of ships of this period were strange to our eyes – short in relation to breadth, for ease of putting about. The length of a sailing vessel about 1800 was often no more than four times her beam: these proportions are reflected in the dimensions of the locks of the Caledonian Canal, which were set in 1804 at 170 ft by 40 ft so that the canal could take a 32-gun frigate.

Wooden ships, like wooden rails, being perishable

things, few actual early vessels remain. The fate of the *Golden Hind*, in which Drake circumnavigated the globe, must surely be an object lesson to all later transport preservationists: put into a dry dock after her return to England in 1580, that she might be preserved for all time, she had, a century later, collapsed from decay. Norse vessels, buried, have been excavated, and the wreck of the fifteenth-century *Mary Rose* is being brought to the surface as I write: but the oldest full-size ship surviving complete in Britain is HMS *Victory*, at Portsmouth, built in 1765 and forty years later Nelson's flagship at Trafalgar. Her length of 226 ft is almost the maximum to which a wooden ship can be built. Two much smaller craft of this period which do survive are the 26 ft 5 in. clinker-built yacht of 1780 at the Windermere Steamboat Museum and the *Peggy*, a 26-ft yacht of 1791 at the Nautical Museum, Castletown, Isle of Man. Apart from these, to appreciate the appearance of pre-1800 shipping one is dependent on the spirited and detailed paintings of contemporary marine artists, and on collections of models – some of them contemporary models – such as those at the National Maritime Museum and the Royal Scottish Museum.

While the design of large ships was gradually evolving, that of small vessels had much less tendency to change. The most striking example is the keel, or small coal-carrying vessel of the East of England. Its survival, in the form of the Humber keels which traded under sail until the 1940s, and still do under power, is so well known as to be almost a cliché; yet it was still a surprise to the author to encounter, in the Royal Scottish Museum, a model of a Tyne coal keel of *c.* 1360 and see at once how closely its proportions, its bluff bow and stern and its square sail, resembled the Humber keel familiar from photographs taken early in the present century. The sight of a square-sailed keel in action has been made reality again by the Humber Keel and Sloop Preservation Society, which in a most worthy effort has purchased the keel *Comrade* (built of steel, but to the traditional pattern, in 1923) and restored her to sail.

As the East Coast coal trade increased, coal was carried in larger vessels and keels came to be used mainly on estuaries and inland waters: on the Humber and waterways radiating from it for general cargo, and on the Tyne tideway to carry coal from waggonway staithes to waiting ships. From the ships on the Thames tideway, lighters carried coal up river; and from them, originally no more than flat-bottomed rectangular boxes, the Thames sailing barge evolved as a general purpose carrier for the Thames estuary. On other large estuaries there evolved sailing barges of similar purpose but distinct design – for builders on each estuary were isolated from the others – trows on the Severn, flats on the Mersey, gabbarts on the Clyde. Many of these worked not only on estuaries but also far inland on navigable rivers.

Navigable Rivers

The largest rivers – such as Severn, Thames and Trent – have been important as highways for the passage of boats containing goods and people since time immemorial. Usually, in the Middle Ages, such large rivers contained enough water to be navigable naturally: for boats to be hauled up them by gangs of men, or later on by horses, and to drift down with the stream. They were assisted in each direction by sails. But navigation was still liable to interruption from floods and droughts, from silting of channels and obstruction by mill dams. To maintain rivers open for navigation, the Crown often put them in the care of city corporations – as early as 1197 the Mayor and Corporation of the City of London were placed in charge of the Thames. In 1424 an Act of Parliament appointed a commission of local landowners to scour and improve the River Lee and levy tolls to pay for the work, a form of administration much used later.

So that boats could pass a mill dam, part of the weir was made to open after sufficient water had been run off for there to be a near level above and below it. The same arrangement – a weir with an opening gate – was used to help boats going upstream over shallows, by shutting the gate to hold up the water after the boat had passed through, and downstream over shallows by riding the 'flash' of water caused by opening the gate. Such was the device called, according to type and district, the flash lock, navigation weir, water gate or staunch. To pass them was slow and time consuming, but they remained in use on the upper Thames until the present century.

In a pound lock the chamber has lock gates at each end communicating with the river above and below the weir, and sluices called paddles to raise or lower the water level in the lock to that of the river upstream or down. It was quicker to use than the flash lock and did not affect water levels in the main river. This is, of course, the type of lock familiar on rivers and canals today. It was introduced to Britain from the Continent in the sixteenth century and

first used on the Exeter Canal which was built, two centuries ahead of its time, in 1564–6 by Exeter Corporation to make the town accessible from the Exe estuary; the River Exe, to which it runs parallel, had become obstructed by weirs and shoals. The first pound lock on a river was probably built on the River Lee in 1577; on the Thames below Oxford three early pound locks were built between 1624 and 1635.

Small rivers and streams were made navigable by means of flash locks, pound locks and dredging. This work was sometimes undertaken by individuals under letters patent from the Crown, such as William Sandys who between 1636 and 1640 made the Warwickshire Avon navigable from its confluence with the Severn, at Tewkesbury, up

to Stratford. More often it was done by commissioners appointed by an Act of Parliament, or by companies of undertakers appointed by one. In return for making or improving their river navigations, and maintaining them, they were empowered to levy tolls on goods carried along them.

In this way a few rivers were made navigable in the seventeenth century, and far more during the first three-quarters of the eighteenth. They included the Wey, the Kennet, the Thames from Oxford up to Lechlade, the Bristol Avon up to Bath, the Weaver, the Mersey and Irwell up to Manchester, the Aire and Calder up to Leeds and Wakefield, the Welland up to Stamford and the Great Ouse up to Bedford. By the 1760s only upland parts of

The River Kennet was made navigable between 1715 and 1723; locks were made with sloping sides of turf, since water was plentiful and seepage unimportant. Later, frameworks of redundant bridge rail from broad gauge track were provided by the GWR to keep boats away from the sides. This is Sheffield lock, OS grid ref. SU 649706.

England were more than a few miles from a navigable river or the sea. A curious survivor from this period is the Linton Lock Navigation – 9¾ miles of the Yorkshire Ouse, with one lock (at OS grid ref. SE 499602) – which has survived two centuries of change elsewhere in the continuing care of commissioners appointed under an Act of 1767. But by that date, although improvement of rivers continued, it must already have begun to seem old-fashioned, for the era of wholly artificial canals had commenced.

CHAPTER THREE

Canals and Tramroads

The Duke and his Canal

As river navigations developed during the eighteenth century, so they came to include longer and longer sections of artificial cut or side canal. These cuts shortened routes and avoided shallows. The year 1742 saw completion of the first canal in the British Isles to cross a watershed: the Newry Canal, in Ireland. It linked Lough Neagh to the Irish Sea and so completed a route for coal mined in County Tyrone to reach Dublin. This canal lasted, in navigable order, until the 1940s and enough still remains for it to be currently the object of an extensive restoration scheme. In 1756 a more ambitious canal, the Grand Canal, was authorised, with the intention of linking Dublin with the River Shannon. But although work started it was to take many years to complete, and the canal which is generally considered to signify the start of the canal era is the one built between 1759 and 1765 by the young Duke of Bridgewater (1736–1803). From his coal mine at Worsley he built it to Manchester, $7\frac{1}{2}$ miles to the east, the better to sell his coal cheaply and advantageously there.

Coal owners elsewhere – such as Brandling at Leeds – had long solved similar problems by building waggonways, and why the duke decided to innovate and build a canal is not clear. He had, however, had ample opportunity to become aware of the potential of canals. He had been educated in part abroad and had inspected the remarkable Canal du Midi in France. This had been built between 1666 and 1681 to connect the Mediterranean with the Atlantic: it was 149 miles long with 101 locks and a summit 620 ft above sea level. Much nearer home the duke was aware that an Act of 1755 to make navigable the Sankey Brook from the Mersey up to St Helens was being used by engineer Henry Berry (who had been a pupil of Thomas Steers, engineer of the Newry Canal) as authority to build

a continuous side canal which used the brook only for water supply; and also that two proposals to bring a waterway to Worsley had already come to nothing. At any rate, despite the need to obtain an Act of Parliament, it was a canal, not a waggonway, that he built.

In this work the duke was much aided by two men – John Gilbert and James Brindley. Gilbert was his factor for the Worsley estate, and since management of an estate in those days included management of any coal mines upon it, he was an experienced mining engineer. He was also, as it happens, a close friend of Matthew Boulton, to whose father he had been apprenticed. It was Gilbert whose brilliant idea it was to kill three birds with one stone: a new sough, or drainage tunnel, was driven into the hillside at Worsley to meet the mine workings within. The canal commenced at the sough exit, so the sough not only drained the mine, it provided the canal with a supply of water and enabled boats to travel up it into the mine to be loaded.

An extensive underground canal network eventually developed, and though the colliery has now long been closed, the canal entrance can still be seen at Worsley Delph (OS grid ref. SD 748005), and water draining from the disused workings still supplies the Bridgewater Canal – conspicuously so for it discolours the canal for considerable distance.

It was also Gilbert who introduced the duke to Brindley. James Brindley (1716–72), brilliant though semi-literate millwright, had already adapted his millwright's experience to drain a coal mine at Clifton, near Worsley, in a scheme which involved both extensive tunnelling and a waterwheel driven pump. In 1758 Earl Gower (1721–1803), politician and the duke's brother-in-law, had employed him to survey a canal from the Trent at Wilden Ferry near Derby up to the Potteries which lay far above the river's navigable limit. Smeaton, already noted for river improvements, had suggested that this might be extended over the watershed to join a river flowing westwards to the sea.

Brindley came to the duke's canal as, in effect, consulting engineer, and before long plans had been changed. Instead of terminating as originally planned in Salford, on the opposite bank of the River Irwell from Manchester, the line of the duke's canal was altered to cross over the Mersey & Irwell Navigation at Barton by an aqueduct, and run into Manchester itself. Brindley's Barton Aqueduct had no precedent in Britain: the spectacle it presented, of boats on the canal passing high in the air over barges on the river, immediately caught the imagination of the public and it became famous. It was eventually replaced in the 1890s, when the course of the Mersey & Irwell Navigation at this point was adopted for the Manchester Ship Canal, by the famous Barton Swing Aqueduct; but the north abutment of Brindley's aqueduct can still be seen, immediately to the west of the Bridgewater Canal on its present alignment, at OS grid reference SJ 766977.

As early as 1761, long before the canal reached Manchester, the duke had started work on a branch which diverged from it at Stretford, a couple of miles on the Manchester side of Barton, and ran in a south-westerly direction. Initially this enabled him to sell his coal in the towns of Cheshire; then, by completing the original line to Manchester and extending the branch to meet the Mersey estuary at Runcorn, the duke provided a canal/estuary route for general trade between Manchester and Liverpool which was independent of the Mersey & Irwell Navigation. But this was not completed until 1776; by then much had happened elsewhere.

A Canal Network

The scheme for a canal from the Trent to the Potteries had taken shape as the Grand Trunk or Trent & Mersey Canal. Josiah Wedgwood was one of the main promoters; Brindley was engineer. It might be best, it was thought, to administer this canal through a trust similar to a turnpike trust; this was the time of the Turnpike Mania and in the region of the Potteries alone demand for improved transport led to establishment of thirteen new turnpike trusts during the period 1761–72. But instead, for the canal, a joint stock company was formed. It was incorporated by Act of Parliament on 14 May 1766, with powers to purchase compulsorily the land needed for the canal, and to levy tolls on goods eventually carried along it; and unlike the powers of turnpike trusts, the powers of the canal company were perpetual. It was to be the precedent in general terms for all subsequent canal companies and, in due course, railway companies.

North-west from the Potteries, the T & M Canal was authorised (and eventually built) to pass beneath the watershed in a 2,880-yard-long tunnel at Harecastle, and then to descend into Cheshire to join not a river but the duke's canal at Preston Brook near Runcorn. The dimensions of the boats to use it, and so of the canal works themselves, were derived from the boats in use on the duke's canal. For although the surface part of this canal was being built large enough and wide enough to take Mersey flats, within the Worsley mine smaller boats, 50 ft long by 7 ft beam, were used and when loaded towed several at a time to Manchester. From these Brindley evolved the concept of the narrow boat, about 70 ft long by 7 ft beam, and the narrow canal, with suitably narrow channel, bridges, tunnels and locks. Not only did this greatly reduce construction costs compared with those for a barge canal twice as wide, but it also minimised water consumption, a point of vital importance where a watershed had to be crossed and supplies were restricted. The boats themselves, in which a load of up to 30 tons could be drawn by a single horse, were still large enough to show substantial economies over road transport. Except for a few miles at each end which were made wide enough for barges from the Mersey and the Trent the T & M Canal was built as a narrow canal.

To live in while supervising construction of the west end of his canal, the Duke of Bridgewater built Bridgewater House, Runcorn (OS grid ref. SJ 504331). The flight of locks beside it by which the canal descended to the Mersey has long since been filled in, but the house still faces the much later, and larger, Manchester Ship Canal and is used by the ship canal company.

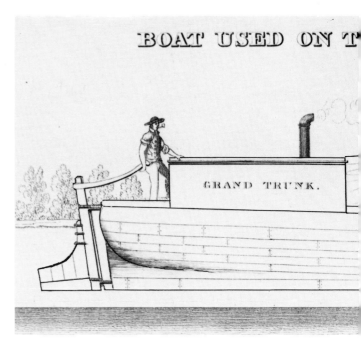

The hull form of this early nineteenth-century narrow boat (above) is more elegant than that of both the starvationers from which it is descended and the later iron- and steel-hulled narrow boats. 'Grand Trunk' was an alternative name for the Trent & Mersey. The plate first appeared in W. Strickland's 1826 Report on Canals, Railways, Roads and other Subjects made to the Pennsylvania Society for the Promotion of Internal Improvement *and was repeated in* F. W. Simm's Public Works of Great Britain *(1838) from which it is here reproduced.*

A Worsley mine boat (left), or 'starvationer' (so nicknamed, probably, from its exposed ribs), is preserved at the National Mining Museum, Lound Hall. Several sizes of boats were used – this is one of the largest, about 48 ft long, and it was from boats of this type that the classic narrow boat of the English canals developed.

Brindley's first aqueduct, at Barton on the Bridgewater Canal, gave him a lot of trouble: his later aqueducts, such as this one (below) by which the Trent & Mersey Canal crosses over the River Dove at OS grid ref. SK 268269, are solid and substantial almost to excess.

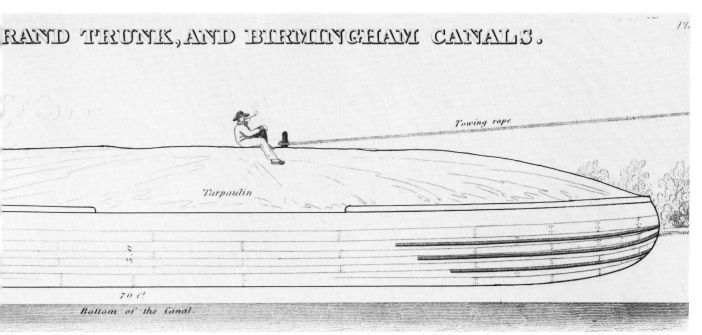

RAND TRUNK, AND BIRMINGHAM CANALS.

Towing rope

Tarpaulin

Bottom of the Canal.

Great Haywood, Staffordshire (below), is a focal point of the canal system: here, at OS grid ref. SJ 995229, the Staffordshire & Worcestershire Canal joins the Trent & Mersey, emerging under the bridge which carries the latter's towpath. The narrow boats, former trading craft, make an interesting comparison with Strickland's engraving and show how little narrow boat design altered throughout the years of canal-borne trade.

To make his artificial canals watertight, Brindley used clay puddle. Much later, this improbable substance was defined by Telford in his autobiography: 'water tight earth, formed by wetting earth to fluidity in an enclosed space, and then turning and working it with a shovel, until it has acquired that alluvial state which experience has shown to be requisite; it is then left to settle, and when the water has evaporated from the sediment, a similar stratum of alluvial earth is superadded from time to time, and this rises with the canal bank, in which it forms a concealed wall of earth, impermeable to water.'

Even while the Trent & Mersey Canal was being planned, there were thoughts of connecting it to the River Severn. These took shape as the Staffordshire & Worcestershire Canal, incorporated on the same day as the T & M, to run from the Trent & Mersey at Great Haywood, Staffs, to the Severn at Stourport near Bewdley. Brindley was surveyor. Then in 1768 and 1769 came Acts for the Coventry and Oxford Canals, to connect the T & M at Fradley near Lichfield with the Thames at Oxford, and so complete what Brindley called the cross, the canal link between Trent, Mersey, Severn and Thames. From these canals there were authorised branch canals, notably the Birmingham Canal from the Staffs & Worcs near Wolverhampton to the town of its name. Many of these canals were laid out by Brindley, and the engineers whom he had taught, as contour canals, hugging hillside contours to minimise earthworks despite increased lengths of route. On the Oxford and Birmingham Canals this principle was followed to an exaggerated extent and can still be noted, conspicuously, in the course of the Oxford Canal in the vicinity of Wormleighton, Warwickshire.

Other important canals were authorised at this period. The Forth & Clyde, its route finally settled, received its Act in 1768. Smeaton was engineer and the canal, to run from the Forth at the place now called Grangemouth to Bowling on the Clyde, was built large enough for small ships – in scale the most ambitious canal so far. The Leeds & Liverpool Canal too, authorised in 1770, was built with wide but short locks to suit the keels using the Aire & Calder Navigation which it joined at Leeds.

With the exception of the last mentioned, all these canals had been authorised before any of them had been completed. The first narrow canal to be opened was a short section from Bedworth to Coventry, needed to supply that city with coal: it was opened in August 1769. But others soon followed, and when Brindley died of diabetes and overwork in September 1772, it was at least with the satisfaction of knowing that the Staffordshire & Worcestershire and Birmingham Canals were open, and so were parts of the Oxford and Coventry Canals, and the Trent & Mersey for $48\frac{1}{2}$ miles from the Trent up to Stone, Staffordshire. It was completed in 1777. The Forth & Clyde was open from Grangemouth to Glasgow (by a short branch from the main line) by 1777 also, but lack of funds prevented its opening through to the Clyde until 1790. Such delays in canal construction were not uncommon: it took until the same year to complete Brindley's cross. The previous year two water routes which linked Birmingham with London had come into being, both of them roundabout. One was by the Staffs & Worcs Canal, the River Severn and the newly-opened Thames & Severn Canal to the Thames at Lechlade; the other, by the Birmingham & Fazeley Canal which joined the Coventry Canal near Tamworth and so gave access via the Oxford Canal to the Thames at Oxford.

Completion of these canals, and their evident success not only in general usefulness but also in return to investors did not go unnoticed by the public. The Duke of Bridgewater, having borrowed astronomically to complete his canals, was reaping an ample reward. The Birmingham Canal paid a 23 per cent dividend for 1789, the little $11\frac{3}{4}$-mile Erewash Canal, running north from the Trent along the Derbyshire–Nottinghamshire border, paid a first dividend of $2\frac{1}{2}$ per cent for 1783, reached 20 per cent for 1787, and 30 per cent for 1794.

The consequence of results such as these was the self-inflating speculative financial bubble called the Canal Mania. During the years 1791 to 1796 inclusive, 51 new canals were authorised by Parliament, 20 of them in 1793 alone. Many more had been proposed. But of those that were authorised, some were not completed or if they were took many years, even decades, to reach completion. The wars with France, which commenced in 1793 following the French Revolution, and the inflation which accompanied them, diverted both attention and resources. Nevertheless the developments of this period, added to the canals and navigable rivers already existing, provided central England with a network of inland waterways extending between Surrey, Somerset, Lancashire and Yorkshire. In Ireland, canals linked Dublin with the Rivers Shannon and Barrow; in the valleys of South Wales and Monmouthshire short canals built to link ironworks with ports became extremely busy.

The Great Canal Engineers

Such rapid expansion of the canal network produced an unprecedented demand for engineering skills. Of the many who were attracted to the profession of canal engineer at this period, the foremost was William Jessop (1745–1814). Jessop had been apprenticed to Smeaton. His first work on his own account was to survey improvements to the Aire & Calder Navigation: these included the Selby Canal, which bypassed a constricted section of river. It was authorised in 1774, built under Jessop's direction and opened in 1778. In the 1780s he improved the navigation of the Trent, to which canals were bringing extra traffic.

The first important canal, independent of a river, for which Jessop was engineer was the Cromford Canal, authorised in 1789 and completed five years later. It extended the Erewash Canal to Sir Richard Arkwright's Derbyshire cotton-mill village of Cromford – Arkwright was one of the promoters. In constructing the Cromford Canal Jessop worked with a local surveyor, Benjamin Outram, as his full-time superintendent, and in 1792 he joined Outram and others in a newly-formed partnership which became the Butterley Company: owners of mines and quarries in the vicinity of the canal and above all iron founders and engineers.

In the mid-1780s Jessop became in effect consulting engineer to the Grand Canal Company in Ireland, and in 1793 he became chief engineer to a canal of comparable significance in England: the Grand Junction Canal. This was to be built with a main line $93\frac{1}{2}$ miles long providing a direct link between London and the Midlands. It joined the Oxford Canal at Braunston, Northants, taking a much more direct route than the roundabout one via the Thames and Oxford. It was eventually completed in 1805; at the London end it joined the Thames at Brentford but a branch approached the edge of central London at Paddington. This canal was built with wide locks, which were able to take a pair of narrow boats, a barge off the Thames, or a barge off the Trent or the Mersey if, as then seemed likely, wide canals were built, or narrow canals widened, to those waterways. Such wide links were never completed, but lengths of wide canal, built in anticipation, remain isolated in the narrow canal network of the Midlands. Leicestershire's Ashby Canal, which branches off the Coventry Canal, is one of them.

Throughout most of the period that Jessop was occupied with construction of the Grand Junction Canal, he was also being consulted about another important canal. This was

John Rennie's canals are notable for the fine architectural treatment given to their main features. This aqueduct carries the Lancaster Canal over the River Lune at OS grid ref. SD 484639.

the Rochdale Canal, authorised in 1794. Here as elsewhere a resident engineer worked under his direction. The Rochdale Canal ran from the Bridgewater Canal at Manchester to Rochdale and then on over the Pennines to Sowerby Bridge; here it met the Calder & Hebble Navigation, where Smeaton had been making rivers navigable at about the same time that Brindley had been engineering the duke's canal. The wide Rochdale Canal was the first of three trans-Pennine canals to be completed, in 1804.

In his work on this canal Jessop had the benefit of earlier surveys done by John Rennie – it had taken the canal company three attempts to get its Act of Parliament. John Rennie (1761–1821), after an education which included a spell at Edinburgh University, had set himself up as a millwright – his activities included construction of steam-driven mills in association with Boulton & Watt. His canals, however, (and the principal ones are the Kennet & Avon, which completed a direct route between London and Bristol, and the Lancaster) are notable for the fine architectural treatment given to features such as aqueducts. His career also came to include design of road bridges, and both he and Jessop dealt also with harbours, docks and land drainage works.

The speculative excesses of the Canal Mania are well exemplified by the Ellesmere Canal, which received its Act of Parliament in 1793. It was intended to provide a link along the Welsh border between the Mersey and the Dee, in the north, and the Severn at Shrewsbury to the south; but it was never completed in this form and what it eventually did provide was a link in a generally east-west direction between the Welsh border country and the main canal network, with a separate section between the Mersey and the Dee at Chester. It would be unimportant today but for two things: it brought Thomas Telford into canal engineering, at first as general agent and engineer under William Jessop who was principal engineer, and later with full responsibility for construction; and the rugged country through which it passed produced the canals' most spectacular and best-known engineering works, the aqueducts at Pontcysyllte, Clwyd (OS grid ref. SJ 271420) and Chirk (SJ 286372). Together with their surrounding scenery they make this the most popular of pleasure cruising canals.

The factual details of Pontcysyllte aqueduct are easily stated: iron trough carried on stone piers, 19 spans, 1,007 ft long, maximum height 121 ft above the River Dee, work commenced in 1795 but most of the structure built between 1800 and 1805. But the origin of the design – and in particular the decision to use relatively light cast iron instead of stone for the spans, which in turn enabled the aqueduct to be built so high and so long, and eliminated the need for seven or eight locks down each side of the valley to a low-level stone aqueduct – the origin of this remains uncertain, and the subject of continuing historical speculation and research.

Use of cast iron for bridges, and also the construction of canal aqueducts, were both then still novelties, so that the combination of the two in a structure so immense, and so self-confident in design, is the more remarkable. Douglas Hague and Stephen Hughes in the *Bulletin* of the Association for Industrial Archaeology (vol. 9, no. 4, 1982) draw attention to Pont-y-Cafnau, a structure still to be seen in Merthyr Tydfil (OS grid ref. SO 037071). Pont-y-Cafnau was a combination of aqueduct (to carry a water channel for water power) and bridge (for an iron-railed tramroad) and was built of iron in 1793 by Cyfarthfa Ironworks. It spans the River Taff, an A-framed structure of design similar to a roof truss.

Pont-y-Cafnau was sketched by the Shropshire ironmaster William Reynolds in 1794, and in 1795 Longdon-on-Tern aqueduct for the Shrewsbury Canal was built on similar principles: Reynolds was one of the promoters of the canal and Telford had recently been appointed engineer. The idea of making it of iron, however, came from the chairman of the canal committee, Thomas Eyton. This aqueduct is still to be seen at OS grid reference SJ 617517 although the canal is abandoned; the aqueduct is scheduled as an ancient monument. In the same year that it was built Telford designed his first road bridge of iron to cross the Severn at Buildwas.

Yet Jessop too was well placed to originate the idea of iron for Pontcysyllte aqueduct. Benjamin Outram, his partner in Butterley Ironworks, was engineer to the Derby Canal and, also in 1795, designed a small iron aqueduct for it. He was, too, engineer to the Peak Forest Canal, then building in Cheshire, and in 1795 an iron aqueduct was proposed for this at Marple; eventually, however, a high masonry aqueduct was built.

What is certain is that Telford regarded successful construction of Longdon aqueduct in iron as establishing the practicability of its use at Pontcysyllte, and furthermore that the bulk of the design and construction work at Pontcysyllte was done under Telford's direction, for Jessop seems to have played little part in the Ellesmere Canal after about 1801.

Robert Fulton and Small Canals

The suggestion for an iron aqueduct at Marple had come not from Outram but from the contractor building part of the canal. This was Robert Fulton, who had just paid a visit to Reynolds's foundry at Coalbrookdale where the plates for Longdon Aqueduct were being cast. Indeed, Philip Cohen suggests (*Transactions* of the Newcomen Society, vol. 51, p. 135) that it was only after this visit that Outram too visited Reynolds's works and then designed his own small Derby Canal iron aqueduct, even though this was completed before Longdon.

So Robert Fulton (1765–1815) enters the story and deserves extended mention – not because of the part he played in construction of British canals which was marginal, but because of the central part he was soon to play in the successful introduction of steam navigation.

He was born in Pennsylvania, still at the time a British colony; he was probably of Irish descent. The American War of Independence took place during his childhood and early teens: an impressionable age, and certainly he grew up to have strong republican sympathies. These did not prevent him from coming to England, however, in about 1786. He had already established himself in Philadelphia as an artist, and one of merit; in England he was successful enough to exhibit at the Royal Academy.

Then, in 1793, at the height of the Canal Mania, he deserted painting for engineering. His attention was first drawn to canals by reading in that year a description of one projected by the Earl of Stanhope. This canal was to carry sea-sand, as a fertiliser, from Bude to the interior of Devon and Cornwall, and with Lord Stanhope Fulton got in touch.

Charles, Third Earl of Stanhope (1753–1816), although a public figure, proved to be a kindred spirit. He was a supporter of reform at home and revolution in France – wits had called him Citizen Stanhope – and he was also a noted scientist and inventor. His experiments on steam boats, and those of Fulton which followed, will be described in the next chapter. Here we are concerned with his ideas on canals.

What Lord Stanhope was proposing was a tub-boat canal. The tub-boat canal was a concept which, like the narrow-boat canal, had its origin in the mines and mine boats of Worsley. Earl Gower, following the example of his brother-in-law the duke, had built, about 1765, a small and level canal to carry coal from his mine at Donnington Wood in east Shropshire for $5\frac{1}{2}$ miles to a point near Newport, Salop, from which it was sold. The boats on this canal were even smaller than those at Worsley and carried only 3 tons each; like the Worsley mine boats, these 'tub boats' were towed in trains.

The Donnington Wood Canal was the first section to be built of what became an intricate little network of tub-boat canals in east Shropshire – the Shrewsbury Canal mentioned above formed part of it – and on another part, the Ketley Canal, William Reynolds built an inclined plane. Between two levels of the canal, one 73 feet above the other, tub-boats were raised or lowered on wheeled cradles which ran on rails on a self-acting inclined plane similar to those on waggonways. The Ketley inclined plane was built about 1788; it was the first built in Britain and the first of several which were built on the Shropshire canals. But the idea was not new: inclined planes for canals had been built on the Continent, and Lord Stanhope's Bude Canal proposal was a revival of an earlier scheme which included them. By 1793 Stanhope's plan was that the levels of the canal would be connected by iron tramroads of such easy gradient that the tub boats, which would be fitted with wheels, could be drawn up them by horses.

It was interest in the Ketley plane which had taken Fulton to visit Reynolds in 1795. By then, building on the foundation of a continuing exchange of ideas with Stanhope, he was rapidly increasing his experience of canals and developing his own ideas about them. He spent some time in the Manchester area, probably initially to study the Bridgewater Canal, and it was then that he successfully tendered for construction of part of the Peak Forest Canal, authorised in 1794. Just how much work he did on it is not clear, for at about the same time he was seeking a contract to cut part of the Gloucester & Berkeley Canal. This canal, authorised in 1793, was a big one: it was intended to enable ships up to 300 tons burden to reach Gloucester.

To cut it, Fulton proposed to use a digging machine of his own devising. It was to be drawn by horses: an endless chain of buckets driven from the front axle was to cut the earth and deliver it to a raised platform, from which rotating arms driven from the rear axle were to bat it sideways on to the growing canal bank. This concept was not transformed into reality, nor was Fulton's tender accepted; but in his ideas can be seen a forerunner of the mechanical excavators of a later age. The canal itself was made, like other canals, by pick and shovel, and took until 1827 to complete.

While Fulton was attempting to design a digging machine for big canals he was also developing his ideas on small ones. They were eventually published in 1796 as his *A Treatise on the Improvement of Canal Navigation . . .*; this was paid for in part by the Peak Forest company. The theme of the book is extension of canals cheaply into poor and hilly districts; the means by which this is to be done, construction of tub-boat canals, wheeled boats, inclined planes, vertical lifts, iron aqueducts and all these in combination. It is in other words a digest of the latest and most advanced ideas on canals, with further developments conceived by Fulton himself. Considering how short a time he had been involved with canals, it was a remarkable feat, and a foretaste of the way in which he would tackle steamboat design a few years later.

By the end of 1796 Fulton's ideas were bringing him attention but little income. He saw them, however, as being applicable to other countries than Britain (a copy of the book was despatched to George Washington); by April

The Hay inclined plane, Ironbridge (OS grid ref. SJ 695027) raised and lowered tub-boats on cradles between two levels of the Shropshire Canal – without it, thirty-seven locks would have been needed. When the weight of an ascending boat exceeded that of a descending one, a steam engine at the top provided power. Track of normal railway type, as used during the canal's last years, has been reinstated by the Ironbridge Gorge Museum Trust. Built in 1792–3, this incline was among the earliest instances of the use of steam power for transport.

Robert Fulton illustrated his book A Treatise on the improvement of Canal Navigation *with engravings made from his own drawings. This is his scheme for an inclined plane for tub-boats with wheels, powered by a cistern of water descending a shaft alongside. Two boats attached to a continuous chain are approaching top and bottom of the incline, and a third has been drawn out of the top canal and over the hump by another chain and awaits its turn to descend.*

In this illustration (right) in his Treatise, *Robert Fulton combined contemporary thinking on inclined planes with that on iron bridges and aqueducts to produce this proposal for crossing rivers and gaining height simultaneously.*

1797 he had obtained the patronage of a wealthy American who considered that Fulton should, before tackling the USA, seek acceptance for his proposals – and a patent – in France. So despite the war it was for France that the American, Fulton, departed, arriving in Paris in the summer of 1797. His subsequent activities are described in the next chapter.

The Bude Canal was eventually built with both inclined planes and wheeled tub-boats which ran on them, though it did not get its Act of Parliament until 1819 and was opened in 1823. It was active until the 1890s; traces of the planes are still visible and one of the wheeled boats is preserved in Exeter Maritime Museum.

Of the Shropshire tub-boat canals and their planes there are substantial traces near Ironbridge, partially restored by the Ironbridge Gorge Museum Trust. The Hay inclined plane, built 1792–3, lowered tub boats of the Shropshire Canal 207 feet down the side of the Severn gorge; it has been cleared of undergrowth and rail tracks have been restored as part of the trust's Blist's Hill open-air museum. The canal level above the plane has also been restored, where it is within the museum, and upon it floats one of the canal's tub boats.

Large Canals

One of the objects of the Gloucester & Berkeley Canal mentioned above was to enable vessels to bypass a particularly meandering and hazardous part of the Severn estuary. The Thames & Medway Canal, authorised in 1800, had a similar purpose: running direct from Gravesend to Strood it much reduced the distance to be travelled by sailing barges passing between the Thames and the Medway. But to do so it needed a tunnel nearly 4,000 yards long, and this was made with a bore 26 ft 6 in. wide and 35 ft high (including 8 ft depth of water). It took until 1824 to complete the canal.

This period of large canals produced also the Caledonian Canal, through the Great Glen of Scotland from one coast near Inverness to the other near Fort William. In 1801 Telford was employed by the government to visit, survey and report on the Highlands and their communications. His recommendations included constructing roads, building bridges, and making the Caledonian Canal.

That name was given to the canal by Telford himself, but the idea was older. Telford consulted Watt over his earlier survey, and the captain of the government galley on Loch Ness, which had originally been placed there by General Wade, provided soundings of the loch. This and three other freshwater lochs occupied a substantial length of the glen: sections of artificial canal were needed to link them together and to the sea. In 1803 two government commissions were set up by Parliament: one to build roads and bridges in the Highlands, the other to build the Caledonian Canal. The activities of the former will be described in chapter five, but it is important to remember that both were at work simultaneously. Telford was engineer to both commissions, with Jessop as consultant over the canal.

The main purpose of the Caledonian Canal was to enable sailing ships – both warships and merchant ships – to pass between the East and West Coasts while avoiding the dangerous passage round the North of Scotland. This is why it was built as a ship canal, and its locks were the largest so far constructed; it was opened in stages between 1818 and 1822.

Soon after work started on the Caledonian Canal, Telford was asked to survey another Scottish canal, the Glasgow, Paisley & Ardrossan. At Ardrossan a harbour was intended, in which ships would transfer Glasgow-bound cargoes to canal barges, for the Clyde was then too shallow for ships to reach Glasgow itself. An Act was obtained in 1806 and the canal was built from Glasgow through Paisley as far as Johnstone by 1811. And there it terminated, unfinished: under an Act of 1809, the Clyde was deepened, ships could come up to Glasgow and the canal carried only local traffic.

At the other end of Britain, a short but important canal was being considered at this period: a link through north London from the Grand Junction at Paddington to the Thames at Limehouse. It was incorporated in 1812 as the Regent's Canal. Part of it was laid out as an enhancement to Regent's Park: the Prince Regent had given his blessing, John Nash was one of the promoters. So were the Earl of Stanhope and Lord Dundas.

Despite this galaxy of talent, it took until 1820 to open the canal throughout, and even this was only achieved as a result of a government loan made to relieve unemployment by the Exchequer Bill Loan Commissioners who had been set up by an Act of 1817. Telford had surveyed the canal works on their behalf and approved.

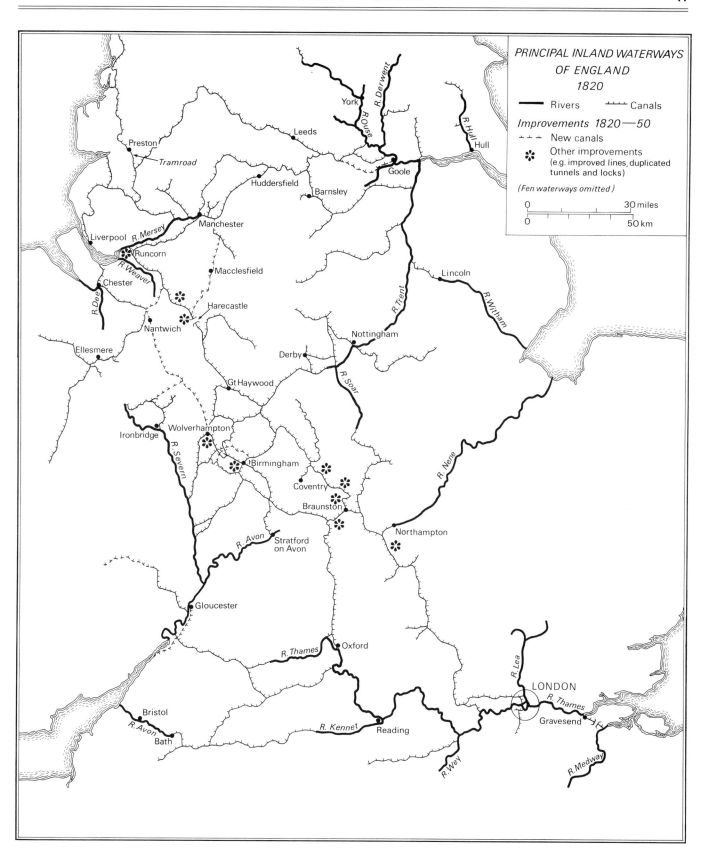

**PRINCIPAL INLAND WATERWAYS
OF ENGLAND
1820**

Rivers ——— Canals ‡‡‡‡

Improvements 1820—50

New canals

Other improvements
(e.g. improved lines, duplicated
tunnels and locks)

(Fen waterways omitted)

0 ———————— 30 miles
0 ———————— 50 km

York

R. Derwent

R. Ouse

Leeds

R. Hull Hull

Preston

Tramroad

Huddersfield

Barnsley

Goole

Liverpool *R. Mersey* Manchester

Runcorn

R. Weaver Macclesfield

Chester

R. Dee

Lincoln

R. Trent

R. Witham

Harecastle

Nantwich

Nottingham

Ellesmere

Derby

Gt Haywood

R. Soar

Wolverhampton

Ironbridge *R. Severn*

R. Nene

Birmingham

Coventry

Braunston

R. Avon

Stratford
on Avon

Northampton

Gloucester

Oxford

R. Thames

R. Lea

LONDON

R. Thames

Bristol

R. Avon *R. Kennet* Reading

Gravesend

Bath

R. Wey

R. Medway

The Duke of Bridgewater's Will

The Act for the Regent's Canal had been helped through Parliament by the Earl of Bridgewater, as chairman of the House of Lords Committee which dealt with it. He was the duke's cousin: the dukedom had died out with the death, in 1803, of the canal duke himself.

He continued however to exert an influence on canals and, as it turned out, the development of railways, through the terms of his will. This set up a trust to take charge of the Worsley colliery and the Bridgewater Canal. One of the trustees was canal superintendent R. H. Bradshaw, and under the will he was not only appointed manager of colliery and canal for life, but given the power to appoint *his* own successor. The beneficiary who received the income from the trust's profits, but had no say in its management, was the duke's nephew, George Leveson Gower, the son of Earl Gower. Earl Gower had been created Marquis of Stafford in 1786, but died himself in 1803 six months after the duke. It is as the second Marquis of Stafford, therefore, that the duke's heir is generally known. His wife was Countess of Sutherland in her own right, and proprietress of much of that county; and eventually, when he was created a duke in 1833, he chose the title Duke of Sutherland.

That was only six months before his death. Income – by then colossal – from the Bridgewater estate was entailed under the old duke's will on his heir's second son. Hugh Malet points out (*Bridgewater The Canal Duke*) that it was the knowledge that his elder son would inherit the title but not the money that led the second marquis to seek to improve the Sutherland estate's profitability, a policy which led to the clearance of many of its inhabitants from their homes in favour of sheep. That is another story, unhappy and indeed horrific; the second Marquis of Stafford's record in matters of transport is better, and we shall meet him again. The Duke of Bridgewater's motive in making his extraordinary will seems to have been to ensure that his enterprise would not be frittered away, but would be maintained as an entity, functioning for public good as well as private gain. This aim was fulfilled.

Canal Traffic

By the second decade of the nineteenth century canals – and, in central England, the canal network – were extensive enough to carry an immense traffic. They carried bulk commodities, of course – coal, timber, limestone, grain – and they also carried great quantities of merchandise in small consignments. Road carriers certainly felt the draught. Here for example is carrier's agent Lydia Sutton, in Liverpool, writing to her principal James Holt in London, as early as 1797:

'. . the Cannals [*sic*] now runs very quick – Mr. R. Hims wanted four piano Fortes down, two he ordered by canal, the other two by our wagon (as 2 of them were immediately wanted) those by Canal arrived 3 days before those by our wagon & were all delivered at the same time. Canal delivered them the 9th day, ours the 12th. The difference in ye carriage was 10/– more by us than those by canal. . . . I trust and hope the Cannal doth not allways bate us in point of time or we shall be quiet [*sic*] don over. – The Irish Tea & Hop merchants tells me they wonder how we get any Businefs as they pay Pickford no more than 6/– P/cwt & I receive 9/6 – As for the Irish linens I do all that lays in my power to get more but it is impossible whilst the canal . . . under carry us.'

The correspondence survives in the Waterways Museum, Stoke Bruerne.

Most traffic on canals was carried by carriers operating their own boats and paying tolls to the canal companies. Some canal carriers were road carriers who had extended their business to the new form of transport: Pickfords was one, and by 1807 James Holt too was carrying by canal, operating fast-moving 'fly boats' for merchandise, comparable to the fly waggons of the roads.

Passengers had travelled by boat for centuries in the Fens, for instance, and on the Bristol Avon. The Duke of Bridgewater introduced a passenger service on his canal, between Worsley, Manchester and Lymm, Cheshire, about 1766 or '67, and subsequently canal-boat travel

Canal paperwork preserved at the Waterways Museum gives an insight into canal traffic and operation. The invoice for a consignment of gin shows it took apparently four days to travel by fly boat from Paddington to Middlewich in 1848. By that date the Grand Junction Canal Co. had taken advantage of an Act of Parliament which allowed canal companies to carry in their own boats (see chapter eight).

Invoice No. *116*		By Boat. No.		**GRAND JUNCTION CANAL CO.**					
								Wednesday Ma	
	Delivery Book.	Consignment.	Residence.	No. of Articles	Species of Goods.	Marks and Numbers.	1st Class. Tons. cwt. qrs. lbs.	2nd Class. Tons. cwt. qrs. lbs.	
Nicholson		*Whitehead*	*Middlewich*	*1*	*Ca. Gin*				

Duchess-Countess, *(above) which once carried passengers along the Bridgewater Canal, survived as a houseboat on the bank of the Shropshire Union Canal until the 1950s. Photographs taken then show her lines to have been much finer than those of the everyday cargo-carrying narrow boat; 'timber-heads' at the bow were deeply worn by towlines.*

IERS BY FLY BOATS.				**From**	*Paddington*	**to**	*Middlewich*						**Time of departure.**	
aster.		*Jno. Leader*												
Rate.	**Paid on.**	**Dr.**		**Dr.** *Main O*	**Cartage.**	**Amount in Porters' Books.**	**Amount Posted.**	**Folio.**	**Under-Charge.**	**Over-charge.**		**REMARKS**		
	s. d.	£ s. d.		£ s. d.		£ s. d.	£ s. d.		s. d.	s. d.				
2/					*10 6*							*March 26/43*		
												Vodow Smith		

became popular there and on many other canals – although never to the point of becoming a national network. That is surprising, for a 'packet boat' or 'passage boat' provided an alternative to stage or mail coach travel which was in many ways preferable: it was smoother and more spacious, and meals and drinks were provided en route. Localities where canals did carry passengers included the canals leading to Manchester and Liverpool, the Wirral line of the Ellesmere Canal (from Chester to Ellesmere Port), the western part of the Kennet & Avon near Bath and the southern part of the Grand Junction Canal. In Ireland there were extensive passenger services on the Grand Canal, and in Scotland on the Forth & Clyde. The Paisley Canal, or rather the section that was built, was laid out on one level by Telford specifically so that passage boats might not be delayed by locks.

The era of the canal passenger boat has sadly left few physical traces. The most substantial, and probably the best known, are the grandiose hotel buildings set up on its banks by the Grand Canal Co. for the benefit of its passengers. Good examples survive at Dublin (Portobello), Robertstown Co. Kildare and, derelict, at Shannon Harbour Co. Offaly. In England, there is the Packet House at Worsley (OS grid ref. SD 748004) a half-timbered building beside the canal from which boat tickets were

Canal boats are still used to a limited extent in the Birmingham area – this one was being loaded with rubbish in 1982 at the foot of Camp Hill locks, Warwick & Birmingham Canal. Entering from the right is the Birmingham & Warwick Junction Canal, completed as late as 1844 as part of the Birmingham Canal Navigations improvements.

sold, and beside Fairfield top lock on the Ashton Canal east of Manchester (OS grid ref. SJ 901979) is a little stone-built boat-house which once sheltered the packet boat. The Waterways Museum, Stoke Bruerne, has a few components from the *Duchess-Countess*, the last passenger boat to survive, notably the large S-shaped, scythe-like blade with which, mounted at the bows, she was entitled to slice through the tow-rope of any lesser boat which obstructed her.

Fortunately, despite the dearth of traces of canal passenger traffic, canals in general are rich in traces of their past. After the coming of the steam railway network in the 1840s canals entered a long period of overall stagnation – the reasons are considered in chapter eight; then in the present century development of motor road transport brought narrow-boat carrying, on anything resembling a large scale, to an end in the 1960s. But a large part of the canal network remains navigable, partly because of increased public awareness of its amenity value, partly just because making a closed canal safe by filling it in and destroying its structures is a difficult and costly business.

The Trent & Mersey's characteristic iron mileposts (left) are a familiar sight to people cruising on that canal. Similar mileposts (right) survive beside former turnpike roads in Cheshire.

For the same reasons many canals and rivers which had become un-navigable have been restored to navigable order.

So to cruise along a navigable canal, or to visit the remains of a closed one, is to encounter a continuing series of eighteenth- or early nineteenth-century structures – locks, hump-backed bridges, flights of locks, aqueducts, tunnels, warehouses, maintenance yards, and engine houses which once contained steam pumps to supply the canal with water. And alongside the canal runs, almost everywhere, the towpath as a constant reminder that when it was built horses were the motive power for transport.

Probably there is no other environment so extensive which contains so much of the past and so little of the present. Surviving narrow boats and similar canal craft, though of recent construction compared with canals themselves, retain the dimensions, and to a large extent the appearance, of their predecessors, and even the present-day canal hire cruiser is in its hull form and proportions directly descended from the boats built by the Duke of Bridgewater for Worsley mine.

The First Iron Canal Railways

In the 1770s the Trent & Mersey Canal Co. decided to build a branch to connect its main line at Etruria with Caldon Low limestone quarries. Caldon Low, despite its name, lies some 1,100 feet above sea level, in those Staffordshire hills which form the southernmost extremity of the Pennines. So the branch was built not wholly as a canal, but partly as a canal, and partly as a horse-and-gravity railway. The canal section terminated at Froghall, 430 ft above sea level and some $3\frac{1}{2}$ miles short of the quarries: a horse railway could overcome the climb to Caldon Low, a canal to all intents and purposes could not. An Act of Parliament for the whole line was obtained in 1776.

A few wooden railways had already been built to feed traffic to canals, but the Caldon line used the latest technology from Coalbrookdale: rails of cast iron, laid on top of the wooden ones. This was the first iron railway authorised by Act of Parliament. Canal and railway were opened about two years later. The canal basin at Froghall (OS grid ref. SK 028477) can still be visited, having been restored to navigability in recent years, but the extent to which traces of the railway can be seen is uncertain, for in its original form it was unsatisfactory, too steep in places, and was rebuilt three times on various sites; in its final form it closed eventually in 1920.

From rails of cast iron laid upon wooden ones, a natural development was rails entirely of cast iron. Deeper than they were wide, such 'edge rails' were first used by South Wales Ironworks about 1791 – the railway over Pont-y-Cafnau was of this type. William Jessop developed the idea further in 1793–4 when he used, on the Forest Line of the Leicester Navigation, iron rails of T-section to combine strength with lightness.

This line had originally been proposed as a canal, but was built partly as canal, partly as railway. The main purpose of the Leicester Navigation, which got its Act in 1791, was to supply Leicester with coal. Derbyshire coal was already reaching Loughborough up the River Soar which had been made navigable from the Trent as the Loughborough Navigation; the new company made the river navigable further upstream, to Leicester, as its 'River Line'. The Forest Line was intended to enable collieries in North-West Leicestershire to compete with those of Derbyshire: it was to run from collieries in the vicinity of Swannington and Coleorton down to the river at Loughborough. Because water supply was inadequate for locks, this line was built with $7\frac{1}{2}$ miles of level contour canal between Thringstone in the west and Nanpantan in the east; from Thringstone steeply graded railways led upwards to the collieries and from Nanpantan another, almost as steep, led down to the wharf at Loughborough.

It is possible that boats were built to carry railway waggons along the canal section; but whether they were or not, the Forest Line had a short life. The coal owners made little attempt to use it – possibly the Ashby Canal, which was authorised in 1794 to serve the same district, offered them a better outlet. The Forest Line seems not to have been used after the turn of the century and by 1819 the rails had been taken up.

Over the years there has been much controversy over the type of rail used and the dates: Jessop has been credited (erroneously) with invention of the edge rail and its first use here. Hadfield and Skempton, however, in *William Jessop, Engineer* (1979) review the evidence and conclude that the rails were (and this was an innovation) of T-section, laid on wooden sleepers like all railways at this period although changes were imminent. It is a pity that this controversy has obscured the Loughborough–Nanpantan section's greater interest in another respect: here for the first time, it seems to me, a railway was built not as an extension at the end of a canal, nor yet as a feeder of traffic to it, but as an integral part of its route. This was a precedent to be much followed during the ensuing two decades.

The site of the canal basin at Nanpantan can be seen as a depression in the ground on the north side of road B5350 at OS grid reference SK 506174. Visiting it in 1982 I could find no obvious trace of the railway, but the former towpath of the canal is indicated as a public footpath, and not far away, at OS grid reference SK 503175, the canal still held water. There were distinct traces of it further west too – near Osgathorpe at OS grid reference SK 430193 for instance, the towpath boundary hedge survived as a field boundary, in places accompanied by the bed of the canal where it has not been filled in, and following a course which is circuitous but, in contrast to other hedgerows, level along a contour on the northern slope of the upland called Charnwood Forest.

Plateways

While the edge rail was thus slowly developing, another development occurred which was for twenty years or so largely to supplant it. This was the L-section rail or plate: on plateways or tramroads laid with these rails, waggons with plain, un-flanged wheels could run.

This type of rail was invented by John Curr and first used in Sheffield colliery when underground tramroads were built; previously the coal had been conveyed, underground, on sledges. Rails were light and gauges narrow. The rails were laid so that their upright flanges ran along their inner edges, between the wheels. Had they been laid with the flanges outside the wheels it would no doubt have been difficult to clear away any stones or other obstructions which lodged on the running surfaces. A 20-in. gauge tramroad of this type was laid on the surface for the first time in 1788 to serve the ironworks of Joseph Butler at Wingerworth, south of Chesterfield, and such tramroads subsequently became popular in the Shropshire iron district. Curr used wooden sleepers but in Shropshire sleepers of cast iron were introduced; plateway of this type has been unearthed within Blist's Hill open-air museum and can be seen there on its original location beside the Shropshire Canal.

Butler of Wingerworth supplied edge rails for construction of Jessop's railways on the Leicester Forest Line, which was planned in 1790 and built between March 1793 and October 1794. From 1792 Jessop was, as has been mentioned, a partner in the Butterley Company, although Benjamin Outram was the active partner, and during 1793 the Butterley Co. built a tramroad to connect its newly opened limestone quarry at Crich, Derbyshire, with the Cromford Canal, then approaching completion. It was laid with rails of Curr's type, L-section: but his gauge was widened, to 3 ft 6 in.

At this period too Benjamin Outram was engineer to the Derby Canal. Originally this was planned to run northwards from a junction with the Trent & Mersey through Derby to collieries near Denby, with a branch from Derby to the Erewash Canal. But Jessop, called in to advise in 1792, suggested that the northern part of the canal should be cut short to terminate at Little Eaton, and that from there to the collieries 'railways of cast iron should be built'. The Act was obtained in 1793 and between December 1793 and May 1795 the railway, called the Little Eaton Gangway, was laid: with L-section plate rails, supplied by Butler of Wingerworth, to a gauge of approximately 4 ft 4 in. between the flanges. The rails were carried not on sleepers of wood, however, but on blocks of stone: the classic horse tramroad or plateway had emerged.

Why blocks of stone were adopted I do not know. Each line of rails was supported on its own individual line of blocks, and it is sometimes suggested that they were used so as to leave a clear pathway between the rails for the horses. This seems most unlikely to me, for horses had walked along cross-sleepered wooden track for almost two centuries without apparent difficulty. My own guess is that Outram, having obtained in cast iron a material for rails very much longer lasting than wood, sought a similarly durable material for sleepers and found it in stone, which was available locally. But cross-sleepers of stone would have been awkwardly heavy to handle, while blocks were heavy enough to keep the track to gauge.

At any rate, from that date forward the concept of the horse tramroad, using L-section plate rails and stone block sleepers, spread far and wide. Such lines were vigorously promoted by Outram and much favoured by Jessop. On them a horse, which could haul a load of 12 cwt excluding the vehicle on an ordinary road at 2 mph or so, could haul a load of about 2½ tons at 3 mph. And although these loads were much less than he could haul on a canal, tramroads were cheaper to build. Telford noted the cost of a 'railroad' at from £3,000 to £5,000 a mile, the cost of a canal at £6,000 to £9,000 – and he held no brief for tramroads, rather the reverse.

Usually horse tramroads were subsidiary to canal transport, and sometimes canal companies built them under blanket powers given by their Acts to build feeder tramroads. Sometimes too they formed part of a combined canal-and-tramroad line – examples have already been mentioned, and Outram's Peak Forest Canal, referred to earlier, was another. In South Wales the mileage of tramroads eventually built (there, earlier edge railways were generally reconstructed with L-section rails) came to exceed, considerably, the mileage of their parent canals.

In some places tramroads were built as temporary links in the line of a canal under construction, pending completion of a particularly difficult engineering feature. The Grand Junction Canal at Jessop's suggestion built a tramroad over Blisworth Hill, Northants, in 1800 and used it until 1805 when Blisworth canal tunnel was completed. The rails were then taken up and used for a branch to Northampton, which in turn was later replaced by a canal. The Lancaster Canal Co. linked northern and southern sections of its canal by a tramroad opened in 1803 across the Ribble valley at Preston. In this instance, the planned aqueduct never was built, and the tramroad lasted well into the steam railway era; today the northern section of the canal remains navigable but isolated from the main canal network.

Only in North-East England, where there was a long tradition of flanged wheels on wooden rails, did tramroads

with L-section rails not become popular: but throughout most of Britain, for two decades or so, the plateway was the usual form of horse railway. At their greatest extent, horse railways of all types probably had a total route mileage of 1,500 miles, the aggregate of many short local lines.

Tramroad Traces

The L-section rail and the stone block sleeper were eventually to prove aberrations from the direct course of railway development, but tramroad engineering was as advanced as contemporary canal engineering and so those tramroads which were not subsequently rebuilt as steam railways have left substantial traces.

Outram's recommendation for track was that stone blocks weighing 150–200 lb should be used, resting on and in a bed of small stones. The top of each block was drilled for an oak plug and the rails were cast with notches in their ends: two rail ends were laid on top of the block and a spike was driven through the hole, formed by adjoining notches, into the oak plug to locate the rails and fasten them down. The rails themselves were 3 ft long, and rested on a block at each end. The gauge recommended was 4 ft 2 in. This was the basic horse tramroad: variations in detail naturally evolved, particularly in the means of supporting and locating rail ends, and it became the practice to make a road surface, usually of small stones, between the rails for the horses to walk on.

When tramroads went out of use – and some of them lasted well into a present century – their rails, having an obvious scrap value, were generally soon removed. Today they can usually be seen only in museums: the Science Museum, London, the National Railway Museum, York, and the Glasgow Museum of Transport all have collections and the National Mining Museum and the Waterways Museum have examples. Coalbrookdale Museum of Iron displays not only plate rails but the wooden patterns from which they were cast.

Stone blocks also often found re-use in buildings, as edgings to canal wharves and so on. But there are places where lines of stone blocks are still to be found in place on their original sites, and highly evocative they are. Recesses for rail ends or supports, and holes for the oak plugs into which spikes were driven, make stone block sleepers instantly recognisable. I mentioned in *The Archaeology of Railways* the Hirwaun–Abernant line, built in 1805, last used in 1900 and for a mile or so eastwards from OS grid reference SN 965052 still apparently intact apart from rails and spikes; and I mentioned also the long run of stone blocks to be found not far away on the course of the Penydarren Tramroad at OS grid reference ST 081977. The Penydarren Tramroad – or, as it is sometimes called, the Merthyr Tramroad – was built by a consortium of Merthyr Tydfil ironmasters with George Overton as their engineer to link their iron works with the Glamorganshire Canal at Abercynon. It was opened in 1802 and last used about 1880 and its importance in the development of steam locomotion is mentioned in the next chapter.

There is another particularly good example of stone blocks surviving *in situ* at Silkstone, South Yorkshire. The Silkstone Railway was built by the Barnsley Canal Co. and opened in 1809 from its terminal basin at Barnby Bridge for about two miles southwards to Silkstone, where coal had been mined for at least 200 years. Its stone blocks were unusually large and laid, for a reason now forgotten, diagonally to the line of route, as shown in the illustration on page 69. For although the line was last used about 1860, many of the blocks are still there. They can be seen at their most complete between OS grid references SE 291055 and 292058: the 1:50,000 map marks a bridleway between these points which is in fact the course of the railway. Or waggonway, as it is called locally: evidently Silkstone is far enough towards the North-East for the term familiar there to be used. According to Baxter (*Stone Blocks and Iron Rails*) the rails were double-flanged, of U-section. North of OS grid reference SE 292058 the course of the tramroad becomes a rough road, the surface of which is in many places broken by stone sleeper blocks: at OS grid reference SE 296069 they can be seen laid out as a passing loop. The tramroad terminus and the canal basin (which is now filled in) lay at OS grid reference SE 302081 just north of main road A635.

Silkstone has another and sombre claim to fame. In its churchyard stands a memorial to twenty-six human beings [*sic*] drowned in 1838 when the coal mine in which they were working – one of those served by the waggonway – was suddenly flooded during a torrential thunderstorm. Only close inspection of the memorial, however, brings the horrifying revelation that of these human beings, who are buried nearby, most were aged 8 or 9 years, the youngest 7 and the oldest of them 17; and that eleven of them were girls.

This tragedy led directly to an official investigation into employment of children in Yorkshire mines (which was widespread) and indirectly to prohibition of employment in mines of boys under 10, and all females, by Act of Parliament in 1842.

The children of Silkstone today have a happier association with the waggonway. So many of the pupils of Silkstone Junior and Infants School asked their teacher, Mr Robert Moore, about the double line of stone blocks that ran along behind the low wall the other side of the road, and showed him bits of coal and pickaxe heads collected along it, that he – and they – got together to find out all they could about the waggonway, its history, route, purpose and remains, as a local history project. The display they mounted as a result won first prize in a schools competition: 'The Place where we Live', organised by a local conservation group, the District of Barnsley Society, and following that, South Yorkshire County Council plans to restore part of the waggonway route, that is to tidy it up by removing rubbish and clearing debris down to the level of the top of the sleeper blocks. It is hoped a small section will be reconstructed with reproduction rails as a display. The part of the waggonway on which this is to be done commences at OS grid reference SE 291055 behind the Ring O'Bells inn and runs in a southerly direction on the east side of Silkstone High Street.

Another restoration scheme which closely involves a tramroad, although it is largely canal-oriented, is that of the Inland Waterways Protection Society for restoration of Buxworth Basin, Derbyshire (OS grid ref. SK 022821). The Peak Forest Canal, coming up from the Manchester area, ceases here and its line was continued as the Peak Forest Tramway to Doveholes and its limestone quarries. The canal/tramroad line was authorised in 1794 and the tramroad itself completed about 1799, the canal a few years later.

There grew up at Buxworth in course of time a canal/tramroad interchange complex of quite remarkable extent – half a mile of wharves, basins, waggon tipplers, warehouses and stables, with a blacksmith's shop and the Navigation Inn. Now, after many years of dereliction, much of the site has been cleared by IWPS volunteers and water re-admitted, so it is particularly regrettable that Buxworth Basin is likely to be adversely affected by works for a new dual carriageway road which is planned to run close beside it.

The Peak Forest Tramway was remarkable in that it had a tunnel, probably the first of its kind: it passed

Buxworth Basin (OS grid ref. SK 022821) was the interchange point between the Peak Forest Canal and the Peak Forest Tramway, the tramroad which continued the canal's line. This is but a small part of it.

The corner house was formerly the Navigation Inn, and the area in front of it where cars are parked was formerly occupied by tramroad sidings.

beneath the road now numbered A624 at OS grid reference SK 058815.

Two other early tramroad tunnels are to be found on the course of the Ashby Canal's Ticknall Tramroad in Derbyshire. The Ashby Canal was authorised in 1794 to run, from a junction with the Coventry Canal, via Ashby de la Zouch to collieries and limeworks in North-East Leicestershire and South Derbyshire. As mentioned earlier, it was planned and in part built as a wide canal: but the expense of doing so caused the substitution in the late 1790s of tramroads for much of the proposed canal line. One of these tramroads led to Ticknall. En route it tunnelled beneath the crown of a low ridge at OS grid reference SK 352232, and both portals of this 50-yard long

tunnel can still be seen. Further on the tramroad passed through another tunnel, which also survives, beneath the driveway to Calke Abbey. It was built to preserve the amenities rather than for engineering reasons. The course of the tramroad at its western approach still exhibits two fine lines of stone blocks between boundary hedges overgrown into twin rows of small trees (OS grid ref. SK 355236). Beyond the tunnel the tramroad curved sharply to the north to cross over the main road (A514) by a stone and brick bridge which remains in place at OS grid reference SK 356240. Its appearance confirms its canal lineage for, as can be seen in the illustration on page 70, it closely resembles the familiar humped bridges of canals.

The greatest engineering structure on canal tramroads must surely have been the viaduct, 50 ft high and with 36 arches, which carried the Monmouthshire Canal Co.'s Sirhowy Tramroad across the valley at Risca, Gwent. This sadly has not survived but a contemporary engraving of it is reproduced on page 71. The Llwydcoed Tramroad's pioneer bridge of iron castings, which dates from 1811, has fared better and still spans the Afon Cynon at OS grid reference SN 997636. It is illustrated in *The Archaeology of Railways*.

With tramroads we have reached a period – unlike that of wooden railways – from which a few vehicles survive. One of the most remarkable is a waggon from the Little Eaton Gangway which is preserved in the National Mining Museum, Lound Hall. Its body is in the form of a detachable container, for transfer into a canal boat. Displayed next to it is a tramroad waggon from a South Wales colliery. The National Railway Museum has a waggon from the Peak Forest Tramway, and at Ironbridge both Coalbrookdale Museum of Iron and Blist's Hill open-air

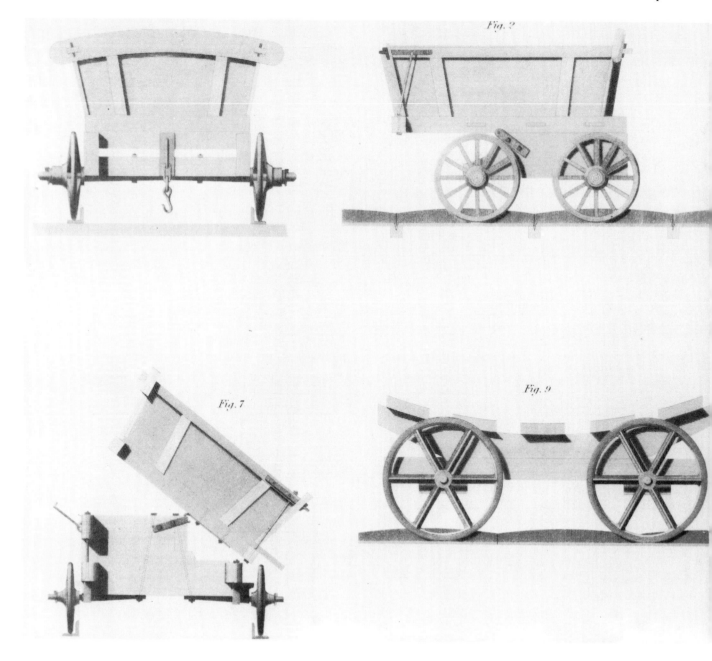

museum exhibit tramroad waggons.

The most distinctive feature of the waggon used on a plateway was its cast-iron wheels: the treads of these were made very narrow, about $1\frac{1}{2}$ in. wide, so that they could crunch their way through any debris which accumulated on the rails. The wheels revolved loose on fixed stub-axles, and their narrow treads presumably precluded the use of brake blocks such as were used on the flanged-wheel waggons of the North-East. Instead, waggons were braked when necessary – and some tramroads such as the Peak Forest Tramway were worked by gravity – by a more primitive method. A short chain with hooks at each end was used: one end was hooked to the waggon and the other thrown against a wheel to catch one of the spokes and make the wheel slide.

In constructing the Caledonian Canal, Jessop and Telford made much use of temporary plateways. These drawings of the waggons used appeared in Telford's Life, although in view of Jessop's much more extensive involvement with tramroads, the waggons probably originated from his experience rather than Telford's. The designs date from c. 1804 and represent good tramroad practice of the period.

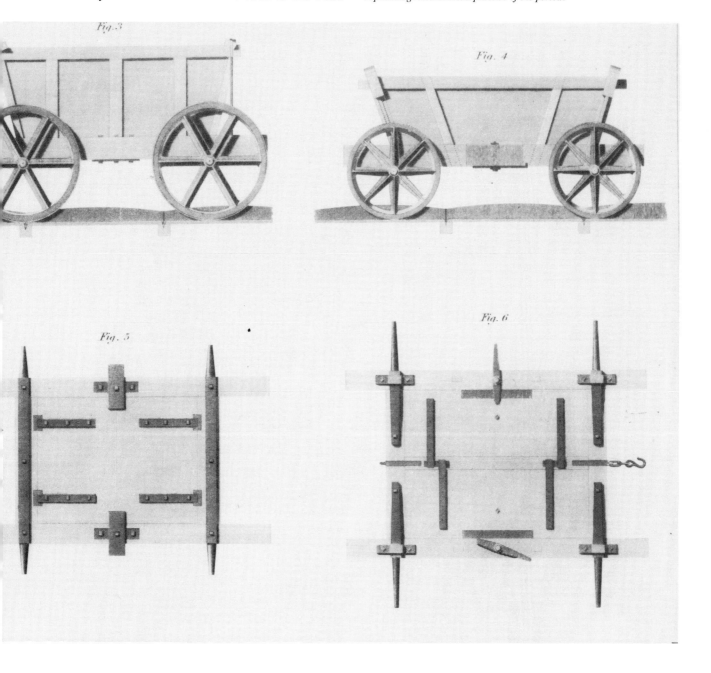

A waggon from the Little Eaton Gangway, as the Derby Canal's tramroad was called, is preserved in the National Mining Museum, Lound Hall. The body is incomplete but it can be seen that it is in the form of a container for transfer to canal boat or road dray. The gauge of this tramroad has often been quoted as 3 ft 6 in., but measurement of this wagon shows that the width between the wheels is approximately 4 ft 6½ in., confirming that it was intended for a track gauge of 4 ft 4 in. between the rails.

The edge railway built from a wharf on the Grantham Canal to Belvoir Castle, Leicestershire (above), in 1815, was used until 1918. In 1980 some rails were still in situ at the point illustrated here (OS grid ref. SK 820341) and on the wooded and steeply graded approach to the castle in the background.

This plateway coal tub (left) was buried by a roof fall in a South Wales coal mine about 1840 and rediscovered in 1973. It is now displayed in the National Mining Museum, Lound Hall.

The tramroad or plateway did not, then, represent the great technical advance that it at first appeared to be, and in due course edge rails came back into favour. Indeed in North-East England they had never really gone out of favour, and in 1797 for the first time a wooden waggonway was rebuilt with iron edge rails. Stone block sleepers were used and, another innovation, cast-iron chairs were mounted on them to locate and support the rails. From this time forward, the wooden railways of the North-East were gradually converted to iron, almost always with edge rails, and new waggonways were built with iron rails.

Elsewhere, too, edge railways started to make a comeback, and it is on the course of one of these that are to be found what are probably the oldest rails still *in situ* on their original site. In 1815 a short horse railway was built from Muston Gorse wharf on the Grantham Canal to Belvoir Castle, Leicestershire, to supply it with coal, and though it was last used about 1918, a section in the castle grounds has never been taken up. The rails are mounted on stone block sleepers and are of the type called, from its shape – deeper, for strength, in the middle than at the ends – fishbelly. Three waggons from the line are preserved in the castle, which is open to the public on certain days, though permission is needed to visit that part of the grounds which includes the railway. Another waggon is preserved in the National Railway Museum.

Inclined Planes

To surmount steep gradients, both plateways and edge railways adopted the self-acting or gravity-operated inclined plane, already in use on wooden railways and on tub-boat canals. The Peak Forest Tramway climbed 209 ft at Chapel-en-le-Frith by such a plane, and its site is still conspicuous – a good viewpoint is the A624 at OS grid reference SK 070803. The Caldon railway was rebuilt in 1802 as a plateway which incorporated several self-acting inclined planes – the engineer was John Rennie, one of his few incursions into this type of work. One of the planes is conspicuous from the A52 at OS grid reference SK 030475.

Then, early in the 1800s, stationary steam engines, which were already in use to power canal inclined planes in Shropshire, were adopted as power for inclined planes on tramroads and edge railways. The precise date seems to be uncertain. Tomlinson in *The North Eastern Railway* states categorically that 'the first fixed engine ever used for hauling waggons was erected at Birtley Fell in 1808'; it began work in 1809. This date has been followed by later writers, such as Dendy Marshall. But it is evidently incorrect, for not only do other writers give other dates and locations, but the Lancaster Canal tramroad had one, or possibly two, steam powered inclined planes and came into use either late in 1803 or early the next year. The inclined plane at Avenham, Preston, is illustrated on this page.

This incline was 115 yd long with a gradient of 1 in 6; today its course (OS grid reference SD 541288) is a tarmac footpath in a public park. So unless further research produces a still earlier instance, it appears that the Lancaster Canal tramroad's inclined planes mark the first successful application of steam power in regular service to a railway – unless of course one counts the Shropshire Canal's inclined planes where boats were carried on rail-borne cradles. For so fundamental a development the uncertainty is surprising.

The Lancaster Canal Tramroad used an inclined plane powered by a steam engine at Avenham, Preston; it was still apparently complete in 1862 when these photographs were taken. It came into use in 1803 or 1804 and was therefore one of the earliest applications of steam power to tramroads on a regular, non-experimental basis. The illustration (right) shows the incline top and engine house, and the illustration shown below shows the foot of the incline on a bridge over the River Ribble. A continuous chain was used to haul the waggons, just as Fulton had recommended for tub-boat inclined planes. The course of the inclined plane is now a footpath at OS grid ref. SD 542287.

Public Railways

Another important trend became evident during the first decade of the nineteenth century, and for this the dates are definite. Canal companies had been showing an increasing tendency to substitute tramroads for parts of their intended canals, so it was almost inevitable that, sooner or later, a tramroad would be substituted for the entire line of a proposed canal.

This eventually happened for the first time during 1801–3. There had been two proposals for canals to link Croydon, then a growing country town with some 5,700 inhabitants, with the Thames. One of these was incorporated in 1801 as the Croydon Canal, to run in a northerly direction from Croydon to join the Grand Surrey Canal – incorporated the same year – near the point at which it entered the Thames at Deptford. The other canal was to run down the valley of the River Wandle to join the Thames further upstream at Wandsworth. But William Jessop, called in in 1799, had found that this canal was impracticable: to take water from the many streams that fed the Wandle would not leave enough for the water-powered mills and factories along that river's course, and there was no other economic source of water. Instead, Jessop recommended construction of an iron railway: railways, he wrote, had 'but lately ... been brought to the degree of perfection, which recommends them as substitute for canals; and in many cases they are much more eligible and useful'.

So, at the recommendation of William Jessop the great canal engineer, the first railway company was formed. The Surrey Iron Railway Company was incorporated by Act of Parliament in 1801, a few weeks before the Croydon Canal. It commenced to have its line built, with Jessop

SURREY
Iron Railway.

The COMMITTEE of the SURREY IRON RAILWAY COMPANY,

HEREBY, GIVE NOTICE,. That the BASON at *Wandsworth*, and the Railway therefrom up to *Croydon* and *Carfhalton*, is now open for the Ufe of the Public, on Payment of the following Tolls, *viz.*

For all Coals entering into or going out of their Bason at Wandsworth,	*per Chaldron,*	3d.
For all other Goods entering into or going out of their Bason at Wandsworth - -	*per Ton,*	3d.

For all GOODS carried on the said RAILWAY, as follows, viz.

For Dung, - -	*per Ton, per Mile,*	1d.
For Lime, and all Manures, (except Dung,) Lime-ftone, Chalk, Clay, Breeze, Afhes, Sand, Bricks, Stone, Flints, and Fuller's Earth,	*per Ton, per Mile,*	2d.
For Coals, - -	*per Chald. per Mile,*	3d.
And, For all other Goods, -	*per Ton, per Mile,*	3d.

By ORDER of the COMMITTEE,

Wandsworth, June 1, 1804.

W. B. LUTTLY,
Clerk of the Company.

BROOKE, PRINTER, No. 35, PATERNOSTER-ROW, LONDON.

The Surrey Iron Railway operated in the same way as contemporary canals and turnpike roads – that is to say anyone could run a suitable waggon on it, provided appropriate tolls were paid. This notice of 1804 (above) announces that the railway is open and indicates the tolls payable on various types of goods.

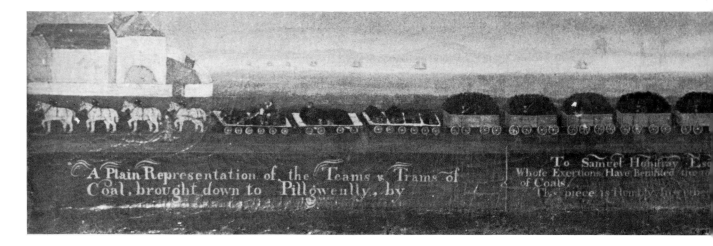

A Plain Reprefentation of the Teams & Trams of Coal brought down to Pillgwenlly, by

as engineer, as a plateway typical of its period, with L-section rails on stone block sleepers. Even while it was still being built, another company, the Croydon, Merstham & Godstone Iron Railway Company, was incorporated in May 1803 to extend it further south. The Surrey Iron Railway was opened in July the same year, from a basin the company had built off the Thames at Wandsworth to Croydon; the Croydon, Merstham & Godstone was opened as far as stone and lime quarries at Merstham in 1805; lack of finance prevented further extensions.

The Surrey Iron Railway was the first public railway independent of a canal, and it was operated in a manner similar to contemporary canals and turnpike roads, by charging tolls upon goods carried along it. Just as canal Acts imposed a public right of navigation, so the Surrey Iron Railway Act stated that 'All persons . . . shall have . . . liberty . . . to pass upon and use the said Railway with waggons'. The Croydon Canal was eventually completed in 1809 and the company built a short tramroad extension from its basin at Croydon to connect with the two railways.

Few physical traces survive of the Surrey or Croydon, Merstham & Godstone Iron Railways, which is scarcely surprising considering how extensively the region through which they passed has subsequently been built up. The course of the Surrey Iron Railway through Mitcham, however, is still indicated by the street called Tramway

Path (OS grid ref. TQ 273681); on the route of the Croydon, Merstham & Godstone part of its substantial embankment across the Chipstead Valley survives at OS grid reference TQ 296595, and at TQ 317622 the course of the line appears as a path across the public park known as the Rotary Field: here, in a railed enclosure, a very short length of track has been reconstructed from original materials, two plate-rails and four stone blocks.

The mention above of the Croydon, Merstham & Godstone line has been slightly out of chronological sequence, for two public tramroads were authorised in 1802 to be built in South Wales and Monmouthshire where the terrain particularly favoured tramroads rather than canals. These were the Carmarthenshire Railroad, from Llanelli to Mynydd Mawr, and the Sirhowy Tramroad. The former replaced a proposed canal branch and was opened during 1803–4. The latter was promoted by ironmaster Samuel Homfray. In 1800 he had been one of the promoters of the Tredegar ironworks: the Sirhowy tramroad was to link these with Newport. Only the upper 15 miles was built by the tramroad company: the lower portion of 9 miles to Pillgwenlly on the Usk estuary near Newport was built by the Monmouthshire Canal Co. and (for one mile) by a landowner. This lower section ran parallel to one of the company's canals and included the 36-arch viaduct at Risca mentioned above. The whole line was built as a plateway and opened during 1805–6.

The Oystermouth Railway or Tram Road Company, as it was called, was incorporated in 1804 to build a plateway from Swansea along the shore of Swansea Bay to Oystermouth; the line was completed in 1806. On it, for the first time, fare-paying passengers were carried by rail. This was the idea of Benjamin French, one of the shareholders.

'The teams and trams of coal', nearly eighty tons of it, brought down to Pillgwenlly by Samuel Homfray on 18 December 1821, are depicted in this painting (below) in the Welsh Industrial & Maritime Museum. The original is ten feet long. Pillgwenlly, on the Usk estuary below Newport, was the terminus of the Monmouthshire Canal Co's tramroads; the trams shown probably originated on the Sirhowy Tramroad.

French provided a vehicle and arranged to pay the company £20 a year in lieu of tolls. His passenger service commenced on 25 March 1807. The earliest known description of the vehicle dates from the following year: it carried twelve people, was made chiefly of iron, ran on four wheels and was drawn by a single horse. Similar passenger services were gradually introduced on other lines, such as the Sirhowy Tramroad as shown in the illustration on page 70.

Of the Oystermouth Railway it seems that no physical remains survive from this period. The next public line to be built, however, the Kilmarnock & Troon Railway (incorporated in 1808) is still represented by the substantial bridge by which it crossed the River Irvine at OS grid reference NS 383369. This line was promoted by the Duke of Portland and William Jessop was principal engineer – one of the last jobs he took on. A new harbour was built at Troon at the same time and the railway built as a double track plateway for 9¾ miles to Kilmarnock. It was opened in 1810. The contractor for the Irvine bridge (see illustration on page 71) was a Mr Simpson, who was probably identical with John Simpson, one of the contractors for the Caledonian Canal. If so, he had been with Telford since his Shropshire bridge-building days, and had been responsible for much of the masonry work on the piers of Pontcysyllte Aqueduct. Much later, when the line was converted into a steam railway, it was diverted in the region of the bridge to avoid sharp curves and a new bridge was built a little way upstream.

About a mile and a half to the west, a stone bridge carried the road which is now the B370 over the tramroad. That a bridge should have beneath it not a watercourse but dry land then seemed so remarkable a phenomenon that it gave its name to the adjoining hamlet: Drybridge. Part of the west portal of this bridge can still be seen, with the date 1811 carved on the keystone, at OS grid reference NS 360365, immediately to the north of the existing railway. The east portal appears to have been obliterated by road widening and even on the west side of the road the cutting by which the tramroad approached the bridge was almost filled with builder's rubble when I saw it during 1982.

The years 1809–10 saw the formation of four tramroad companies all connected with exploitation of the collieries of the Forest of Dean, Gloucestershire. It was a branch of one of these – the Bixslade branch of the Severn & Wye Railway & Canal Company – that eventually became, as Baxter puts it, 'probably the last horse-drawn tramroad

to survive in open country between two fixed points'. Stone was carried along it from Bixhead quarries to dressing sheds at Cannop until the mid-1940s, and in 1982, although the rails had gone, two well-preserved lines of stone blocks still stretched enticingly away into the forest at OS grid reference SO 605100.

A National Tramroad Network?

During the decade following 1810, the trend continued: formation at intervals of companies to build public horse tramroads, often now called railways. Many were connected with canals. Some that reached the stage of getting an Act of Parliament remained unbuilt because of difficulty in raising the necessary money, or were built only in part – this was to be a continuing feature of railway promotion. All those that were built were, at this period, of local importance only. But that was not for want of dreams by their promoters. As early as 1802 it was proposed that the Surrey Iron Railway might be extended to Portsmouth. There was a rival scheme which would have extended the Croydon Canal. Neither was successful.

About 1808 William James proposed formation of a General Railroad Company with a capital of £1 million. William James (1771–1837), perhaps the most flamboyant of all the individuals to be connected with the introduction of railways, was the son of a once-wealthy Warwickshire solicitor who had lost money speculating in canal shares. He himself entered the profession of land agent and surveyor. At this he was successful and prospered. Being a land agent to the nobility meant managing their estates: these included coal mines and the tramroads which served them, which enabled James to develop a knowledge of both. James was involved in tramroad projects from the turn of the century onwards; during 1802–3 he was active in Lancashire, surveying mines and tramroads proposed to connect them with the Bridgewater Canal, and at that period he first considered the possibility of a tramroad from Liverpool to Manchester. Other railway projects followed, culminating in the general railroad proposal of 1808. This was premature, not to say over-ambitious: James seems to have turned his attention, for a few years, back to land agency, and to coal mining on his own account. His eventual return to railway promotion was closely linked with the development of steam locomotives; and to the first attempts to apply steam power to vehicles and vessels we must now turn.

Most of the bridges on the military roads built by General Wade and his successors are plain and unadorned, but the bridge at Aberfeldy (above) which carried his road from Crieff to the north over the River Tay symbolised completion of Wade's basic network. So this triumphant structure was designed by noted architect William Adam and built in 1732; it still carries a B road. OS grid ref. NN 851494.

General Wade's military road to Fort Augustus (above), built in 1731, climbs out of the upper Spey Valley to cross the 2,507-ft Corrieyairack pass. Its layout is typical of Wade's work: climbing straight and steadily along the flank of the far ridge, then turning towards the pass and running as straight as possible until the steepening slope forces it to rise by zigzags to maintain the same overall direction. The photograph was taken in July 1982 from OS grid ref. NN 427984, looking east.

Pontcysyllte aqueduct (below), designed by Jessop and Telford, was built between 1795 and 1805; the canal system's greatest structure. Nineteen iron spans on stone piers carry the Ellesmere Canal 121 feet above the River Dee, at OS grid ref. SJ 271420. Yet the canal line it was built for, which was intended to link the Severn with the Mersey, was never completed.

In the early 1820s, canals were at their zenith—extensive, busy and unchallenged. This picture, from the original painting by T. H. Shepherd, epitomises the period. The Regent's Canal's locks are not only wide, but duplicated for heavy traffic; the boats are Pickford's fly boats loaded with general merchandise. A top-hatted clerk is gauging the boat on the right—that is, measuring how low it floats in the water so that the load it carries, and from that the toll payable, may be calculated.

In Georgian Bath, Cleveland House (above) was built over the Kennet & Avon Canal, and was formerly the canal company's offices.

Close to its junction with the Trent, the Trent & Mersey Canal passes Shardlow, Derbyshire, where an inland port grew up. The warehouse seen here was built in 1780 with access for boats beneath it. It was restored in the late 1970s to house a canal exhibition.

Most British canals today are too small to take barges large enough to carry economic loads: instead, they are valued for amenity and recreation. This is the bottom lock of Jessop's and Outram's Cromford Canal at Langley Mill, on the Derbyshire/Nottinghamshire border, where it joined

the Erewash Canal. All the canal seen here was formerly derelict and has been restored through the efforts of the Erewash Canal Preservation and Development Association.

Stone block sleepers of the Silkstone Waggonway in South Yorkshire are still prominent along its course, as here at OS grid ref. SE 292057. This tramroad was built by the Barnsley Canal Company in about 1809, and last used in 1860. Positioning the blocks diagonally to the line of route was unusual.

Narrow gauge plateway track (above), of the type developed by John Curr and subsequently much used in Shropshire, is seen here in its original position alongside the Shropshire Canal—a tub-boat canal—within Blist's Hill Open Air Museum, Ironbridge. The boat is an icebreaker.

James Brindley evolved a system of carrying coal by boat in small containers: it was used on the Bridgewater Canal and the neighbouring Manchester, Bolton & Bury Canal. A boat of this type from the M.B. & B. Canal with two of its containers (left) has been recovered by the Boat Museum, Ellesmere Port, and contrasts with the modern container depot in the background.

The bridge which carried the Ashby Canal's Ticknall Tramroad over the main road at Ticknall, Derbyshire (above), shows a strong affinity of style with the usual humped bridges of canals. OS grid ref. SK 356240.

Miller, Taylor, Symington and (perhaps) Robert Burns steam across Dalswinton Loch in October 1788 (below). Also present was Alexander Nasmyth, on whose sketch this lithograph by J. C. Bourne was very closely based. Although it was published much later, there is every likelihood of its accuracy. The boat was moving under power: there is no wind, for there is no ripple on the water, so the smoke trail results from her own motion.

A typical Telford-style road foundation of carefully positioned upright stones, built as late as the 1860s, is revealed by roadworks at Kingshouse, Perthshire in 1982. See also page 99.

The horse railway at its greatest (left): the Monmouthshire Canal Co.'s section of the Sirhowy Tramroad crossed the valley of the Ebbw River at Risca by this viaduct of thirty-six arches. A train of trams of coal is shown, with a horse-drawn passenger vehicle in the foreground. The viaduct was built c. 1805; it is now demolished.

The Kilmarnock & Troon Railway crossed the River Irvine by this bridge (below) of four arches each of 40ft span. The railway company was incorporated in 1808, built its line as a horse tramroad and appears to have brought it into use late in 1811. Despite its neglected 1982 appearance, the bridge is a substantial relic not only of Scotland's first public railway but also of the first decade of public railways anywhere. OS grid ref. NS 383369.

Un-tarred road, wrought-iron tollgate barring the way, tollkeeper's house alongside: a scene familiar to travellers on Telford's Holyhead Road is re-created within Blist's Hill Open Air Museum, Ironbridge. Gate and tollhouse were designed by Telford; the tollhouse was originally at Shelton, near Shrewsbury, before removal to the museum.

A stage coach enters an inn yard (above): an occurrence well-known throughout the coaching era. The coach office is on the right; on the left a waiter descends to solicit passengers' custom.

On a summer evening the Quicksilver *Devonport Royal Mail Coach—the fastest of them all—passes the Star & Garter Inn, Kew Bridge, c. 1835. In the background is a turnpike gate and, on the River Thames, a steam*

boat. Early development of steam-boat services on rivers and estuaries was contemporary with development of good roads and fast coaching on land. A picture of this same location in 1982 appears on page 108.

CHAPTER FOUR

Steam Carriages, Boats and Locomotives: the First Pioneers

Dreamers and Schemers

As the preceding chapters have shown, transport developed rapidly during the second half of the eighteenth century, but remained dependent on traditional forms of power – animals, wind, gravity. Yet at the same time the old atmospheric pump was evolving into the steam engine as a stationary provider of power. The prospect of making self-propelled steam boats and carriages was attractive, and many people attempted to do so. Such attempts were to be successful during the early part of the nineteenth century.

They had originated long before, in the ideas of dreamers and schemers whose ideas were too far advanced for contemporary technology to turn them into practical reality. Papin, mentioned on page 12, about 1690 suggested a steam ship and the way in which it would work, and Jonathan Hulls had in 1736 patented a tug boat propelled by a Newcomen engine. It was to be used for towing sailing ships in and out of harbour during calms and contrary winds, to solve a constantly recurring problem. Hulls may perhaps have built a small experimental steam boat and tried it out on the River Avon at Evesham.

There is no doubt, however, that in 1769–70 Nicholas Joseph Cugnot, French military engineer, built a steam road vehicle intended to transport artillery. It had three wheels of which the front one was driven through a pawl-and-ratchet arrangement from a steam engine supplied with steam by a copper boiler. Although it worked, it did not do so successfully enough to be used as intended: but the actual vehicle is preserved in Paris.

James Watt at this period, in the intervals of laying out the Monkland Canal and developing the separate condenser, was already aware of the potential of steam power for driving vehicles, although he did not pursue it; and

in 1770 he was approached by Dr William Small, associate of Matthew Boulton (with whom Watt was not yet in partnership) about the possibility of applying his proposed rotary steam engine to power boats on the newly-opened Birmingham Canal. Watt suggested they might be driven by a 'spiral oar' rather than paddle wheels. This anticipation of the screw propeller was far ahead of its time.

Several French pioneers attempted to build steam boats during the 1770s; one of them, the Marquis Claude de Jouffroy d'Abbans was eventually successful in 1783. His *Pyroscaphe*, nearly 150 ft long, had a double-acting horizontal cylinder $25\frac{1}{2}$ in. diameter by 77 in. stroke, enclosed within the boiler; the piston rod was connected with the paddle shaft by a ratchet mechanism. This vessel succeeded in ascending the River Saône against the current for fifteen minutes; but government support for continued experiments was not forthcoming.

William Murdock

Foremost among the pioneers of this period – though as things turned out a frustrated one – was William Murdock. Murdock (1754–1839) spent his entire working life with Boulton & Watt's firm, and spent twenty years of it in Cornwall – for the partners regarded him rightly as the best of their engine erectors, and so did the mine adventurers. To build a steam carriage was long his dream and, about 1784, fearful that others might forestall him, he considered building one in reality. Watt's reaction was to protect the idea of the steam carriage in *his* own patent of 1784, although his opinion expressed in a letter to Boulton was that it 'will cost much time to bring it to any tolerable degree of perfection, and that for me to interrupt the career of our business to bestow my attention on it would be

William Murdock's model steam carriage: the simplicity of the design confirms the genius of the designer. It is now displayed in Birmingham Museum of Science & Industry; it was built probably, during the years 1784–6. The rectangular copper boiler is heated by a spirit lamp and the vertical upright cylinder and valve chest are partly set within it; the piston rod is connected to an overhead beam which in turn drives the 9¼ in. diameter rear wheels by a connecting rod and crank.

imprudent'. He and Boulton did not want Murdock wasting his time on steam carriages either, for he was far too valuable to them as an erector of stationary engines. Nevertheless Murdock did build a model steam carriage, and it worked well. It was the first self-propelled vehicle to run in Britain.

The upshot was the famous chance meeting of 1786 when Boulton, travelling by coach down to Cornwall, encountered near Exeter another coach containing Murdock travelling in the opposite direction. It soon transpired that Murdock was on his way to London with his model to seek his own patent. Somehow – just how seems not to be recorded – Boulton persuaded Murdock to abandon his journey and return to Cornwall. So Murdock never did build a full-size steam carriage – but his model survives (or perhaps it is a later one built *c.* 1791) and is displayed in the Birmingham Science Museum. It is illustrated on this page. Other notable inventions for which Murdock was later responsible were the D-slide valve for steam engines which he patented in 1799, and lighting by coal gas.

Symington and Miller

One of the earliest tasks which Murdock undertook for Boulton & Watt, even before he went to Cornwall, was to travel to Wanlockhead, on the Dumfriesshire/ Lanarkshire border, in 1779 to help commission a Watt engine. This had been set up to drain a lead mine, and had been erected by mine engineer George Symington assisted by his young brother William. During the intervals in the work of commissioning the engine, there seems little doubt that Murdock's dream of a steam propelled carriage entered the conversation. Certainly, about 1784, William Symington (1764–1831) himself started to think seriously about a steam carriage, and by the middle of 1786 he too had completed a working model. It was driven by a pawl-and-ratchet arrangement but the cylinder, unusually for the period, was positioned horizontally. This model impressed Gilbert Meason, the active partner in the Wanlockhead Mining Company, so much that he had it demonstrated to visitors to his house in Edinburgh. Symington, with associates, then set about finding a backer for a full-size version (among those to whom they wrote was Thomas Gilbert, the Duke of Bridgewater's general land agent and elder brother of John Gilbert who had played a large part in building the Bridgewater Canal).

Simultaneously, Symington had been working on another development. At Wanlockhead, in a remote upland area, an economic steam engine was particularly advantageous, for there were no coal mines in the immediate vicinity and the cost of coal was inflated by transport charges. To Meason, however, the payment of premiums to Watt under his patent was particularly irksome, for there were no Newcomen engines locally with which Watt's engine might be compared to confirm estimated savings in coal consumption. So Symington was encouraged to design his own improved atmospheric engine. This he did and, by the autumn of 1786, had completed a working model; he was granted a patent the following June.

The cylinder of Symington's atmospheric engine was extended downwards and its lower part was separated from the main part by an extra piston, to form a condensing chamber into which the exhaust steam was admitted. When fresh steam was let into the cylinder, it not only allowed the main piston to rise, but forced the extra piston downwards to expel the condensate. This piston was connected by a downward rod, a beam and a chain to a balance weight which made it rise again towards the main piston descending under atmospheric pressure. The wall of the upper part of the cylinder was kept hot – it was contained in a chamber through which passed not steam but hot gases from the fire; and rotary motion could be obtained by pawls and ratchets.

Symington's engine was therefore highly ingenious. It achieved much of the benefit of the separate condenser as applied to an atmospheric engine, it was simpler than Watt's arrangement, and it almost – but not quite – evaded Watt's 1769 patent. It saw its first use, however, not as a pump but, in slightly developed form and at the instance of Patrick Miller, to power a boat.

Patrick Miller (1731–1815) was among those who saw the model steam carriage in Edinburgh. As a young man he had been to sea, but by 1786 he had been a banker for many years and had prospered greatly. Much later his great-great-great granddaughter was to describe him as 'the best meaning man in the world, perhaps even in Scotland'* and whether the transposal of words was deliberate or not the description sums him up. Except in one respect: he was also impulsive, quick to take people (and things) up, as quick to drop them again. In 1785 he had purchased unseen an estate at Dalswinton, Dumfriesshire, which had proved on inspection to be depressingly neglected. He was inclined, too, to patronise the arts: in 1788 the newly-famous ploughboy-poet Robert Burns was persuaded, rather against his own better judgement, to become a tenant of one of the Dalswinton farms, and Miller was already employing Alexander Nasmyth. Nasmyth had originally been apprenticed to a coachbuilder, but had shown such talent in painting coats-of-arms on carriages that he had become a successful portrait painter.

In 1786 Miller's preoccupation was to find a means of propelling ships – particularly warships in battle – independently of the wind; and this, he thought, might be accomplished by the use of paddle wheels driven by capstans turned by the crew. Several successive experimental ships were built, with either two or three hulls and the paddle wheels mounted between them. During trials the paddle wheels worked satisfactorily but the sailors soon became exhausted.

Miller employed as tutor to his sons James Taylor, a Wanlockhead man and an old acquaintance of William Symington. It was Taylor (who had taken his turn at the paddle capstans) who suggested to Miller that a steam engine would be better than manpower, and who introduced him to Symington; and after initial scepticism on Miller's

*C. Carswell, *The Life of Robert Burns*

part it was arranged in 1788 that Symington should build a small engine and fit it into a double-hulled boat which was already at Dalswinton for a trial on the loch there.

The engine was built according to Symington's latest ideas, and had – indeed has, for it can be seen to this day in the Science Museum – two vertical cylinders, 4 in. diameter by about 18 in. stroke, in which the pistons rose and fell alternately; the rods of the extra pistons were linked by a rocking beam beneath, so that each extra piston could act in place of a balance weight for the other. The chain, pawl and ratchet drive converted the alternating motion of the pistons into continuous rotation of two paddle wheels mounted one astern of the other between the two hulls. One hull contained the engine and the other the boiler. The boat itself was 25 ft long by 7 ft beam.

The steam boat was completed and tried out on Dals-

Symington's steam boat engine of 1788 is preserved in the Science Museum. It was kept at Dalswinton House for many years, but later dismantled; it was eventually re-erected, and some missing parts replaced, in 1854. It is an atmospheric engine and two cylinders, in which pistons rise and fall alternately, are used in the absence of a flywheel to give continuous motion. Chains, pawls and ratchets transmit power to the paddle shafts.

This is how Dalswinton Loch (above right) looked in June 1976 when visited by the author, by kind permission of the owner Mr. D. W. N. Landale. It was here that Miller, Taylor and Symington made their first steam boat trials in 1788, as shown on page 70.

winton Loch before numerous spectators over several days in October 1788. Burns was there (possibly on board, probably on the shore) but sadly did not see fit to record the event in verse. Alexander Nasmyth, who acted as Miller's draughtsman, did on the other hand record the scene in

a detailed sketch which was later to form the basis for the lithograph reproduced on page 70. The boat, in Symington's words (*A Brief History of Steam Navigation*), 'was propelled in a manner which gave such satisfaction that it was immediately determined to commence another experiment on a larger scale'.

This experiment, it was decided, should be carried out on the Forth & Clyde Canal, with an engine built under Symington's direction by the Carron Company. The Carron works had their own dock close to the eastern entrance to the canal. Miller was a substantial shareholder in Carron, and also one of the 136 proprietors of (i.e., shareholders in) the canal company. But work did not start until the following summer and then went forward slowly – probably, in part, because Symington was by then building a full-size pumping engine to his design at Wanlockhead – and although Taylor, who was assisting Symington at Carron, told Miller in July that it was hoped to have the vessel ready in about six weeks, it was early December before she was complete enough for trials. This boat also

was double-hulled – it was one that Miller had used for earlier paddle wheel experiments – and was 60 ft long; the engine was in effect a larger version of the Dalswinton one with cylinders of 1 ft 6 in. diameter by 3 ft stroke.

With Miller and others on board, the boat was tried out and found to go well at slow speeds. When full speed was attempted the paddle floats started to break off one after another, for the arms of the wheels were not strong enough. Presumably they had been provided for capstan propulsion. New wheels were therefore made and fitted and with these, when tried out on 26 and 27 December 1789, the boat ran successfully at nearly 7 mph.

But Miller was not present. He had gone back to Dalswinton after the first trial. Justifiably angered and impatient over the delays in construction – he had wanted a summer trial – the business of the paddle floats was perhaps the last straw. At any rate, his mind was made up. '. . . Mr Symington's engine is the most improper of all steam engines for giving motion to a vessel . . . do as you will, a great deal of the power of the engine must be lost in friction . . .' he had written to Taylor. He did not alter his opinion after the second, successful, experiment; and to the extent that Symington's boat engine did need extensive development before it would be satisfactory in commercial use, he was right. Miller did make an approach through an intermediary to James Watt about possible use of a Watt engine in a steam boat, but the engine of the 1789 boat had already been described to Watt by John Rennie (who happened to see it at Carron), and Watt regarded Symington's engines as infringing his patent. Miller got the usual discouraging response. After that his interest in steam boats evaporated and agricultural improvements, initially a Dalswinton necessity, became his consuming passion. Symington for the time being went back to constructing stationary engines and pumps, often with parts supplied by Carron, and in this he was by no means unsuccessful.

Fitch and Rumsey in the USA

While Miller, Taylor and Symington had been carrying out their experiments, steam boat pioneers had been at work in the USA, which had recently declared itself independent. John Fitch in 1785–6 had designed and built a steam boat which he tried out on the River Delaware: it was propelled by twelve vertical oars or paddles, six on each side, which were made to reciprocate by the steam engine. Fitch developed his ideas and by 1790 had built a steam boat reliable enough to operate a scheduled passenger service for the first time. This ran on the Delaware River throughout the summer of that year but attracted too few passengers to be a commercial success.

Contemporaneously, from 1785 onwards, James Rumsey had been experimenting on the Potomac River with a steam boat driven by a water jet: an atmospheric steam engine was used to draw water from the river and expel it from the stern of the boat. Trials went on over three years and eventually the boat was able to move at a speed of 4 mph.

In 1788 Rumsey came to England and started to negotiate an agreement with Boulton & Watt – or, rather, with Boulton acting on behalf of the partnership. Rumsey would build Watt engines in the USA and Boulton & Watt would back his steam boat in England and provide expertise. But then Rumsey sought improved terms and the agreement fell through. He was however able to have a boat built to his design but before trials were complete – indeed, before the boat had moved under its own power – Rumsey had collapsed suddenly and died.

The boat was completed nevertheless and demonstrated on the Thames in 1793. It reached a speed of 4 knots.

Lord Stanhope

One of the witnesses of the experiments with Rumsey's boat was Lord Stanhope, the same Lord Stanhope who was mentioned in chapter three. In 1790, before he became involved with the Bude Canal proposal, Stanhope had taken out a patent for a steam boat to be driven by a propeller shaped like the foot of an aquatic bird. After trials with models, he arranged for a full-size vessel called the *Kent* to be built at Deptford during 1792–3; it was intended for the Navy. The propellers – there were two – were made of wood and iron plates; they reciprocated and opened and shut like a duck's feet. The vessel had only limited success: it reached a speed of about 3 mph. The steam engine was later taken out and, as it had been paid for from public funds, placed in store in Deptford Naval dockyard.

It was not forgotten. Several years later, in 1800, General Samuel Bentham (1757–1831) persuaded the Admiralty to have a steam-driven bucket dredger built to his design. The engine left over from Stanhope's experiments was then thriftily removed from store (according to the *Mechanic's Magazine* of 23 August 1845) and used to power its endless chain of buckets. In this task it was far more successful than in its earlier application. Bentham's dredger was completed and set to work dredging Portsmouth Harbour in 1802: there had earlier been a steam-driven spoon dredger, and a horse-driven bucket dredger, but this was the first steam-driven bucket-chain dredger to be built. Another was built on Bentham's recommendation in 1804–6 at Deptford for use in Woolwich Dockyard.

In 1804 too William Jessop designed a steam bucket-dredger, and engine and machinery were built by the Butterley Company, sent north to Inverness and installed in a hull with the intention that they should be used to dredge Loch Dochfour and Loch Oich, two of the natural lochs which formed part of the line of the Caledonian Canal. However this dredger sank before it could be used and was not salvaged. Nevertheless steam dredgers did become an important product of the Butterley Co. and it did eventually supply about 1814 the first of two steam dredgers used to deepen the Caledonian Canal lochs.

Fulton in England

It was while Lord Stanhope was experimenting with steam boats in 1793 that Robert Fulton started to correspond with him. That November, Fulton wrote in a letter: '. . . In June '93 I began the experiments on the steamship; my first design was to imitate the spring in the tail of a salmon: for this purpose I supposed a large bow to be wound up by the steam engine and the collected force attached to the end of a paddle [at the stern] . . . which would urge the vessel forward. This model I had made . . . and I found it to spring forward in proportion to the strength of the bow, about 20 yards, but by the return of the paddle the continuity of the motion would be stopped. I then endeavoured to give it a circular motion . . . by applying two paddles on an axis, then the boat moved forward by jerks. There was too great a space between the strokes; I then applied three paddles forming an equilateral triangle to which I gave circular motion by winding up the bow. I then found it to move in a gradual and even motion 100 yards with the same bow which before drove it but 20 yards.' A second model had been fitted with two 'equilateral triangles' of paddles, one each side of the hull.

Fulton worked out the paddle wheel from first principles. Evidently neither he nor Stanhope knew at that stage of Miller's and Symington's experiments; but Stanhope did not put the paddle wheel to practical test, and Fulton took up canal engineering and moved near Manchester.

Here he must surely have heard of, and perhaps seen, experiments carried out by John Smith of St Helens, which commenced in 1793. Smith fitted a boat with a Newcomen-principle engine and paddles, and steamed it (at about 2 mph) down the Sankey Brook Navigation, across the Mersey to Runcorn and up the Duke of Bridgewater's canal to Manchester. In November 1794 Fulton addressed an enquiry to Boulton & Watt, asking whether they could supply a 3 or 4 hp engine to be placed in a boat; the engine was to have 'rotative movement' and occupy as little space as possible. Boulton & Watt, it seems, did not condescend to reply.

About 1796 the Duke of Bridgewater himself decided to have a steam tug built for trials on his canal. Fulton seems to have been involved, though just how closely is not clear: authorities differ widely. Probably he did no more than tell the duke of his ideas; in any case, he left for France late in the spring of 1797.

The engine of the duke's steam tug was provided by Salford engineers Bateman & Sherratt, who at that time were doing a roaring trade in stationary atmospheric engines with separate condensers – until Boulton & Watt served injunctions on them. Sherratt had seen John Smith's steam boat on the canal. According to Malet (*Bridgewater The Canal Duke*) the duke himself got Capt. Shanks RN to supervise construction of the boat at Worsley. It was driven by paddle wheels and named – or more probably nicknamed – *Buonaparte*; and when completed it towed eight 25-ton starvationers from Worsley to Manchester – but only at about 1 mph which was slower than horses, and with such commotion from the paddle wheels that it was feared they would damage the clay puddle lining of the canal. Experiments ceased in 1799 though the engine was used for many years as a pump.

The Captain Shanks who supervised construction of the Worsley steam boat is probably identical with Captain John Schank RN (or Schanck: all three spellings are known), 1740–1823, who was noted for his mechanical ingenuity: he had gained the nickname 'Old Purchase' from construction of a seaman's cot fitted with pulleys so that it could be raised or lowered by the person lying in it, and in the 1780s he had successfully persuaded the Admiralty to adopt the sliding, or drop, keel in vessels for use in shallow water. During the mid-1790s he was in charge of East Coast defence against invasion, a task which included construction or adaptation of small craft to take cannon. That sounds useful experience for fitting a boat with a boiler and steam engine. He retired from active service in 1802.

Charlotte Dundas

What is certain is that when, on 5 June 1800, Lord Dundas, governor (i.e. chairman) of the Forth & Clyde Canal Company, and some of its directors at an ill-attended meeting agreed that a steam tug-boat should be built at the company's expense, it was to be built to a design by Captain Schank (of Worsley) – and fitted with an engine by William Symington.

This was the start of the succession of experiments which resulted in the highly successful performance of the *Charlotte Dundas* on 28 March 1803. Detailed knowledge of these experiments has for many years been clouded by confusion. Symington himself, in his own account *A Brief History of Steam Navigation*, wrote much of the results but little of the experiments, and gave no hint at all that not one but two successive vessels were involved. Most later writers have naturally therefore assumed that there was only one, and became muddled over the dates. Yet the fact that there were two boats was known at the time but subsequently forgotten; it was mentioned, briefly, by J. & W. H. Rankine in their *Biography of William Symington* (1862) and has now been confirmed by W. S. Harvey and G. Downs Rose: the results of their extensive research are contained in their recent biography *William Symington*.

The original cause of the confusion is probably lost among the un-minuted internal politics and jealousies of the canal's administrators. For one thing, administration was divided between a governor and council meeting in London and a committee of management meeting in Scotland, which seems unlikely to make for harmony. Furthermore, Dundas was by far the largest shareholder. Family papers which survive in North Yorkshire Record Office make it clear that in 1788 he had held 90 shares against the next largest shareholder's 30 (while Patrick Miller, for instance, held 5): the eastern entry to the canal had been built across Dundas estates and it was sometimes supposed that he tended to exploit the canal to his own advantage rather than that of the proprietors as a whole. Whether or not this was justified, he did serve the canal well as governor for many years, and became a commissioner of the Caledonian Canal when that commission was established in 1803.

Symington had started to build, about 1793, stationary atmospheric engines in which a crank instead of ratchets and pawls was used to produce rotary motion. About the same time, to prevent the piston rod slopping to and fro sideways, he started to use a crosshead and slidebar arrangement. It was probably an engine of this type, with vertical single cylinder and overhead beam, which was installed in the spring of 1801 in the boat which had been built to Schank's design by Alexander Hart of Grangemouth. Hart was then in his early twenties and his yard newly established (it later became the Grangemouth Dockyard Company and closed down as recently as 1980).

The boat was named *Charlotte Dundas* after Lord Dundas's daughter and during 1801 it ran trials, towing vessels on the River Carron, on the Firth of Forth and on the canal. It was unsatisfactory: the boat with its large beam engine was simultaneously unstable and underpowered, and its wash seemed likely to damage the banks. The latter criticism echoes that made against Schank's Bridgewater Canal boat. In January 1802 the committee of management, alarmed at the expense and the evident unsuitability of the boat, expressed the opinion that Dundas should direct Symington to send in his final account, so that it could be settled and the boat and apparatus put to best use – not, presumably, in combination as a steam tug.

But Symington was already working on an improved engine and boat, and some of the parts had already been invoiced. My guess is that, on first being approached by Dundas, he put forward his latest type of stationary engine for use in Schank's vessel. Then, even as the detailed work of designing and building it turned his mind more closely to the subject, he gradually realised that great improvement could be made – particularly since he was now free from the constraint of Watt's patent, which had expired. So the horizontal cylinder thought of long before for the steam carriage was revived, and made double-acting, Watt's separate condenser was used, and his own recent crosshead and slide bars were adopted to prevent vertical movement of the piston rod, which was connected by another rod direct to a crankshaft. Symington obtained a patent for this design in October 1801, for stationary use on land as well as in boats.

In the improved boat, Symington planned, the engine would drive a single paddle wheel set within the stern of the boat. This arrangement would minimise wash and bank damage. During the winter of 1801–2 he had a detailed model made of the proposed boat, and early in 1802 he took this to London to show Lord Dundas. Dundas was so impressed with it that he introduced Symington to the Duke of Bridgewater: and the duke, after initial doubts resulting from the failure of his own experiments three years earlier, was in turn so much impressed by the model that, as mentioned in chapter one, he ordered Symington to build eight full-size boats for his canal, as soon as possible.

So the second *Charlotte Dundas* was built to the improved design during 1802. The name was transferred from the earlier vessel, which was eventually converted into a ballast lighter. The hull of the new boat was built by John Allan, the engine, which had a cylinder of 22 in. diameter by 48 in. stroke, from parts supplied by Carron.

The new boat was built under difficult conditions, for the management committee, concerned at the continuing expense, ceased to meet Carron's accounts in August 1802. (They were eventually settled in 1804: meanwhile Symington had been attempting to raise funds by, for instance, returning unused parts as scrap to be credited.) The new boat was completed late in 1802. She was demonstrated in public for the first time in Glasgow on 4 January 1803; then, with altered gear wheels between crank- and paddle-shafts, she made on 28 March the outstanding trial described in chapter one.

And then, the rewards of success were snatched away from Symington just when they must have seemed within his grasp: on the very day of the successful trial, Symington records, he heard of the death of the Duke of Bridgewater which had taken place on 8 March 1803; the order for tug boats for the Bridgewater Canal was subsequently cancelled by R. H. Bradshaw, all-powerful superintendent and trustee of the canal under the duke's will. The management committee of the Forth & Clyde remained unimpressed by steam boats, and although *Charlotte Dundas* was probably maintained for a short time, she does not seem to have gone into regular service. In 1808, steam plant and

William Symington 1763–1831, sketched in his old age: saddened, it appears, rather than embittered.

Although it seems that no pictures of Charlotte Dundas *survive which are precisely contemporary with her successful performance as a steam tug, there are several which were prepared a few years later when her full significance was realised. As can be expected, they all differ in detail. This diagram was sent to the* Mechanics' Magazine *in 1832, after Symington's death, by his son William, so has a fair likelihood of accuracy.*

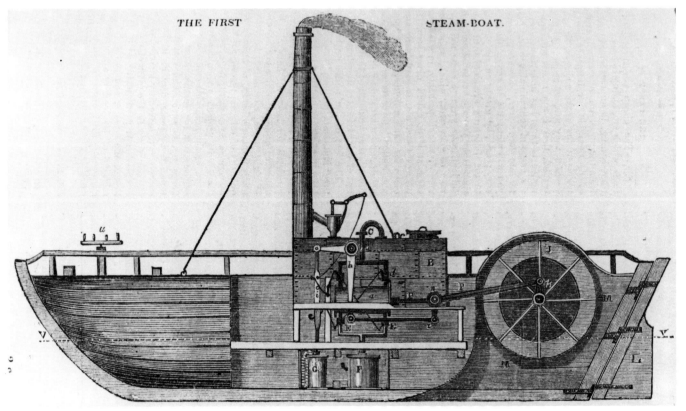

THE FIRST STEAM-BOAT.

paddle wheel were removed and she was converted into a dredger, hand powered; in the 1860s the rotting remains of this eventually disintegrated at the edge of the canal. Part of one of her rudders is preserved in Grangemouth Museum, along with other material relating to canals in the vicinity. Symington, a disappointed man, built no more steam boats; but *Charlotte Dundas*, in one or other version, was seen at work and closely examined by at least three people – Robert Fulton, Henry Bell and David Napier – who were to play prominent parts in their future development.

Richard Trevithick

There was another inventor who was active at the same period as Symington: he was, perhaps, the greatest of them all – Richard Trevithick (1771–1833). His work to some extent paralleled Symington's, particularly in use of horizontal cylinders; but Cornwall, where Trevithick did his early work, is a long way from central Scotland, and it does not appear that either was aware in detail of what the other was doing.

Trevithick's father, also Richard Trevithick, was a noted tin mine manager in Cornwall, and the son grew up with mines and Newcomen engines as familiar surroundings. He seems to have gained little from formal education, far more from being able to wander at will among the mines and mine machinery. It was during his childhood that a Watt patent engine was set up in Cornwall for the first time, in 1777: the first doubts of Cornish mine managers, with Trevithick senior prominent among them, gave way to enthusiasm at the savings to be gained. There was a rush to install Watt engines and within a few years they had virtually supplanted the Newcomen type. But payment of royalties to Watt was if anything even less popular in Cornwall than in Wanlockhead.

Meanwhile Richard Trevithick junior was growing up, to become in due course a young man of immense stature and strength – he was 6 ft 2 in. tall. Yet he was unassuming and gentle, but high spirited too, and with a reputation for threatening those who contradicted him that he would fling them down the engine shaft. He was also becoming an engineer of skill and repute. In the early 1790s he entered into an informal association with Edward Bull, formerly an engine erector for Boulton & Watt, to build beamless pumping engines of a type which Bull had developed. The cylinder was inverted directly over the pump shaft,

and the piston connected directly to the pump rod. However these engines infringed Watt's patent and attracted an injunction from Boulton & Watt in 1796.

Then, probably in 1797, it occurred to Trevithick that there was indeed a simple way to evade Watt's patent. By using what was then called 'strong steam', high pressure steam that is, at a pressure considerably greater than that of the atmosphere, and letting the used steam exhaust into the air, he could simply eliminate the condenser. Just how this thought occurred to him is not recorded. It is quite probable that Trevithick had seen Murdock's model steam carriage which worked on this principle; but when Trevithick himself had working model steam carriages made in 1797–8 he used a different layout. He had realised that although a boiler for strong steam must be made stronger than those then generally used, it could also be made much smaller, and so was well suited for incorporation into a vehicle. One of these models, built in 1798, is now preserved in the Science Museum. It has, unusually for its period, a cylindrical boiler with an internal flue which was heated by insertion of a pre-heated cast iron block. The cylinder is upright, vertical and set into the boiler; the piston rod is attached to a wide crosshead from which dual connecting rods, one on each side of the boiler, descend to crank pins on the road wheels. Retractable legs enabled this little road locomotive to be run as a stationary engine.

Trevithick's first full-size application of strong steam was in construction of mine winding engines with beams and cranks from 1799 onwards; but by late 1800 he was working on a full-size steam road carriage. To confirm that powered wheels would have sufficient adhesion with the road to propel a vehicle and would not, as many thought, simply spin round, he and a friend propelled a one-horse chaise up hill by turning the wheels by hand. The steam carriage was built in a smith's workshop near Camborne with Trevithick working, mostly, in his spare time. It was completed ready for trials over Christmas 1801.

Trevithick's first steam carriage made its first successful run with several passengers on Christmas Eve; it ran again on Christmas Day, and possibly on other days, until on 28 December Trevithick and some friends set out on it to visit other friends who lived two and a half miles away. But they had travelled only 300 yards or so, with the carriage going well, when it struck a gulley, an open water course across the road: the steering handle was jerked out of the hand of the steerer, Andrew Vivian, and the carriage overturned and was damaged.

The damage, evidently, was beyond immediate repair, for the would-be travellers, although they were expected at their destination, pushed the carriage under cover at a nearby hotel: and then, deciding perhaps that Christmas so far had been all work and no play, proceeded to drown their sorrows, and in due course they sat down to a roast goose. But the fire in the carriage had not been extinguished: the water boiled away and as its level fell, the iron boiler became red hot and set fire both to the carriage and to the shed in which it had been placed: everything that would burn was burned away.

The next step taken by Trevithick and Vivian was to go to London to obtain a patent to cover Trevithick's concept of a rotary steam engine using strong steam, together with its application to drive a sugar mill and a road carriage. In both the mill and the carriage a cylindrical boiler was to be used with an integral furnace: the fire was contained in a large cylindrical flue which made a U-bend at the far end of the boiler from the fire door and returned to a chimney beside it. The cylinder too was set within the boiler and in these two applications was to be horizontal. This patent came into force in March 1802 – approximately a year after Symington's patent of 1801 for an engine which was horizontal and direct acting but still low pressure and condensing.

Trevithick had been advised to build a full-size steam carriage and exhibit it in London; but first he went to Coalbrookdale in August 1802 to experiment with a high pressure pumping engine. This, which had a 4 ft diameter boiler, was working at pressures from 60 lb per sq. in. up to as high as 145 lb, and Trevithick had thoughts of taking the pressure higher still.

At the same time, the Coalbrookdale Company started to build a steam carriage, or locomotive, on Trevithick's principle for use on its tramroads. Of this, the first attempt to build a railway locomotive, tantalisingly little is known. A scale drawing survives at the Science Museum, and the illustration on page 11 is derived from this. It seems unlikely that the original ever did any useful work, if indeed it was completed. It is possible that a fatal accident during trials led to their abandonment, and the dismantling of the locomotive.

Early in 1803, while Symington far away in the north was showing off the second *Charlotte Dundas* to the public, the boiler and cylinder for Trevithick's second steam carriage were being built in Cornwall. When complete they were sent by sea to London where they arrived late in the

spring, and were fitted into the specially built carriage which was waiting to receive them. This vehicle had driving wheels some ten feet in diameter, the better, I assume, to overcome road surface irregularities of the sort which had upset the first carriage. The coach body was mounted high up between these wheels, the boiler also between them, low down at the rear. It worked at a pressure of about 30 lb per sq. in., a more usual pressure for Trevithick's engines than those of the experimental engine mentioned above, and the exhaust steam was turned up the chimney to draw the fire. The single cylinder was set horizontally within the boiler, the piston drove the wheels through rods, a crankshaft and gears. The coach was steered by a pair of small wheels pivoted at the front. In this vehicle Trevithick and Vivian successfully and extensively steamed about the streets of London during 1803.

Unfortunately no commercial interest was shown. By now, however, Trevithick's high pressure engines were becoming popular for stationary use. The boiler of one of them exploded with fatal results in 1803 – the boy supposed to be in charge of it had gone off to catch eels, in the foundations of a mill under construction which the engine was draining – but even this proved only a temporary setback, although it did discourage General Bentham from installing one of Trevithick's engines in the dredger which was being built for use in Woolwich Dockyard. Trevithick in subsequent engines fitted two safety valves, and developed a lead rivet, or fusible plug as it is now known, to be fitted into the furnace. If it overheated from lack of water, the lead would melt, releasing the steam and extinguishing the fire. Trevithick engines were built, in return for an agreed royalty payment, by engineering firms such as the Coalbrookdale Co., and they were installed for winding, pumping and other purposes in places as far apart as Cornwall, London and Manchester.

Penydarren

In the course of promoting his stationary engines, Trevithick encountered Samuel Homfray, the ironmaster, of Merthyr Tydfil. Ironworks had made Merthyr at this period a boom town, greater in population than Swansea and considerably greater than Cardiff. Homfray wanted Trevithick's engines initially for his ironworks and collieries; he was admitted to a half-share in the patent and started to build them at Penydarren Ironworks, Merthyr. This ironworks was one of those which used the Penydarren Tramroad completed in 1802, as mentioned in the previous chapter, according to the best of Outram's principles with plate rails and stone blocks. Furthermore, Homfray was a man of sporting character. By late in 1803 not only was Trevithick building a locomotive for him at Penydarren, but Homfray had laid a wager of as much as 500 guineas with an unconvinced and rival ironmaster that it would haul a load of 10 tons of iron down the $9\frac{3}{4}$-mile length of the tramroad to Abercynon.

The locomotive was ready early in 1804. After a trial of the engine without wheels, it was completed and ran first on rails, under its own steam, on 13 February 1804: the first occasion on which a railway locomotive is known to have worked satisfactorily. Further trials followed, and then the locomotive set out on 21 February to haul, with success, down the tramroad to Abercynon not merely 10 tons of iron, loaded into five waggons, but also seventy men who jumped aboard for the ride. Subsequent trials showed it able to haul a load of at least 25 tons.

This locomotive had its single cylinder set horizontally in the boiler; the diameter of the cylinder was $8\frac{1}{2}$ in., its stroke $4\frac{1}{2}$ ft. The weight of the locomotive was about 5 tons and that, though not great by later standards, was its downfall: although it worked satisfactorily, running at 4–5 mph, it damaged the track and broke the brittle cast-iron rails. It was converted into a stationary engine and used as such for many years; but its eventual fate is unknown.

In view of this, the Welsh Industrial & Maritime Museum – part of the National Museum of Wales – has had a full-size working replica constructed. This project originated in 1978 and has been led by the museum's assistant keeper, Dr E. S. Owen Jones. Because no drawings of the original locomotive survive, the design of the replica was based on the drawings which do survive of the 1803 Coalbrookdale locomotive and, more particularly, the Trevithick locomotive built at Gateshead in 1805, which will be mentioned shortly. There were of course some modifications needed – for instance present-day safety requirements necessitated a boiler of welded steel rather than Trevithick's original cast iron. Many of the components were provided by industrial undertakings in South Wales and a track on which to run the locomotive was laid in Cardiff at the museum, as part of a Youth Opportunities Programme. New rails were cast, using an original Penydarren Tramroad plate as a pattern, but sleeper blocks were made from concrete not stone.

The completed replica locomotive was commissioned in 1981 and is steamed regularly at the museum. During 1982, it and the museum's stationary engines were being steamed on the first Saturday of each month, and additionally for school parties. It is a strange and remarkable sight, this locomotive, as it lumbers up and down its track, a reminder that the original, so primitive compared with what came after, was yet far advanced compared with what had gone before. It is also interesting to observe that the locomotive is indeed hard on the track: plates judder as the wheels strike them, and securing spikes are jerked upwards. An incautious comment by the author to his escort in the spring of 1982 produced the response that although inconspicuous precautions had been taken to make the track stronger than the original, by enlarging the bearing surfaces between rails and sleepers, and these had initially seemed wholly successful, there had recently been seven cases of broken rails.

The summer of 1804 was a period of serious danger that Britain would be invaded by Napoleon: a French fleet assembled at Boulogne for this purpose. Trevithick, then at Coalbrookdale, was approached by the second Marquis of Stafford and other gentlemen who enquired whether one of his engines could power a steam boat which could be used to tow fireships in among the French fleet. The marquis may well have been aware of the interest in steam boats of his late uncle the Duke of Bridgewater, and possibly of Symington's approach in connection with the *Charlotte Dundas* in 1802, but he was not of course responsible for cancelling the duke's order to Symington for steam tugs.

At any rate the Marquis of Stafford despatched Trevithick to London to call on the Admiralty: but the Admiralty kept him waiting day after day for so long that he eventually grew tired of this and returned to Coalbrookdale. There he found one of his stationary engines loaded for despatch into a barge on the Severn: he promptly adapted it, by way of experiment, as temporary power for the barge. A paddle wheel was fitted each side of the vessel and the engine connected to them. It was found that it could propel the barge, of between 60 and 70 tons burden, in still water at about 7 mph. This, probably, was late in 1804; and nothing came of it, for the invasion threat was already receding.

Meanwhile, far away in the North-East, a man called Christopher Blackett had in 1800 inherited his family's estate at Wylam, and the colliery that it included. Wylam lies on the north bank of the Tyne, about five miles above its navigable limit at Lemington, and for over fifty years a wooden waggonway had followed the river to carry coal from colliery to keels waiting at Lemington.

The Wylam Waggonway was therefore nearly level, and even included a gradient against the load. Generally Tyneside waggonways had a sufficiently steep descent to the river for loaded waggons to run down by gravity, but on the Wylam Waggonway horses had to haul the loaded waggons as well as the empties. This must have given Blackett a powerful incentive to find a cheaper alternative. Of course, anywhere else but in the waggonway-conscious North-East, the river itself would have been made navigable up to the colliery, or a lateral canal dug; and indeed estimates had been made as early as 1764 for a navigable cut between Lemington and Wylam. But it had not been made.

Blackett had been impressed by the performance of Trevithick's Penydarren locomotive and, according to Samuel Smiles in *Lives of the Engineers* he 'formed the acquaintance of Trevithick in London', though Smiles is not always a source to be trusted. At any rate, when in 1805 another Trevithick-type locomotive was built, Blackett had an option to purchase it on completion. This is the locomotive built at Gateshead, at Whinfield's Foundry, following Trevithick's instructions. Drawings survive and appear as an illustration on page 86.

This working full-size replica of Trevithick's 1804 Penydarren locomotive was completed in 1981. It is seen here in action on the length of plateway built for it at the Welsh Industrial & Maritime Museum, Cardiff.

As the drawings clearly show, this locomotive was intended for wooden track: but Blackett never took delivery. It seems that on seeing the completed locomotive on trial at the builder he realised, what is obvious to us now, that his track was not nearly strong enough. The locomotive was put to use by the builder as a stationary engine; Blackett (who seems to have been unusually well-informed on tramroad developments away from the north-east) had re-laid his waggonway by 1808 with plate rails – most unusual on Tyneside – which enabled a horse to haul two loaded waggons where previously it had hauled only one.

From 1806 onwards, Trevithick was again busy in and about London. Towards the end of the previous year, Trinity House had invited Homfray and Trevithick to make an offer for raising ballast from the bed of the Thames tideway by means of Trevithick's steam engine. At this period large amounts of ballast were dredged for use in ships; spoon dredgers operated by men were used. Trevithick hoped for a fourteen-year contract, but Trinity House wanted to see satisfactory trials first. So Trevithick fitted out the gun brig *Blazer* as a dredger with one of his engines, completing the work in July 1806, and she was used to raise ballast during the autumn. But he found this dredger was not sufficiently powerful; and although he proposed to build a much more powerful dredger, the price he asked Trinity House for ballast to be raised by it was greater, at 9d a ton, than the $7\frac{1}{2}$d a ton which manual dredging contractors charged. So the project lapsed, though the *Blazer* continued to be used on various dredging tasks on the Thames for several years.

In August 1807 Trevithick, because of his mining background, became engineer to a project for driving a tunnel beneath the Thames at Limehouse Reach. Work had been commenced by the Thames Archway Company (incorporated for the purpose in 1805) with Cornishman Robert Vazie, the original promoter, as engineer. Vazie succeeded only in sinking a vertical shaft 76 ft deep on the south bank before quicksands brought the work to a halt. It was at this stage that Trevithick was brought in and, with a team of skilled Cornish miners, started to drive a small-bore trial level or driftway (intended to drain the eventual main tunnel) northwards from the shaft and beneath the river. At first all went well, but the winter of 1807–8 brought problems – of more quicksands, of water bursting through into the driftway from the river, of wrangling among the proprietors. By July 1808, with 1,000 ft driven and only 200 ft to go, work was at a standstill. Trevithick proposed a mov-

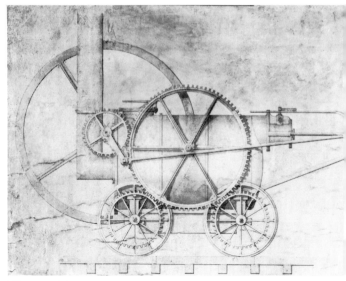

The original drawings for the Trevithick locomotive built at Gateshead in 1805 survive at the Science Museum. The locomotive was intended for Christopher Blackett's wooden-railed Wylam Waggonway; it was never used there, probably because it would have been too heavy for the track. It was converted into a stationary engine and used as such for many years.

able caisson to build a brick- or iron-lined main tunnel on the bed of the river, but was turned down. So this project, too, eventually lapsed.

Catch me who can

By July 1808 however Trevithick's attention was already being claimed by something else – construction of a steam locomotive which, so *The Times* reported, would be raced against any mare, horse or gelding produced at the forthcoming October meeting at Newmarket – with £10,000 already (by July) wagered on the result. The locomotive was to be run on a circular track for twenty-four hours, the horse to start at the same time, the winner to be whichever travelled farthest.

The locomotive, which in due course was given the name *Catch me who can*, was built at Hazledine & Rastrick's foundry at Bridgnorth, Shropshire. This firm had built many Trevithick stationary engines. The Hazledine of the partnership was John Hazledine, elder brother of William Hazledine whose foundry, set up at Plas Kynaston, Ruabon, in the late 1790s, had provided the ironwork for Pontcysyllte aqueduct. The Rastrick partner was John

Urpeth Rastrick (1780–1856) who though born in Northumberland had gained experience of the use of cast iron in Shropshire before becoming Hazledine's partner. He also practised as a civil engineer; in the spring or early summer of 1808 he worked for a time under Trevithick on the abortive Thames tunnel project.

Trevithick laid a circular track for this locomotive, not without difficulty from subsidence due to soft ground, on an open space on the south side of the street then known as New Road and now called Euston Road. Here the public paid to view it running, and those who were not too timid rode behind it in an open carriage. The locomotive had a single vertical cylinder set into the top of the boiler at the opposite end to the chimney and firedoor; the wide crosshead ran between slide bars mounted vertically above the boiler and from it connecting rods descended either side of the boiler to crank pins on the driving wheels: a much neater layout than the horizontal slide-bar arrangement which projected at one end of earlier locomotives. Unlike them, too, it had no flywheel: Trevithick must have realised that, once it got going, its own momentum would carry the cranks over dead centre. This locomotive was, in effect, Trevithick's usual stationary engine of the period mounted on four wheels, of which the driven pair replaced the crankshaft and flywheel.

A Trevithick stationary engine of this type, built by Hazledine & Co., is preserved in the Science Museum, and J. T. van Riemsdijk, Keeper of Mechanical Engineering of the Science Museum, suggests (*The Pictorial History of Steam Power*) that this may be the actual *Catch me who can* engine converted for stationary use. Both of its connecting rods are cranked outwards, and while one of them clears the flywheel in this way, there is no obvious reason for the other to be so cranked. It is possible that both were made in this way originally to clear the driving wheels of the engine when used as a locomotive.

The grand contest between the locomotive and competing horses was announced in the press for late September – and then, silence. One is reminded of the earlier contrast between the absence of information about the Coalbrookdale locomotive and the glowing reports of the Penydarren one – if the contest had been a resounding success for *Catch me who can*, then surely this would have been widely publicised. So presumably for some reason or other it did not win. What did actually happen to it is recorded, however: after it had run successfully for several weeks, a rail broke (the ground was still soft), the locomotive flew off at a

A Trevithick high pressure stationary steam engine built by Hazeldine & Co. of Bridgnorth is preserved in the Science Museum. It is possible that this was originally mounted on wheels to form Trevithick's 1808 locomotive Catch me who can.

tangent and overturned. Whether this was before, during or after the contest I do not know: but admission charges were not meeting the expense of running the locomotive and it was not set to work on rails again.

Trevithick made no more direct contributions to the development of steam transport although, as we shall see, indirectly he was still to have great influence on the application of steam power to both railways and ships, so it is worth summarising the later career of this remarkable man. He seems to have used up most of his financial resources on *Catch me who can*. He had earlier won a large wager for Homfray with the Penydarren locomotive, and I am inclined to see the whole episode as a grand gamble to restore his fortunes, already failing after several disappointments. In fact, after the demonstrations of this locomotive were over, he was a poor man; he had been progressively disposing of shares in his interest in the engine patent, and sold his last remaining interest in it in 1808.

He was still, however, rich in ideas. In July 1808 he had patented, jointly with merchant and inventor Robert Dickinson, a 'nautical labourer', a steam boat which would act as both tug boat and floating crane. It was never completed, but Trevithick's and Dickinson's next patent did take practical form: this was the construction of large iron tanks to replace wooden casks for carrying liquid cargoes and water aboard ships. These the partners started to manufacture in Limehouse. In 1810 a third joint patent covered the use of iron in shipbuilding and many associated ideas.

In May 1810 Trevithick was hit by a serious illness, probably typhus, and incapacitated for six months or more. He was eventually taken by sea back to Cornwall to recuperate. During this period his business affairs deteriorated and Dickinson, a shady character, proved to be a false friend. Calamity followed calamity when in February 1811 the partners were declared bankrupt.

Trevithick was eventually discharged from bankruptcy at the beginning of 1814. In the meantime he remained in Cornwall, setting up, in effect, an engineering consultancy. He developed improved boilers for mine engines, and single-acting high-pressure steam engines which worked expansively – that is to say, steam was cut off from entering the cylinder when the piston had made only part of its stroke, the pressure of the steam expanding within the cylinder propelling it the rest of the way. He adapted such engines for agricultural use to power threshing machines, and he did much else besides.

Then in 1813 he was approached by Francisco Uvillé, who had come from Peru (then a Spanish colony) to find him, with a proposal that engines of his type should be used to drain the rich but flooded silver mines of Cerro de Pasco. The point was that, because the mines lay 14,000 feet above sea level, engines dependent on low-altitude atmospheric pressure could not be used – only high pressure engines were suitable.

The following year nine engines built by Hazledine Rastrick & Co. were shipped to Peru. Because of difficulties of transporting machinery to a remote spot in the Andes (approached only by a precipitous mule track in places no more than $2\frac{1}{2}$ feet wide) and in setting it up there, and of the deaths of two of the English erectors who accompanied it, Trevithick himself set out for Peru in 1816. As with the Thames tunnel, the physical difficulties with which he found himself confronted on arrival were matched by the internal political differences within the mining company; but in Peru he found in addition that he had arrived during the opening stages of a civil war, which eventually led to the country's independence from Spain. It was only after many further ventures and adventures in South and Central America that he finally returned home to England and his family in 1827. He was as inventive as ever. In 1832 Trevithick proposed a tower of cast iron 1,000 feet high to celebrate the Reform Act; but the following year, while experimenting with water jet propulsion for ships, he contracted pneumonia and within a week had died, at the age of sixty-six.

Fulton in France

We left Robert Fulton arriving in Paris in June or July 1797 with the intention of promoting in France his ideas on small canals. He was granted a French patent for them in 1798 and his book about his proposals was published in French translation the same year (and in Portuguese in 1800) but by the end of 1797 he was already working on something else – a scheme for a submersible boat, a submarine. This was a remarkable episode and although it bears only indirectly on his steam boat work, it is worth mentioning at length because it marks Fulton's transition from visionary to one who could in fact make the wildest dreams take practical form.

There had been previous attempts to design submarines and one had been built and used by the Americans, with very little success, during the American War of

Robert Fulton 1765–1815 (left): British by birth, American by course of events, republican by conviction, cosmopolitan in outlook – artist turned visionary turned practical engineer turned the world's first successful steam boat operator.

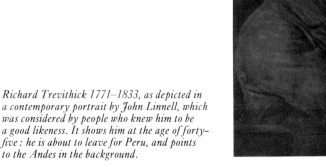

Richard Trevithick 1771–1833, as depicted in a contemporary portrait by John Linnell, which was considered by people who knew him to be a good likeness. It shows him at the age of forty-five: he is about to leave for Peru, and points to the Andes in the background.

Independence. Fulton's plan was that his submarine, to be called the *Nautilus*, would submerge by taking in water ballast. It would be just over 21 feet long, and propelled by a screw propeller half a century ahead of its time, driven through gearing from cranks turned by the crew. Or, on the surface, it would sail.

It was to be armed with a mine, which Fulton called a torpedo, though it was not a self-propelled torpedo in the modern sense. Rather, the *Nautilus* itself was to navigate beneath the ship being attacked. To position the mine and fire it, a shaft passed upwards through the conning tower by means of a stuffing box, and terminated in a screw eye; through this eye there passed a tow rope from the mine, which was carried on the outside of the submarine, to a winch, also on the outside. The screw eye was to be embedded in the wooden hull of the ship being attacked by blows on the opposite end of the shaft by the submarine crew, who would then turn the shaft to screw the eye firmly into the wood. *Nautilus* would then set off again, paying out the rope from the winch until it was fully extended at which stage, since it passed through the screw eye, it would bring the mine into contact with the ship and explode it.

Fulton's proposal to the French government was that it should enter into a contract with the Nautilus Company, which he would set up to develop the submarine, and which would be rewarded according to the number and armament of British ships destroyed.

Such a proposal from one who had recently been enjoying the friendship and hospitality of British people seems barbarous in the extreme. Fulton seems to have been actuated partly by a desire to make his fortune, and partly by a belief that it was in the best interests of the USA to redress the balance of power of European navies, then heavily weighted towards the British.

At any rate he succeeded in building his *Nautilus* (at his own expense); he launched this amazing vessel in July 1800, and carried out trials, with himself in command, in the river Seine and at sea, with remarkable success. The following March, after some procrastination by the French government, and a meeting between Fulton and Napoleon, he got an agreement approximating to what he wanted.

The spring and summer of 1801 he spent at Brest carrying out further trials. He successfully sailed the submarine on the surface. He obtained light for the interior by inserting small windows. He made the submarine plunge and rise vertically, and steer to port and starboard; he steered it under water by compass, and he provided a reservoir of compressed air to replenish used oxygen. He also successfully used his mine on trial to blow up a sloop at anchor. But when Fulton attempted to use his submarine to approach British ships blockading Brest harbour, he was frustrated. The British had been warned, had look-outs at their mast-heads and boats rowing round their ships.

The submarine was not, however, taken up by the French authorities, possibly because of a change in the Minister of Marine to an admiral of the old school who did not approve, possibly just because the likely results from using it seemed insufficiently advantageous to be worth while for the authorities to pursue. In any case, overtures for peace had been going on since March 1801: a preliminary treaty between France and Britain was signed on 1 October and hostilities ceased. The definitive treaty, the Treaty of Amiens, was concluded on 25 March 1802 and for all that anyone knew at the time the peace would be permanent. At the end of its trials the submarine was dismantled. Technologically it had been a brilliant achievement.

The end of the submarine scheme and the cessation of hostilities prompted Fulton to turn again to the line of development in which he was eventually to achieve success as a world pioneer: propulsion of ships by steam on a commercial scale. Perhaps the effort needed to propel a vessel – in his case the *Nautilus* – by human power had impressed on him, as it had earlier on James Taylor and Patrick Miller, the superiority of an alternative such as steam.

He was much aided by the providential arrival in Paris in November 1801 of Chancellor Robert R. Livingston as Minister Plenipotentiary of the United States to France. Livingston had earlier in the USA conducted steam boat experiments of his own; in them he had been helped by, among others, a young French royalist emigré called Marc Brunel (later to become the famous father of an even more famous son, Isambard Kingdom Brunel). The experiments were not successful, but nevertheless in 1798 Livingston had obtained an exclusive right for twenty years to operate steam boats within the state of New York – provided that he built within a twelvemonth a boat that would go at a speed of not less than 4 mph. In North America, the incentive to develop the steam boat was greater than in Britain for, while highways were comparatively few and poor, rivers were extensive and broad.

In October 1802 Livingston and Fulton entered into an agreement of which the principal points were: a steam boat 120 feet long should be built able to carry 60 passengers and run on the Hudson River between New York and Albany at 8 mph in still water; a US patent should be taken out by Fulton and the profits shared equally; and Fulton should go to England to construct an experimental steam boat at Livingston's expense.

Things did not work out quite like that, of course; but Livingston's 1798 right to operate steam boats in New York state, which had lapsed, was re-established and extended jointly to Livingston and Fulton. Proof was to be produced within two years; the date was subsequently extended.

It was in France that Fulton then built a steam boat,

for trials on the Seine at Paris. It was 66 ft 6 in. long, and had a single upright cylinder and side paddle wheels, and it seems to have been completed in the early spring of 1803. While it was moored awaiting trials there was a violent storm during the night, in the course of which the heavy steam plant dropped through the hull to the bed of the river. This must have been very close to the date (28 March 1803) on which *Charlotte Dundas* successfully steamed against a gale on the Forth & Clyde Canal: perhaps it was a bad spring. Fulton, by working all day without food or rest, succeeded in raising the engine and boiler. A new and stronger hull was built and the steam plant installed in it. After at least one private trial for his friends, Fulton demonstrated the boat in public on 9 August 1803. The demonstration was wholly successful: the steam boat towed two other boats and during a period of one and a half hours ascended and descended a reach of the Seine four times.

Three days earlier, Fulton had written to Boulton, Watt & Co. asking them to supply engine components – cylinder, piston, piston rod with 4 ft stroke, valves, air pump, condenser – for despatch to New York. He does not appear to have indicated the purpose for which they were needed. James Watt had retired from business by this date, succeeded by his son, also James Watt; and his firm had set up the Soho Foundry to manufacture engines and components. But in this case it was unable to get government permission to export Fulton's requirements to the USA.

Fulton in England again

At this point the story takes a distinct cloak-and-dagger turn. The Peace of Amiens, following the 1802 treaty, was a fragile one, and on 18 May 1803 war between Britain and France had broken out again. Lord Stanhope, as early as the spring of 1802, had told the House of Lords that submarine navigation had been brought to such perfection by a person in France as to render the destruction of ships absolutely sure. The British government evidently took Fulton's submarine activities seriously enough to want him, so to speak, on our side rather than theirs. So Fulton was approached by British agents in 1804, induced to transfer his allegiance to the British government, and spirited out of France to England. He reached London again on 19 May 1804.

Fulton had been treated none too well by the French

Fulton adapted beam engine layout for the steam engine of his boat the Clermont. *The drive, as usual, was from crosshead to beam to connecting rod to crank; but the familiar overhead beam was replaced, so that the vessel would not be top heavy, by two beams low down in the form of bell cranks. Cylinder, condenser and associated parts were built by Boulton, Watt & Co. in 1804; the vessel was eventually built in 1807.*

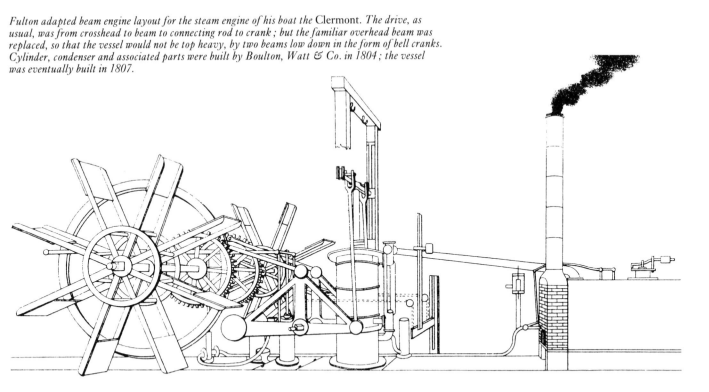

government; he had never been in its pay, though some of his submarine expenses had been reimbursed. As a staunch republican he was probably disappointed in the direction which the form of government in France was taking. Napoleon, previously first consul, had himself crowned emperor on 18 May 1804.

One of Fulton's first actions on arriving in England was to travel to Birmingham to visit Boulton, Watt & Co. For their subsequent correspondence, most friendly in tone, one may refer to H. W. Dickinson's biography of Fulton, where it is quoted in full. This time there was neither concealment of the purpose of the engine he wanted, nor hesitation by the manufacturers. Fulton's order was accepted against a guarantee by the American consul in London, and towards the end of the year the parts for a steam engine and associated fittings were ready for him. The single cylinder, 2 ft diameter and 4 ft stroke, was to be positioned upright; from its crosshead, working in vertical guides, connecting rods were to descend to bell cranks positioned low down, and from these the drive would be taken by connecting rods and spur gears to the paddle shaft. Fulton had established this layout in his trial boat on the Seine the previous year.

The engine and associated parts were packed up and despatched by canal boat to Fulton in London, after some delay caused by ice. The eventual cost of the engine was £548. Fulton obtained permission to ship the engine to America, and he had an externally fired boiler built of copper in London.

Despite all this, to have steam boat engines built was not the purpose for which he had been brought to England. The year 1804 was the year of Napoleon's invasion threat. Fulton was able to reach agreement with the British government to disclose his plans for attacking fleets by 'submarine bombs'. Of his submarine boat no more was heard, but the 'torpedo' side was developed: the intention now was to use floating mines with clockwork timers, linked to a grapnel and line which would be attached to the anchor cable of the ship attacked so that the tide would carry the mine beneath the ship.

Three expeditions were mounted, one against the French fleet in Calais, two against the fleet in Boulogne. (It was at this period that Trevithick was approached about the possibility of a steam tug to tow fireships in among the French fleet: while Boulton, Watt & Co. were completing Fulton's engine in Birmingham, Trevithick was carrying out his steam boat experiment over at Coalbrookdale.)

The three expeditions, however, met only limited success, which prompted Fulton to hold a demonstration to show that the method of attack, not the mine, was at fault. The target was the captured brig *Dorothea*, anchored off Deal. Two boats, each with a mine in the stern, rowed towards her, approaching with the tide. The mines were linked by a long line; as the boats separated to pass one each side of the *Dorothea*, the line caught on her anchor cable, and the mines were swept beneath her. In the explosion which followed the brig was almost totally destroyed.

A further expedition was made against Boulogne in October 1805 and successfully blew up shipping in the harbour; but by then the invasion threat was much reduced and Nelson's victory at Trafalgar the same month removed it altogether. Fulton's mines were no longer needed, but the British government rewarded him by a payment of £10,000 plus £5,000 salary and released him from his contract. Fulton eventually left England in 1806, arriving in New York in December of that year after nineteen years away from his native country.

Fulton and Symington

Before he left Britain in 1806, Fulton visited William Symington and inspected the *Charlotte Dundas*: but the precise date at which he did so continues to puzzle historians. Fulton himself admitted to the visit but appears to have left no detailed record of it. Symington, however, in his *A Brief History of Steam Navigation* (published in 1829, long after the event) states that 'during the period that I was employed in constructing the experiments under the patronage of Lord Dundas, viz., in July 1801 . . . a stranger came to the bank of the canal and requested to see me. He very politely announced himself as Mr Fulton, a native of North America . . .'. Symington admits he was flattered, and had the fire of the boat lit, and took Fulton on it for four miles along the canal and back again. During this cruise, Fulton took out a memorandum book, put several pointed questions about the machinery and noted down the answers. A similar account of this incident is included in Bowie's *A Brief Narrative proving . . . Symington to be . . . the inventor of . . . Steam Navigation* (1833) but he dates it to '1801 or 1802'. A different account is quoted in Bennet Woodcroft's *A Sketch of the Origin and Progress of Steam Navigation* (1848): it is that of Robert Weir and was made under oath in 1824. Weir said he was employed by Symington for several years, and in 1801

remembered Symington erecting a boat with a steam engine in it and dragging two vessels along the Forth & Clyde Canal. He was employed as engine fireman on board. 'Some time after the first experiment' [*sic*] while the boat was lying at Lock 16, it was visited by a stranger; Symington got Weir to light the furnace and the stranger was carried about four miles along the canal and back. Weir heard him say his name was Fulton, and that he was a native of the USA. Weir also remembered Symington remarking that the boat was much impeded by the narrowness of the channel, to which Fulton replied that the objection would not apply on the large rivers of North America. The same affidavit is quoted by the Rankines in their 1862 biography of Symington; and they, like Bowie, are confused over the date of Fulton's visit, giving it in one place as 1801 and in another as 1802.

The snag to all these accounts is of course the dates. Fulton did not arrive back in England from France until mid-May 1804; he then promptly arranged for Boulton, Watt & Co. to build engine components, and involved himself in mine trials for the British government. So, unless he paid a very hurried visit to Scotland in June 1804, he is unlikely to have had the time to spare for a visit there before the spring of 1805. Historians have generally assumed that Fulton did visit Symington in 1804 or later and that Symington's memory was at fault over the date.

Even June 1804, though, is a long time after the successful *Charlotte Dundas* trial of March 1803, and 1805 is longer still. Although Symington was still in the district, it is unlikely that he would be found by a stranger 'coming to the bank of the canal', and it is probable that *Charlotte Dundas* was no longer in commission. Earlier, in 1801, the date given by Symington, Fulton was fully committed with the submarine schemes at Brest, and Symington's memory was clearly at fault to that extent. But 1802, however, would be a different matter. France and Britain were at peace: many British people took the opportunity to visit France, and there was presumably no hindrance to an American's leaving France to visit Scotland. Fulton was thinking of steam boats again, and it would be at this stage of his project that he would wish to see what others were doing.

It is notable too that the layout of Fulton's boats owes nothing to the *Charlotte Dundas* of 1803: but this vessel was being built in 1802 and if Symington took Fulton on board a steam boat then, it must have been the Schank/Symington boat of 1801. This, according to Harvey and

Downs Rose, was driven by a beam engine: in Fulton's boats, although the familiar upright cylinder of the beam engine was retained, the overhead beam, which would tend to make the boat top heavy, was replaced by rocking bell cranks (Fulton called them beams) at low level, which would much improve the boat's stability: just the sort of step forward which might be expected.

There is however another important point in favour of an 1802 visit by Fulton to Symington: it is this, that it provides a motive for something otherwise inexplicable, Symington's omission to mention, in his own account of the 1801–3 trials, that two successive boats were involved, an omission which has confused and baffled historians ever since. Symington's account originally formed part of a petition to Parliament made in the hope that he would receive a financial reward as the originator of steam navigation, and in it he is at pains to emphasise that Fulton minutely examined the *Charlotte Dundas* at work several years before his own steam vessel appeared on the Hudson River. If in fact it was the unsuccessful 1801 boat that Fulton examined, and not the successful 1803 one, then the validity of Symington's claim is reduced almost to nothing. How great a motive Symington would have had to conceal the existence of two successive boats, and blur their identities into one!

According to H. W. Dickinson, Joel Barlow, an American in whose Paris house Fulton was a frequent and long-term guest, does seem to have visited England in, probably, June 1802, and consulted William Chapman on Fulton's behalf about steam engines for boats. William Chapman (1749–1832) was a native of North-East England, and had a long and distinguished career as a canal engineer, much of it in association with William Jessop and the early part of it in Ireland where, about 1788 on the Kildare Canal, he originated the skew bridge. He returned to England in 1794 and in 1797 he recommended construction of a steam dredger to improve the channel of the River Orwell down stream from Ipswich. When this was eventually built in 1805–6 it incorporated a Boulton, Watt & Co. bell-crank engine.

After visiting Chapman in 1802 Barlow immediately recommended to Fulton that he should go directly to England 'silent and steady' and get Chapman to build him an engine while Fulton built a boat for it, for trials prior to the New York venture. Barlow offered to find the funds 'without any noise' for the English operation. As we know, the trial boat was eventually built in France, that winter.

Fulton passed the whole summer of 1802, says Dickinson, at the spa of Plombières in the east of France as escort to Barlow's wife. There is no apparent record of his leaving France and going to Scotland and back during that period: though the temptation to suppose that he may have done so, silent and steady, is a strong one. It remains a fascinating enigma.

The *Clermont*

On his return to the USA late in 1806 Fulton was at last able to set about having the boat built for which his Boulton, Watt & Co. engine was intended. This was no sudden impulse – on the contrary, and in this Fulton had perhaps learned from previous ventures – he had researched the subject thoroughly. He had investigated the work of earlier steam boat pioneers, he had studied recent works on resistance of solids to passage through water, he had concluded that his vessel should be long, narrow, shallow and flat-bottomed, he had carefully calculated the power and dimensions of the engine needed, and he had obtained the components of it from the best known and most experienced maker.

The general public, of course, knew little if anything of this: what it did know, as the boat took shape during the spring of 1807, was that a great many people had previously attempted to build steam boats, that no one had been really successful, and that probably no one ever would be. Fulton's steam boat acquired the nickname *Fulton's Folly*.

Robert Fulton, of course, was vindicated. The boat ran for the first time, experimentally, on 10 August 1807, with encouraging results. Then, after what Fulton described as 'corrections, and the finishing of cabins', she was ready for her main trial on 17 August. On that day she set out from New York for Albany, 150 miles upstream. She took 24 hours to reach Clermont, the seat of Chancellor Livingston, 110 miles above New York, and after an overnight stop continued to Albany, 40 miles, reached in a further 8 hours. The following day she started south again, reaching Clermont in 9 hours, and continued after a halt of only one hour to New York, reached after a 21-hour voyage from Clermont. In each direction there was a slight head wind: no sails were used, and the average speed was 5 mph. Clearly, the age of the steam boat had arrived.

After further modifications and improvements, the boat left New York on her first voyage as a commercial venture, with fourteen passengers, on 4 September 1807. She continued to run until late November, when the river started to freeze over. She commenced running again the following May, at which date her accommodation was said to comprise 3 excellent cabins, 54 berths, kitchen, larder, pantry, bar and steward's room.

There now began a well-deserved period of success for Fulton and Livingston – despite the attempts of owners of other vessels on the river who, suddenly realising what they were up against, attempted to hinder the progress of the steam boat by obstructing her and even colliding with her. A second and similar steam boat was ready for the 1810 season and was called the *Car of Neptune*; the first boat, till then known simply as the *Steamboat* or *North River Steamboat*, was named the *Clermont*. Several other vessels followed; in 1811 Fulton and Livingston extended their operations to the Mississippi with construction of the *New Orleans*, the first steam boat on that river, and about the same date Fulton designed steam ferries to take horses and carriages as well as foot-passengers across the Hudson River between New York and Jersey City, the river being about $1\frac{1}{2}$ miles wide at that point.

In 1814 relations between Great Britain and the USA had deteriorated to the point of war. Fulton designed the *Demologos*, a double-hulled steam warship with her single paddle wheel central, for protection; but the war ended in December 1814 before *Demologos* could see action. The following February Fulton got wet through while examining her and other boats under repair. His lungs became inflamed (they had been weak ever since the episode of raising the sunken steam engine from the bed of the Seine in Paris), and shortly afterwards he died at the age of 49, a sadly premature end.

After Fulton's success in operating *Clermont*, others soon followed his example. Some indeed had already been working independently – such as Livingston's brother-in-law John Stevens, who had been interested in steam boats since the 1780s, experimented with launches driven by screw propellers in the 1800s, declined to join the Livingston-Fulton partnership in the spring of 1807 and launched his own paddle steamer *Phoenix* on to the Hudson River in 1808. Because of Livingston's and Fulton's rights on the Hudson, however, she was sent down to Philadelphia, by sea – the first steamer to make a sea passage. The first steam boat in Canada was built in 1809, and from then on their spread, in North America, was rapid: there were said to be 300 steam boats in use there in 1822. Their introduction to commercial use in Europe is described in chapter six.

With his paddle steamer Clermont, *completed in 1807, Robert Fulton became the first person to operate, successfully in commercial service, a steam boat – or, for that matter, any vessel or vehicle with a self-contained steam plant. Her route lay on the Hudson River from New York to Albany, 150 miles.*

CHAPTER FIVE

Roads and Coaching: the Heyday

Highland Roads

In terms of transport, the significance of the first three decades of the nineteenth century is that it was the period when steam boats and railways were successfully developed. Yet that judgement can only be made with the benefit of hindsight, of knowledge of what came later. To most of those living in Britain at the time, this was the great period of road improvements: of surfaces which were at last made smooth, firm and to a large extent water resistant, of better alignments and bridges, of effective administration, and of quicker, more frequent and more extensive mail and stage coach services, made possible by these improvements. The two interacted: better coach services fed the demand for still better roads. Indeed ever since introduction of the mail coach system, the Post Office had been diligently pressing turnpike trusts to keep their roads in order, and county authorities to maintain their bridges well.

The turnpike system was continuing to expand and during its heyday, the 1820s and 1830s, over 1,100 trusts were responsible for some 25,000 miles of road in England and Wales – a route mileage greater than that of the railway network at its most extensive a century later. But although the establishment of the turnpike system had provided the financial basis for maintaining roads used by long-distance traffic, it had done little, before 1800, to improve the actual methods of maintenance.

It was however the Highlands of Scotland that were to see the first important developments in road construction of the new century. In 1800, there were no public coaches, or other public vehicles, in the Highlands, and when an attempt was made in that year to introduce coach services between Perth and Inverness, and Aberdeen and Inverness, the roads were so bad and the traffic so limited that they were soon discontinued. Roads in the Highlands meant either the 600 miles of military roads which were still maintained for civil use, their military purpose having ended, or drove roads for cattle and sheep on the hoof, interrupted by innumerable fords which were often rendered impassable by heavy rain. It was against this background that Telford reported, as mentioned in chapter three, and that the 'Commission for making Roads and building Bridges in the Highlands of Scotland' was set up by Parliament in 1803 to work in parallel with the Caledonian Canal Commission.

To finance these new roads and bridges, a new principle was established: that Parliament would defray half their estimated cost, provided that landowners or others who would benefit defrayed the other half. It was from them rather than the government that proposals for particular roads and bridges were to come.

These arrangements continued until 1816, after which year no more proposals were entertained although construction continued, and under them over a total period of eighteen years there were built some 920 miles of new roads and 1,117 bridges. Most of these were in the counties of Inverness-shire, Ross-shire, Caithness and Sutherland: one of the landowners who had responded handsomely had been the second Marquis of Stafford. The commission continued in existence to maintain these roads and bridges and 300 or so miles of military roads which had been placed in its charge about 1814. In consequence of its activities, mail coach services reached not merely Inverness but, from 1819, Wick and Thurso.

The success of the programme was due largely to the men appointed to carry it out: even though Telford's first choice for general superintendent seems to have proved a failure, his assistant superintendents John Mitchell and

Alexander Easton were sound, and Mitchell became general superintendent in 1809, which he remained until his death in 1824. He was then succeeded in 1825 by his son Joseph Mitchell (1803–1883) who held the post of Chief Inspector and Superintendent of Highland Roads and Bridges for the next thirty-nine years. His *Reminiscences of my Life in the Highlands* is a fruitful source of information.

Telford's 'General Specification for Highland Roads' is included in his *Life*. 'On dry-bottomed ground' he stipulates 'gravel of a proper quality, out of which all stones above the size of a hen's egg shall have been previously taken, shall be laid to a depth of fourteen inches in the middle, and nine inches at the sides [the roads were to be twenty feet wide]; but the stones which are taken out of the gravel and do not exceed four inches in size, may be laid for that thickness below the gravel, and in that case ten inches only of cleaned gravel will be required.' The specification also details the extensive drainage works to be provided, the stone 'breastworks' to be built to support the downhill sides of roads which ran along slopes, the 'retaining walls' on the uphill side, parapets, cuttings and embankments.

Despite the straightenings and widenings of recent years, many of Telford's Highland roads continue to carry traffic today, their foundations disguised by a surface of tarmac. During 1982 the author noted that long sections of the A890, between Achnasheen and Strathcarron, appeared to be the original Lochcarron road, and similarly much of the A831 between Beauly and Cannich appeared to be the original Strathglass Road: even though the construction of the road itself was hidden, it appeared that original alignments, earthworks and bridges were still in use. The bridges on the Highland roads were, for the most part, arches of stone, unadorned and serviceable – and in many cases still in service. Of large bridges of this type, the five-arched bridge at Struy, Strathglass Road OS grid ref. NH 403404) is typical. Two famous bridges were made of cast iron: that at Bonar Bridge was swept away late in the nineteenth century; that at Craigellachie (OS grid ref. NJ 285452), built during 1812–15, was reconstructed in steel in the 1960s, though the original appearance was largely retained.

During 1814 the mail-coach road between Glasgow and Carlisle became nearly impassable and Telford was appointed by the government to survey it. Following his report, an Act of 1816 authorised reconstruction of 69 miles

of it under the Commissioners for Highland Roads and Bridges. This road presented Telford with a different problem to the Highland roads, for its principal traffic was not cattle on the hoof but mail and other heavy coaches, and carts carrying from one to four tons. So the central part of the road, to a width of 18 ft out of a total of 30–34 ft, was built on a solid foundation. A 'bottom course of stones, each seven inches in depth' instructed Telford, was 'to be carefully set by the hand with broadest ends downwards, all cross-bonded . . . and no stone to be more than three inches wide on the top'. Above this there was to be a seven-inch course of broken stones 'each to pass through a circular ring two inches and a half diameter in their largest dimensions'. Above this in turn was to be a layer of gravel one inch thick. The surface was to be curved, 'a curvature of six inches in the middle eighteen feet'. This type of construction was used also on the Lanarkshire and Holyhead Roads, which are mentioned shortly, and elsewhere.

Today the Glasgow-Carlisle road is the A74, an extremely busy dual carriageway: and although traces of earlier alignments can be seen from it, to establish just how much of Telford's work survives, and how much is pre-Telford, and how much post-, would be a matter for close investigation. Telford's improvement of this road, however, prompted improvement of other roads in Lanarkshire, notably the one from Cumbernauld south to the Carlisle road at Abington, now the A73. The work was financed by a loan from the Exchequer Bill Loan Commissioners, administered by the Highland Roads and Bridges Commissioners, and engineered by Telford.

It is on this road, at the northern approach to Lanark, that one of Telford's greatest road bridges remains in use. This is Cartland Craigs bridge, which carries the road across the narrow gorge of the Mouse Water at OS grid reference NS 869445. The gorge is so narrow that three arches of 50 ft radius suffice; yet the height from the bed of the stream to the underside of the middle arch is 120 ft, which is comparable with the tallest arches of Pontcysyllte aqueduct. The bridge was completed in 1822. Downstream where the gorge opens out are two older bridges – one still in use, the other not – approached from both directions by gradients of between 1 in 7 and 1 in 5. It seems clear that Telford realigned a considerable length of the old road to provide a gradient acceptable to coach horses, taking his new line gently upwards by traversing hillsides and encountering the Mouse Water ravine in the process. So narrow is this, and so short the bridge, and so suddenly encountered, that today's motorist can easily speed across without realising what lies beneath. Examination on foot reveals suddenly a wooded ravine with rocky sides of vertiginous steepness: the location unfortunately renders it impossible to produce a satisfactory photograph conveying to the full the appearance of the bridge in its surroundings.

The Holyhead Road

It was geographically convenient rather than chronologically correct to consider Cartland Craigs bridge at this point, for prior to its construction Telford had long been engaged on another great work of road building – the Holyhead Road.

Ireland, with some five million inhabitants at this period when the population of Great Britain was only twelve million, was relatively much more important then than now, and the union of Ireland with Great Britain in 1801 had meant that Irish Members of Parliament had to travel to and from Westminster rather than Dublin. So the inadequacies of the route from Dublin to London and back had been thrown into sharp relief.

Originally the mail coach route from London to Holyhead ran via Chester and the North Wales coast, with ferry crossings of the Conwy estuary and the Menai Strait. About 1805, however, it seems that a turnpike road was made through North Wales from Shrewsbury to Bangor; it avoided the Conwy ferry crossing and the mail coach was diverted on to it. But it was a steep, narrow and dangerous road: on the western approach to its summit, over 1,000 feet above sea level near Llyn Ogwen, it was in places as narrow as 15 feet and as steep as 1 in 13. It was the accidents that the Irish MPs met with when travelling over this road by mail coach that, according to Edmund Vale (*The Mail Coach Men . . .*), forced the government to employ Telford to survey it. His report, which was included as an appendix to the report of the House of Commons Committee on Holyhead Roads published in May 1811, included a detailed description, with maps, of the road as then existing and Telford's suggested improvements.

Very little was done, however, until in 1815 the cause of the Holyhead Road was taken up by Sir Henry Parnell, MP for Queen's County, and as a result the Holyhead Road Commission was set up by Parliament in the same year,

with Telford as engineer. The work which followed under his direction continued over the next fifteen years. West of Shrewsbury the seven small and impoverished turnpike trusts responsible for the route were so little able to cope with improvements, or to maintain them once completed, that in 1819 at the instance of Telford and Parnell they were consolidated by Act of Parliament into a single trust and subsequently this section of the road was in effect managed directly by the commission. Between Shrewsbury and London the existing turnpike trusts were left in control: but the many improvements needed were laid out and built by the commission, which handed them over when complete to the trusts against reimbursement from the increased tolls they were authorised to charge.

So it was on the North Wales section that Telford's improvements were most numerous, and here today, happily, there are many traces of them to be found. Time has dealt kindly with this section of the Holyhead Road: the brief period when Dublin was the second city of the United Kingdom is long since past, and the road is relatively much less important now than it was when it was built. Despite the arrival and increase of motor traffic, the A5 as it is now numbered has seen nothing like the drastic reconstruction that has been the lot of, for instance, the A74 Glasgow-Carlisle road.

Telford's alignment remains in use for mile after mile, with the tarmac presumably carried on his foundation buried beneath; and that alignment, one comes to realise, is typical of a road built to meet the demands of transport by horse-drawn coaches. There are two main features. Firstly steep hills were eliminated: they slowed the horses down to an unacceptable walk both uphill and, for safety, down. James McAdam's opinion was that a gradient of 1 in $22\frac{1}{2}$ was an easy trotting slope for a coach horse. He was son, and pupil, of J. L. McAdam, who was Telford's great contemporary in road improvement and will be mentioned shortly. In the point of gradients, if in little else, Telford agreed with the McAdams: through the Nant Ffrancon pass of the 1,000 ft summit, the Holyhead Road was laid out with ruling gradient of 1 in 22. Modern cars, of course, find this easy. Secondly, coach horses at their best could not exceed speeds of about 15 mph and so the road – particularly the bends – was laid out for speeds of this sort. The bends are not sudden sharp corners, such as are met with on roads of earlier origin, but they are continuing curves of radii far smaller than are usual in a road built or improved for motor vehicles.

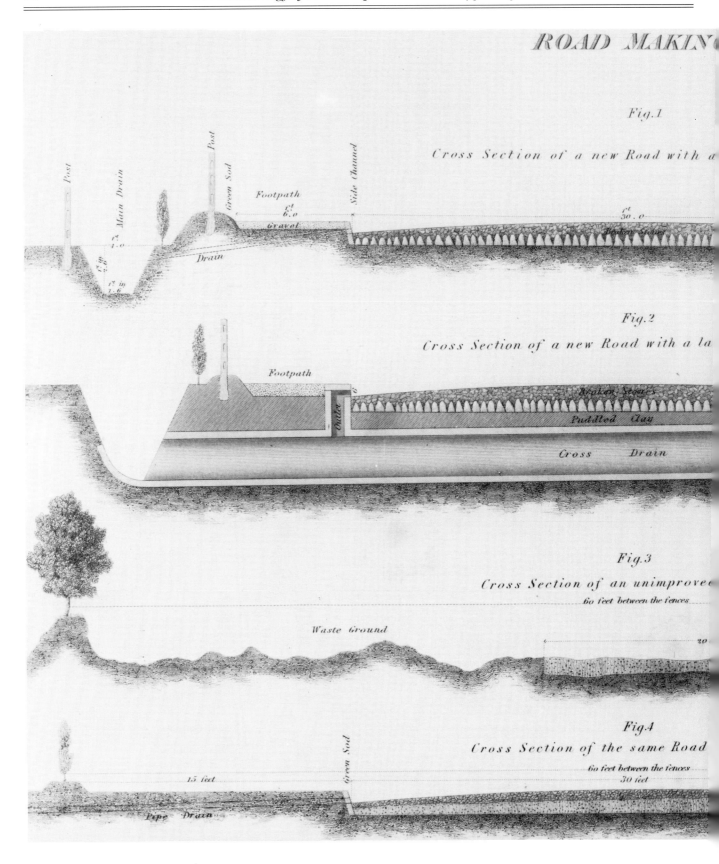

ROAD MAKING

Fig.1

Cross Section of a new Road with a

Fig.2

Cross Section of a new Road with a la

Fig.3

Cross Section of an unimprove

60 feet between the fences

Fig.4

Cross Section of the same Road

60 feet between the fences

30 feet

Along the Holyhead Road, Telford designed not only the roadway itself, but also details: turnpike gates, cottages and mileposts like this, iron plates mounted on granite. Many of them, including this one, are still in place in their correct positions.

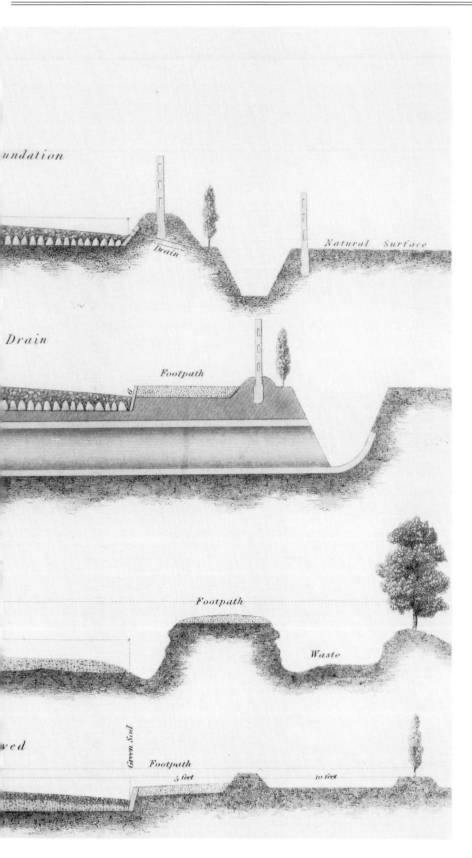

Foundation

Drain

Natural Surface

Drain

Footpath

Footpath

Waste

Green Seal

Footpath

5 feet   *10 feet*

Road making (left): how Telford built new roads and improved old ones. This method (top) originated on the Glasgow–Carlisle road, was used on the Holyhead Road and endured long after Telford's death – see colour illustration on page 71.

The consequence is that the motorist driving through North Wales along the A5 finds long straight stretches which are fast indeed: but they are succeeded at intervals, where for instance the road has to descend into a valley or climb out of one, by a succession of reverse curves, many of them blind and all of uncomfortably small radius. But always the gradients are easy – top gear stuff, or at worst third through the curves. Which considering the mountainous nature of the district, and the hills to be encountered on the other roads within it, is remarkable.

The Holyhead Road was made 30 ft wide and the techniques developed on the Highland and Glasgow & Carlisle roads were used on it – retaining walls, breastworks, masonry bridges, good drainage. One large and handsome cast-iron bridge was provided – one of the first structures to be built – to carry it across the River Conwy near Bettws-y-Coed at OS grid reference SH 798557. It was built, as the cast-in lettering proudly proclaims, in the same year that the Battle of Waterloo was fought, 1815. Cast-iron bridge construction was developing. Other cast iron bridges of this period which are still in use are Tickford Bridge at Newport Pagnell (OS grid ref. SP 877457) built in 1810 to Rowland Burdon's patented system in which cast iron voussoirs are held together by wrought iron straps, and J. U. Rastrick's bridge over the Wye at Chepstow (OS grid ref. ST 536944) which was built in 1816. The culmination of Telford's work on the Holyhead Road was his suspension bridge over the Menai Strait, but this is mentioned later in this chapter for work on it did not start until 1818 and it was not completed until 1826: there are other things to be mentioned first.

A pleasant feature of the Holyhead Road was the standardised but elegant roadside 'furniture' designed for it by Telford himself – iron mileposts, many of which survive in place, toll houses, some of which do (at, for instance, Lôn-isaf, OS grid ref. SH 602693) and iron turnpike gates none of which of course survives as such on its original site, though some are still in roadside use in the immediate vicinity of the Menai Bridge, on the mainland shore.

Something of how the road appeared when built, with tarmac and motor cars equally absent, may be gathered from a visit to Blist's Hill open air museum, Ironbridge. Here a short length of road has been built to the authentic Telford specification, with a part left unfinished to show its construction. Barring the way along it is an original Holyhead Road turnpike gate; beside this is an original toll house, reconstructed. This stood beside the road at Shelton, a mile from Shrewsbury, from 1829 until 1972; then its site was needed for road widening, and it was dismantled and removed to the museum.

As well as its work on the Shrewsbury-Holyhead road, the Holyhead Road Commission improved the roads between Chester and Bangor, Howth and Dublin, and, in twenty-two places, London and Shrewsbury. The route was via Coventry, Birmingham and Wolverhampton; Telford's description of one of these improvements, probably a typical one, at Braunston, Northants, is worth quoting for – among other reasons – Braunston is well known to many people interested in canals who are probably unaware of a great canal engineer's other work in the vicinity.

The improvement was '. . . to commence on the present mail road, between Braunston toll-bar and Berry bridge over the Oxford Canal . . . to continue upon the said road across the canal a second time at Mr Pickford's office, and through the village called Braunston wharf, to the point where the [old] road bends a little to the south; it [i.e. the improved line] then enters the fields on the northern side of the present road, passes through the same by easy [upward] inclinations, and in a gently curving direction, to near the bridle road to Little Braunston, where it bends a little more to the south, and runs in a nearly straight line to the present road . . . a distance of 1 mile 396 yards'.

The A45 at Braunston still follows Telford's line, which can be clearly followed on the map and on the ground from his description. The old line of the road can be traced too from the point at which they diverge – it survives as a narrow and relatively steep lane with name boards 'Old Road'. 'Mr Pickfords's office' is today the location of a hire cruiser base, and those who know their canals will have realised that Telford's references to the Oxford Canal relate to its original route, prior to alterations made in the early 1830s.

Tickford Bridge, Newport Pagnell, Buckinghamshire, (OS grid ref. SP 877457) was built in 1810 and is one of the oldest iron bridges still in use by road traffic.

McAdam

Telford's improvements to the Holyhead Road had been superimposed on existing turnpike-trust administration, but during the period that they were taking shape another great figure was working not only at improved methods of road construction, but also at reform of the turnpike trusts themselves. This was J. L. McAdam.

John Loudon McAdam (1756–1836) had been born of minor Scottish gentry; in 1770 after his father's death he moved to colonial New York, where his uncle had established himself as a merchant. His reaction to the War of Independence was the opposite of that of his republican contemporary Robert Fulton: McAdam was a loyalist and it was as such that he returned to Scotland in 1783 after the Declaration of Independence. In Scotland for some years he led the life of a country gentleman – which included, in 1787, becoming a trustee of the Ayrshire turnpike roads. Then, in the mid-1790s he seems to have had business problems (he was later reticent about this period of his life) and moved to Bristol, and for a time Falmouth. He had, however, to return to Scotland from time to time, and it was probably experience of these long journeys which impressed upon him the inadequacies of the turnpike roads over which he travelled. Certainly from that time onwards, as his fortunes recovered, he seems to have dissipated them again in travelling as far and wide as possible to examine roads and interview those trustees and trust employees who were prepared to talk. He claimed to have travelled 30,000 miles between 1798 and 1814 on this self-imposed task.

By 1811 McAdam was giving evidence, based on his conclusions, to the House of Commons Select Committee on Highways and Turnpike Roads in England and Wales. This formed the basis of his subsequent book *Remarks on the Present System of Road Making*, and in 1816 at the age of sixty he was appointed surveyor to the Bristol Turnpike Trust, of which he was already a trustee. This was an unusually extensive trust: the appointment put McAdam in charge of about 149 miles of road, on which to put his theories into practice.

What McAdam had concluded from his travels was that it was not the type of material in a road surface that mattered – satisfactory roads could be made from most types of readily available stone – but the sizes of individual stones and particles. Large stones were obstacles for wheels to bump over and then crash down on to the road, producing holes in the road surface which were rapidly enlarged into ruts; and where clay was used to bind stones together it absorbed water and was broken up by frost. What was needed was stones of size corresponding to the area of contact of a carriage wheel with the road, which he considered to be about one inch across. Stones broken to this size, and laid without any clay or binding material on a pre-drained foundation to a depth of one foot or so, would soon compact into a firm impenetrable surface.

Lest there by any confusion in readers' minds, there was no question of any tar in McAdam's (or Telford's) roads. Tar came later, with the motor car. What McAdam produced was what became known, in due course, as water-bound macadam. According to J. W. Gregory (*The Story of the Road*) the feature that made the road so firm, though McAdam did not know it, was the surface tension of water surrounding each particle of dust within it between the stones. This cemented them together, just as wet sand at the sea's edge is firmer under foot than dry sand further up the beach. The dust in the road was produced by the traffic itself, by the grinding action of iron-tyred vehicles drawn along it; they also compacted the surface. The effect was the same in the surface of Telford's roads. Tar was eventually needed when pneumatic tyres started to suck the dust out.

Most roads were repaired, McAdam noted, by dumping more and more road material on them; this meant that if the existing material of a road were lifted, sifted and, after dirt had been removed and large stones broken down, replaced, then a good surface would be produced without the expense of obtaining more material.

Related to all this was another aspect. As McAdam put it, the orders of turnpike trustees 'fall . . . for execution into the hands of surveyors, selected not infrequently from the lowest class of the community . . . want of science in the surveyors has gone hand in hand with improvident expenditure, injury of the roads and derangement of the finances.' Financial mismanagement was allied with corrupt practices. What was needed administratively was a 'respectable and efficient executive officer' – and to achieve that it might be necessary to unite small trusts together to form larger ones. In the already extensive Bristol trust McAdam was in effect in that position: his title was General Surveyor and he was paid appropriately. One of his earliest actions was to sack five of his fifteen sub-surveyors and double, approximately, the pay of the rest.

The effect of McAdam's appointment was dramatic. Previously, the Bristol turnpike roads had been getting

worse and worse while the trust was approaching insolvency. Now, year by year the condition of the roads improved, year by year expenditure on them fell and the trust's debt was reduced. McAdam's influence rapidly spread far and wide: by 1819 he had been consulted by 34 trusts in 13 counties responsible for 637 miles of road, and there were more to come. Since small trusts remained reluctant to unite with each other, he – and members of his family – instead accepted multiple appointments as surveyor with several trusts adjoining one another. By 1837, fifty-eight trusts employed a member of the family. McAdam did not consider himself an engineer but he was rapidly founding a new profession, general road surveyor. By the mid-1820s, the word 'macadamise' had entered the language.

What all this meant on the ground, or rather how it appeared to one inhabitant of a typical village, can very well be extracted from *Our Village* by Mary Russell Mitford. The village in which she lived was Three Mile Cross, near Reading, the date about 1820.

Here is the turnpike road through the village, pre-macadam, in a hot dry summer: 'What a dusty world it was . . . No foot could make three plunges into that abyss of pulverised gravel, which had the impudence to call itself a hard road, without being clothed with a coat [of dust] a quarter of an inch thick . . . And if we happened to meet a carriage coming along the middle of the road – the bottomless middle – what a sandy whirlwind it was!'

In winter, though, hard frost improved things: 'The very waggons as they come down the hill along the beaten track of crisp, yellowish frost-dust, glide along like shadows'. A thaw, inevitably, follows: 'The road is alive again. Noise is re-born. Waggons creak, horses splash, carts rattle and pattens paddle through the dirt with more than their usual clink.'

A few months later, however, we read: 'The road has been adjusted on the plan of Mr Macadam; and a tremendous operation it is. I do not know what good may ensue; but for the last six months some part or other of the highway has been impassable for any feet, except such as are shod by the blacksmith. . . . However, the business is nearly done now; we are covered with short sharp flints every inch of us . . . the Macadam ways are warranted not to wear out. So be it; I never wish to see a road mender again.'

From the lack of subsequent criticism, the warranty seems to have been justified. Instead, and perhaps with delighted exaggeration: 'The macadamised roads, and the light open carriages lately introduced, have so abridged, I had well nigh said annihilated distances in this fair island, that what used to be judged a journey is now a drive; . . . we think nothing of thirty miles for a morning call, or forty for a dinner party; Richmond is quite within visiting distance, and London will shortly be our market-town.'

It is unfortunate that from the nature of McAdam's activities little if any physical trace of them can be seen today, for on the roads of England his influence was far greater than that of Telford. But in the still-current term 'County Surveyor' (of roads) there is an echo of his General Surveyor for turnpike trusts, and in the word tarmac, contracted from tarmacadam, the first syllable of his name is still familiar.

Road Engineering in the 1820s

The years 1824–6 were boom years for speculation and saw creation of fifty-nine new turnpike trusts. The mileage of turnpike roads was still increasing. In 1826 however action was at last taken to consolidate one group of trusts, a consequence of the strictures of McAdam and the example of the Holyhead Road: the Metropolis Roads Commission was set up by Parliament to take over fourteen turnpike trusts in Middlesex and with them 56 toll houses, 47 gates, 44 bars and 133 miles of road. James McAdam became surveyor-general. It was anticipated that flints for road repairs could be obtained via the Surrey Iron Railway; they would have been an improvement on the gravel mixed with clay that was usual.

Road engineering continued to develop. For years cuttings had been made through high ground: now engineers started to make road tunnels through ridges. One of the earliest, which still survives, was made during 1823–4 beneath Castle Mound in the centre of Reigate, Surrey. It was built privately by local landowner Lord Somers, but formed part of the turnpike road network of the district. It enabled coaches to avoid a quarter-mile detour and was equipped with a turnpike gate at the south end. The tunnel (OS grid ref. TQ 254503) is now used by pedestrians and bicyclists only; motor road traffic has

During the 1820s and 1830s road engineering had reached the stage that tunnels were built to improve the alignments of turnpike roads. This tunnel in the centre of Reigate (OS grid ref. TQ 254503) was built privately in 1823–4 but formed part of the turnpike road network of the district.

reverted to, presumably, the original route.

Writing in the *Bulletin* of the Association for Industrial Archaeology (Vol. 9 no. 2 1982) Paul W. Sowan reported the continuing use for road traffic of two tunnels made in the early 1830s by the Bridport Turnpike Trust, on what is now the A35 road at OS grid reference SY 349948 and the A357 at OS grid reference ST 467032.

Construction of bridges with spans far greater than masonry or cast iron could provide was made possible by the development of suspension bridges, with chains of wrought iron links. One of the earliest to be completed, and one which is still in use, is the Union Chain Bridge over the River Tweed at OS grid reference NT 934510. It was designed by chain manufacturer Captain Samuel Brown, with modifications by consulting engineer John Rennie, and built in 1819–20. Its span, 437 ft between suspension points, is remarkably large for its time.

The Union Bridge was built very quickly, in less than a year; before work on it started, Telford had commenced building the Menai Bridge, but this was not completed until much later.

There had been several proposals for bridging the Menai Strait: two designs for cast iron bridges had been prepared by Rennie in 1801, and Telford himself prepared designs for cast iron bridges in 1810. A problem, however, was the requirement of the Admiralty for unobstructed clearance for sailing ships beneath the bridge, not merely when it was complete, but even while it was being built.

During the period 1814–17 Telford designed a wrought iron suspension bridge intended to cross the Mersey at Runcorn; the project did not come to fruition, but it brought him into contact with Captain Brown and the two pooled their knowledge. So when, in 1818, the Holyhead Road Commissioners decided to grasp the nettle of bridging the strait, it was a suspension bridge that Telford designed for the purpose.

The breadth of the Menai Strait at high water at the point selected was 306 yards. The bridge as designed, and built, had four masonry approach spans on the Anglesea side and three on the mainland side; the main span between them was 579 ft long between its points of suspension. The main piers were 100 ft high to the roadway, and thence to the apex 53 ft more. There were two parallel roadways 12 ft wide with a 4 ft wide footpath between them. The road surface was of fir planking, with wheel guides, which were longitudinal timbers of oak, 7 ft 6 in. apart.

Masonry work and underground anchorages on each shore for the chains were built first, and the chains themselves prepared and extensively tested. The first chain was slung in April 1825, towed across the strait by boat and hoisted into position (the Admiralty, presumably, had temporarily relaxed its prohibition on obstructions to navigation). The remaining fifteen chains were slung during the summer and the bridge completed the following winter. After inspection by Telford and Sir Henry Parnell, it came into use without ceremony in the dark and stormy small hours of 30 January 1826. At 1.30 am the London–Holyhead mail coach, occupied by the Superintendent of the Mail Coaches and members of Telford's staff, was the first vehicle to cross. As Telford himself wrote, it passed 'at the level of 100 ft above that tideway which heretofore had presented a decisive obstruction to travellers'. It was the turnpike era's greatest triumph.

The turnpike era's greatest triumph: the Menai Bridge, designed and engineered by Telford to carry the Holyhead Road – the main route between London and Dublin, two principal cities of a kingdom recently united – across the Menai Strait. The bridge was opened in January 1826. Less than four months later, Parliament passed an Act authorising construction of the Liverpool & Manchester Railway, the first trunk line, and within ten years a network of steam railways was being built that would render the turnpike road obsolete.

The Menai Bridge still stands (OS grid ref. SH 556714) and carries traffic to and from Anglesea, though the suspension chains are now of steel, the road surface is of tarmac, the central footpath has gone and tolls are no longer collected, as they once were, at its approaches.

According to Edmund Vale (*The Mail Coach Men . . .*) the effect of Telford's Holyhead Road improvements, including the Menai Bridge, was that the schedule for the London–Holyhead mail coach was reduced from 44 hours 50 minutes to, eventually, 26 hours 55 minutes. So marked an improvement prompted emulation elsewhere. Even before the Holyhead Road improvements were complete, Telford was employed to direct surveys for similar improvements to the road through South Wales to Milford Haven, the port for the crossing to the south of Ireland, and in the late 1820s he was employed by the Post Office to make surveys of the roads between London and Edinburgh. These eventually produced a proposal for an improved line for the Great North Road, 362 miles long, compared with the 392 miles of the then existing road, and for parliamentary commissioners similar to the Holyhead Road Commissioners to oversee it.

Going south from Edinburgh, Telford had commenced his surveys eleven miles from the city, at Pathhead – he considered that the intervening stretch might be 'left to the inhabitants of that rich and prosperous vicinity'. But when those inhabitants failed to agree on an improved line for their section of the road, Telford was instructed by the GPO in 1827 to survey it. The consequence was the construction of a new alignment north of Pathhead which included the Pathhead or Lothian Bridge (OS grid ref. NT 391645). This is not so much a bridge as a road viaduct – it carries the road at high level across the valley of the Tyne Water and avoids a steep descent into the valley. Its five sandstone arches still carry the traffic of the A68; although as ever one gets little idea of the nature of the bridge when crossing it, and it is best appreciated from a by-road which does descend into the valley immediately to the west and which, it seems probable, is the original line of the turnpike road.

Lothian Bridge should, therefore, have stood in the same relationship to the Great North Road as did the Waterloo Bridge, Bettws-y-Coed, to the Holyhead Road: the fore-runner of far more extensive improvements to follow. But, in fact, for reasons explained in chapter eight, few of these were carried out.

There came, in 1835, a fundamental reform: the age-old

The Menai Bridge (above) as it appeared in 1981, carrying heavy traffic to and from Anglesey. The suspension chains are now of steel.

Pathhead Bridge (OS grid ref. NT 391645) was designed by Telford and completed in 1831; it carries a main road running south from Edinburgh high above the Tyne Water, and forms part of a road diversion laid out by Telford to avoid steep hills. This might have formed part of an improved route all the way from Edinburgh to London, but the project to reconstruct the entire Great North Road in a manner similar to the Holyhead Road was overtaken by the construction of the steam railway system and so lapsed.

practice of statute labour on roads was abolished, and replaced by a system of rates, by the General Highway Act of that year. It still left responsibility for maintenance of local roads with parishes, though. Two other and successive clauses of the same Act provide an indication of concerns of the time: one obliges proprietors of railroads to provide gates and gatekeepers at level crossings, the next prohibits the baiting of bulls on the highway against a penalty of forty shillings.

Fast Coaching

Thomas Telford records that the consequence of road improvements such as his was that the usual rate of travel by coach was increased from 5 or 6 mph to 9 or 10 mph. Looking back from the second half of the twentieth century, of course, travel at 10 mph seems as comical as travel at 5; but the subject should not be dismissed so lightly. A near-doubling of the speed of communications means a near-halving of travel times, and that is remarkable whatever the period. In our own time, construction of the motorway network has had that effect on road travel, increasing average car-journey speed from 30 mph to 60 or so. The effect of Telford's and McAdam's road improvements, in their era, was comparable to that of construction of the motorway network in our own.

It was similarly accompanied by a great increase in the amount of traffic, though statistics on any comparable basis are hard to come by. However a contemporary list of mail coach routes in Great Britain in 1814 survives in the GPO archives: it details 20 services which radiated from London and a further 62 in the provinces (some of them evidently in effect branches of the London coaches and not all of them using patent mail coaches). The total number of mail coach routes was thus 82. By the eve of the railway era, in 1836, the number of mail coaches, wrote Capt. Malet (*Annals of the Road*), which left London 'every night punctually at 8 o'clock' was 27; the total number of mail coach services had risen to 109. To maintain these services it seems that no less than 700 individual coaches were needed.

And the mail coaches were but the cream on the coffee. In 1828 some 600 long-distance coach services were based on London, and in addition there were many more to nearby villages. To give some examples from the provinces, at the same date there were 80 coach services radiating from Bristol; a few years earlier, in 1823, J. L.

McAdam recorded 50 stage coach journeys made daily between Bristol and Bath. From Brighton, in 1829, 23 coaches left daily for London, 21 of them between 6 am and 3 pm and then 2 more at 10 pm; and from Manchester in 1832 there were 14 coaches to London, most of them running daily. Even a comparatively small market town, Hitchin, Hertfordshire, had at this period its own coach to and from London, three days a week; and coaches between London and Bedford, Kettering and Leeds also called there. In the mid-1830s there were some 3,300 stage coaches on the road.

Coaching evidently was meeting a popular need, and the point about coach travel at this period is not that it was paralytically slow by later standards, but that it had suddenly become incredibly quick by any standard known previously. Stage and mail coach operation was a spectacular performance in which great skills were obvious and great effort evident. It is extraordinarily difficult now to describe coaching without descending into too-familiar clichés; besides in our present-day experience of travel nothing remotely resembles it. Something of what it was like can, however, be discerned from the works of contemporary or near-contemporary writers.

'Nimrod' (C. J. Apperley) in *The Chace, The Turf and The Road* had the happy thought of describing coaching of this period as though seen through the eyes of a traveller of a century or so before, who has slept, Rip van Winkle style, for that length of time and now wishes to return home from London to Exeter. He expects the journey to take a fortnight.

In London, as he waits for the coach, a vehicle so smart that it seems to be a gentleman's carriage approaches. This is indeed his coach, the *Comet*. He boards ('You must be as quick as lightning' he is told) and takes a seat, as it happens, opposite the coach proprietor. When the coach stops at Hounslow he expresses a wish for breakfast; but before he has finished speaking, the coach is off again – the change of horses took fifty seconds only. So fast is the coach's speed that he is convinced the horses are running away.

The roads are perfection, remarks the proprietor – no horse walks a yard between London and Exeter, it's all trotting ground now. The traveller leaves the coach at Bagshot, want of breakfast having won. Here, from an innwaiter, he learns another point of view: 'These fast drags be the ruin of us. 'Tis all hurry and scurry and no gentleman has time to have nothing on the road . . . mutton chops, veal cutlets, beef-steaks or a fowl, sir?'

The traveller later continues on the *Regulator* which, though considered a slow coach with 16 passengers instead of 14 is still timed at 8 mph through much of the country. At such speeds the amount of luggage carried on the roof alarms the traveller who fears the coach will overturn and

On page 72 the Quicksilver *mail is depicted in colour passing the Star & Garter, Kew Bridge. This is the scene from the same viewpoint in 1982 – during a brief lull in the traffic.*

In pre-dawn moonlight, the turnpike keeper at Stamford Hill allows the up Edinburgh mail its mandatory toll-free passage. It is on the last stage of its journey to the GPO, and when it arrives it will have covered some 400 miles in a little over 40 hours. Allowing for stops, this meant an average speed when on the move of about 11 mph, even though the greater part of the journey was done by lamplight.

he descends again at the end of a stage. Here another conversation with an inn-waiter ensues:

'Have you a coach which does not carry luggage on top?'

'Oh yes sir' replies the waiter, 'we shall have one to-night that is not allowed to carry a band-box on the roof.'

'That's the one for me; pray, what do you call it?'

'The *Quicksilver* mail, sir, one of the best out of London. . . .'

'Guarded and lighted?'

'Both, sir; blunderbus and pistols in the sword case; a lamp each side of the coach and one under the foot-board – see to pick up a pin on the darkest night of the year.'

'Very fast?'

'Oh no, sir; *just keeps time and that's all.*'

'That's the coach for me, then,' replies the traveller.

Nimrod's readers were in on the joke, of course: if the mails were the cream of coaching, then the cream of the mails was the Devonport Mail, named (unusually among mail coaches) the *Quicksilver*. It was half a mile in the hour faster (as Nimrod puts it) than most mails in England, one mile an hour faster than the *Comet*, three faster than the *Regulator*. For the $170\frac{1}{2}$ miles between London and Exeter, this predecessor of the Cornish Riviera Express was scheduled to take 17 hours, an amazing performance for a horse-drawn vehicle.

Just how deeply the mail coach system imprinted itself upon people's consciousness is revealed by Thomas de Quincey's *The English Mail Coach*. He was impressed, firstly, by the coaches' velocity; secondly, by the 'grand effects for the eye between lamplight and darkness upon solitary roads'; thirdly, by the 'beauty and power so often displayed in the . . . horses'; fourthly, by the 'conscious presence of a central intellect, that, in the midst of vast

distances – of storms, of darkness, of danger – over-ruled all obstacles into one steady co-operation to a national result'; but finally and particularly by the '*political* [his italics] mission which they fulfilled'. For it was the mail coaches which distributed over the face of the land the news of the victories – of Trafalgar, of Salamanca, of Vittoria, of Waterloo. The spectacle of the nightly departure of the mail coaches from the General Post Office was a grand one on any evening: but when there was news of a victory to distribute, to the usual immaculate appearance of horses, men and coaches were added elaborate decorations of laurels, flowers, oak leaves and ribbons. As the coaches headed out of London on a warm summer evening (all the land victories were won in summer) the passengers saw 'heads of every age crowd to the windows – young and old understand . . . our victorious symbols – and rolling volleys of . . . cheers run along us, behind and before us'. Yet good news of a victory was also bad news, of a battle which might mean loved ones lost.

Dickens, too, put vivid descriptions of coaching into *David Copperfield* and *Pickwick Papers*. Just the sort of coach he was writing about is preserved in the form of the London–Rochester *Commodore*, in Bath Carriage Museum. This coach was built in 1839.

Coach Organisation and Operation

What does fascinate and indeed astound the present author is the degree and complexity of the organisation needed to support the networks of mail and stage coaches – particularly since they could be administered only by written commands sent out by the coaches themselves.

The length of a stage, the distance, that is, which a horse could travel at speed daily as part of a team hauling a coach, was about ten miles. This meant that a fresh relay of four horses had to be provided promptly for every four-horse coach at intervals of approximately ten miles throughout its route, night and day. Nimrod's account of teams' being changed in fifty seconds is perhaps exaggerated: Thomas Hasker, Superintendent of the Mail Coaches, originally allowed five minutes, though with practice this was reduced to one and a half. That was a highly creditable performance and, as L. T. C. Rolt points out (*George and Robert Stephenson*), the scene at a coaching inn when horses were being changed was far from being the leisurely one of popular tradition, and had more in common with (in our own time) the activity at a pit stop during a grand prix motor race where every second counts.

For each team of four horses there was an additional horse spare: each horse worked hard for about one hour a day for four days, and rested on the fifth. Because five horses had to be provided to haul a coach over each 10-mile stage, and there was a coach in each direction daily, the number of horses needed for each route was closely equivalent to its length in miles. To work the Shrewsbury *Wonder* from London over its route of 158 miles, 150 horses were kept. The total number of horses involved in coaching was enormous – Anthony Bird (*Roads and Vehicles*) gives a figure of 150,000 for the year 1835, and that was just the number needed actually to draw the coaches. More again were needed to cart fodder and dung. Economists began to doubt the ability of the land to feed enough horses if traffic continued to grow as it had.

Coach horses themselves were, on the crack coaches, well bred and according to Nimrod 'sumptuously fed and kindly treated . . . we often see [a coach horse] kick up his heels when taken from the coach after having performed his stage of ten miles in five minutes under the hour'. Yet their lives were short, other accounts suggest horses on less important coaches were not too well treated and standards of cruelty to animals were much harsher then than now: I am inclined to think that fast coaching may well have involved a degree of ill-treatment to the horses that would be unacceptable today.

The mail coaches were hired by the Post Office from their builder, the horses and drivers were provided by contractors. The Post Office representative was the mail guard, in sole charge of the coach, a young man resplendent in royal uniform of scarlet and gold braid, and accustomed to the discharge of firearms. This, his blunderbuss and pistols seem to have acted successfully as a deterrent – there are few records of mail coaches being held up by highwaymen. The guard's seat was raised at the rear of the vehicle, facing forwards; his feet rested on the mail box, the rear boot. Seated there, at intervals he blew his horn to announce the coming of the mail – for all other traffic had to give way to it, and turnpike keepers had to be ready with their gates open as the mails paid no tolls. That was a constant irritation to turnpike trustees, but seems to have been alleviated, to any great extent, only in Scotland after Telford's improvements to the Glasgow to Carlisle road. During journeys, postmasters had to complete a timebill, carried by the guard, inserting the coach's actual time of arrival at points of call as recorded by the guard's locked timepiece. The guard added his explana-

General Post-Office.

The Earl of CHESTERFIELD, } Postmaster-
                        AND
The Earl of LEICESTER,   } General.

London to Exeter Time-Bill.

	Miles	Time allowed H. M.		
			Dispatched from the General Post-Office, the of 179	
			at	
			Coach No sent out { With a Time-Piece safe No to	
			Arrived at the Gloucester Coffee-house, Piccadilly,	
			at	
Wilson	3½	3 55	Arrived at Bagshot at	11 . 55
Demezy	20	2 30	Arrived at Basingstoke at	2 . 25
W. Wilson	8½	1 10	Arrived at Overton at	3 . 35
Weeks	28½	3 40	Arrived at Salisbury at	7 . 15
			Coach No gone forward Delivered the Time-Piece safe to	
		30	*To be at Salisbury by a Quarter past Seven, where Thirty Minutes are allowed for Breakfast*	
Shergold	10	1 20	Arrived at Woodyeats at	9 . 5
Wood	12½	1 40	Arrived at Blandford at	10 . 55
Bryer	16	2 10	Arrived at Dorchester at	12 . 55
		30	*Thirty Minutes allowed for Dinner, &c.*	
Warre	27½	4 0	Arrived at Axminster at	5 . 25
Pine	9½	1 15	Arrived at Honiton at	6 . 40
Land	16	2 10	Arrived at the Post-Office, Exeter, the of 179	
			at	
	179	24 50	*The Mail to be delivered at the Post-Office, Exeter, Fifty Minutes past Eight in the Evening*	
			Coach No arrived { Delivered the Time-Piece safe No to	

THE Time of working each Stage is to be reckoned from the Coach's Arrival. Five Minutes for changing four Horses, is as much as is necessary, and as the Time whether more or less, is to be fetched up in the Course of the Stage, it is the Coachman's Duty to be as expeditious as possible, and to report the Horse-keepers if they are not always ready when the Coach arrives, and active in getting it off.

By Command of the Postmaster-General,

T. HASKER.

A mail coach timepiece (above) : this was carried by a mail guard and used by postmasters when entering times on mail coach timebills. When mail coaches were introduced, the time was not standardised throughout Great Britain, and timepieces were regulated to gain or lose according to the journey being made.

A specimen mail coach timebill (left) : on this unused example, the scheduled times of arrival at the various stops have been inked in. In normal use, postmasters filled in the actual times of arrival of the coach, and the mail guard returned the completed form to the Superintendent of Mail Coaches, who thus had a constant and detailed check on each coach's performance.

This standard mail coach (below), as used throughout most of the life of the mail coach service. This example dates from c. 1820. The telegraph springs (see page 28) on which the body is mounted can be seen : the skid (see page 31) and its chain hang from the body to the rear of the step.

tions for delay and returned the timebill to the superintendent.

Each mail guard was in charge of the running of his coach, and the safety of both the coach and the mails it carried; mail guards developed, as might be expected, considerable esprit de corps. This must have been particularly valuable at times of flood or snow. When a coach was halted by deep water or drifts, or indeed from breakdown or any other cause, the guard's first priority was to get the mail bags forward – by taking one or both leading horses, by going on foot if snow drifts were impassable for them, by hiring a post chaise as soon as he succeeded in reaching a town. The very hard winter of 1836–7 put mail guards particularly to the test: there was an exceptionally heavy snowfall, with extensive drifting, on the night of Christmas Day: by 27 December fourteen mail coaches were abandoned up and down the country.

Coach bodies were of wood and subject to constant jolting and stress: this meant that they had to be well protected by paint to prevent ingress of water and consequent rot, and the paint in turn needed to be protected against mud and stones thrown up by the wheels and the horses' hoofs. As many as fifty coats of paint and varnish might be applied: and of necessity was made a virtue, for the finishes were superb, of quality which had seldom been equalled let alone excelled. Mail coaches themselves in their livery of deep maroon and black with red wheels exemplified how sober colours can produce a striking effect. Mail coach design remained static throughout the main coaching era, a consequence of the contract held by Vidler and his successors until 1836. Its eventual loss was a result of Parliamentary rather than Post Office pressure.

A few mail coaches are preserved in museums, where one may see that famous livery and remark on the large size of the lamps, a reminder that much of their travelling was done by night. The Science Museum has a mail coach of 1827; the Glasgow Museum of Transport has one of the post-Vidler era dating from *c.* 1840; and Bath Carriage Museum has a third example. Others remain in private ownership.

Fast Day Coaches

The success of the mail coach system encouraged operators of stage coaches to improve their own services using coaches of the same general pattern but brightly painted, named and carrying in some instances as many as fourteen people on top in addition to those inside. Then, as McAdam's and Telford's road improvements began to have effect, the speed of coaches increased. Journey times were reduced so much that it became practicable to institute fast day coaches to reach places which had previously been accessible from London only overnight. The first of such coaches was the Shrewsbury *Wonder*, already mentioned, which was put on in 1825, by which date presumably Telford's twenty-two improvements to the road between Shrewsbury and London were far enough advanced to make it feasible. The distance was 158 miles: the *Wonder* was scheduled to leave Shrewsbury at 5.45 am and reach London at 9.15 pm.

By the mid-1830s fast day coaches such as this were running between London and most places of importance up to 140 miles away. The mail coaches, timed to leave London in the early evening, and to arrive there in the early morning, began to feel the draught of competition: the GPO increased its mileage rate to contractors.

Stage coaches were operated by proprietors, who generally did not own the actual vehicles but hired them from coachmakers. Nimrod gives an example of the way in which the system worked: Proprietors A, B, C and D would enter into a contract to horse a coach over 80 miles, each doing so for 20. At the end of a month they would make a settlement: if the gross earnings were £5 a mile these would total £400 from which would have to be deducted: tolls, stage coach duty to the government, mileage (i.e., payment to a coachmaker for hire of the coaches), two coachmen's wages, porters' wages, rent of booking offices (sic), and cost of washing the coaches. These might amount to £100, which left £300 to be divided between the proprietors; out of their shares they would have to keep 80 horses and pay horse keepers.

Many of the coach proprietors were also contractors who horsed and operated mail coaches for the Post Office. The greatest of them all was William Chaplin (1787–1859). Chaplin was the son of a coachman and in due course became a coachman himself. Then having turned coach proprietor he built up his business into the largest of its kind with 1,300 horses and five 'yards' in London, of which the principal was at the Swan with Two Necks in Gresham Street, not far from the GPO. Chaplin horsed fourteen mail coaches on their first stages out of London; places served by stage coaches, of which he was a proprietor, included Manchester, Birmingham and Bristol.

Next in importance among coach proprietors were

Four in hand : driver's view in 1982 (above). Powerful short-legged Welsh cobs like these are horses of just the sort which would have pulled coaches in their heyday.

With the skid in use beneath the near-side rear wheel as a primitive brake, a mail coach descends a hill. The guard is blowing his horn to announce arrival at a town and warn other traffic to keep clear.

Edward Sherman and Benjamin Horne, both with some 700 horses. It was Sherman who originated the Shrewsbury *Wonder*; Horne put on an opposition coach in competition, and Sherman was also in competition with Chaplin for the Manchester traffic.

At the other end of the scale were a great many small proprietors. They based themselves on the coaching inns, where passengers booked tickets, horses were changed, and passengers briefly ate when coaches halted for slightly longer than usual. Former coaching inns such as the Sugar Loaf at Dunstable on the Holyhead Road and the George at Stamford on the Great North Road, are still a familiar sight in country towns. R. E. and J. M. Anderson's *Quicksilver* includes a list of over 100 of them.

The Driver's Art

The coachman's art of driving four horses in hand, instead of having a postillion on the near side leader, seems to have originated late in the eighteenth century. It was a skilled performance, carried out in the public eye by a larger than life character riding high up on his box seat: the most famous coachmen became heroes, the pop stars of their day to be imitated in their slang, mannerisms and dress by other young men, poor or rich. Some of the latter on privileged occasions might be allowed to take the reins briefly themselves. In 1807 the first club was set up for those wishing to drive four-in-hand as a sport: and as a sport it has continued, with ups and downs, to this day, so that the coachman's art is still practised and may be observed.

John Richards of the British Driving Society recently kindly took me with him when exercising four-in-hand: and although webbing reins and nylon traces have replaced those made of leather, the skill needed is observably still as great as ever. The positive steering of a motor vehicle controlled by a steering wheel is so familiar that it comes as a shock to be reminded in practice of what one well knows in theory, that the direction taken by this horse-drawn vehicle really does depend on the direction taken by the four trained animals that are pulling it, and in turn on the skill of the driver in controlling them. One marvels afresh that a comprehensive transport network was based on such a system.

Present-day four-in-hand drivers do have the advantage of brakes. Throughout the era of long distance coaching, coaches were braked either by making the horses hold them

back or, on steep hills, by slipping the skid beneath one of the rear wheels, as described on page 31. No doubt as roads were improved and steep hills avoided it became easier for horses to hold back coaches and there was less demand than ever for improved brakes.

Indeed such technical developments as there were in carriage design at this period were slow to see adoption. Carriages were steered by centre-pivoted front axles, which meant that the front wheels had to be small to clear the driver's box. Large front wheels, of similar size to the rear wheels, would have produced a vehicle which was easier to pull and more stable, and were made possible by the invention of Ackermann steering in 1816. (Print-seller Rudolph Ackermann was English agent for the German inventor.) But no coach builder would use it: it had to wait for the introduction of the motor car – in which the arrangement is still familiar – to see general use.

Another solution to the problem which did see limited use in coaching days was the 'equirotal' vehicle, invented by W. Bridges Adams. The vehicle body itself was hinged, or articulated, behind the front wheels so that all four wheels could be of equal size. The author was able to inspect an equirotal phaeton of *c.* 1830 which once belonged to the Duke of Wellington, in Dodington Carriage Museum in 1982; it is in effect a gig (front part) hinged to, and separable from, a cabriolet (rear part).

The invention of elliptical springs in 1804, which made it possible to eliminate the perch (the central longitudinal frame member) and mount a coach body directly on the axles, seems to have been ignored by builders of mail and stage coaches, but such springs were used by builders of light private carriages. In general, though, the first four decades of the nineteenth century were a period not of radical innovation in carriage design, but rather, now that the basics were well-established, of the introduction of minor variations of style – of both four-wheeled and two-wheeled vehicles – according to the whims of owners and the commercial judgement of coachbuilders. Much the same thing was happening to sailing vessels, where several centuries of gradual development were resulting in vessels of more-or-less uniform efficiency but great divergence in detail

A travelling chariot of c. 1800: in such vehicles, the wealthy travelled post, hiring successive teams of horses at posting inns. When no longer wanted by their owners, travelling chariots were often sold for use as post chaises.

according to their purpose and the area in which they were built. Phaeton, curricle, gig, dormeuse, travelling chariot and cabriolet on land were matched in diversity by bark, brig, snow, brigantine, schooner, smack, hoy and wherry on the water.

The aristocracy still stuck to their travelling chariots, posting from town to town – though it seems unlikely that by the late 1820s such a mode of travel could compare for speed with the fastest scheduled day stage coaches with hand-picked horses ready and waiting at the start of each stage: which in turn may help to explain the appeal of coaching at this period of young men of fashion. Their elders, no doubt, continued to prefer the privacy and convenience of their own vehicle to the speed of the public one: certainly to open the door of a travelling chariot, such as that dating from 1820 seen in Dodington Carriage Museum, is to reveal an interior as luxurious as the excellent furnishing standards of the time could make it. Furthermore the noble occupants had a view to the front as well as to the sides: the body was cut off short, so to speak, ahead of the doors, the travellers faced forwards and in front of them were windows rather than, as in a public coach, other travellers facing back.

Such vehicles, when no longer required by their owners, were sold for use as post chaises. Even then their use remained exclusive: the rate of hire for a post chaise and two horses in 1826 was from 1s to 1s 6d a mile, at a period when a mail guard's wage was 10s 6d a week plus tips and uniform. Extremes of wealth were indeed far greater then than now.

Vans and Waggons

Improved road surfaces brought benefit for freight traffic too. They enabled 'fly vans' to be established, by carriers such as Pickford, for light goods; they were fast, for their horses trotted, and they ran to fixed schedules, night and day. Throughout the turnpike era, though, the stage waggon continued to be the staple of road freight transport, lumbering along as it always had with goods and a few passengers too poor to travel by coach but preferring the waggon to Shanks's pony. Services were widespread: waggons from Manchester for instance regularly visited places as remote as Bristol, London and Edinburgh; and Birmingham had communication by waggon with 168 other towns. For a smaller town, let us again consider Hitchin. The Hitchin stage waggon set out every Monday and Thursday at noon, and arrived in London at 7 am the next morning. Three waggons from Bedford also passed through the town on their way to London; and four more served villages round about.

Throughout the turnpike era the stage waggon was the principal means of transport for goods by road. It also carried a few passengers.

CHAPTER SIX

Steam Boats and Locomotives in Commercial Use

Henry Bell

Despite Fulton's successful construction and operation in the USA of the *Clermont* (with British-made machinery) and subsequent steam boats, there was no rush in Britain to follow his example. In 1811, for instance, J. C. Dyer arrived from the USA armed with descriptions and drawings of Fulton's steam boat inventions, but found it impossible to convince leading engineers of their practicability here.

Then, in 1812, at a date when Telford's road improvements were still confined to the Highlands of Scotland, and McAdam had yet to have an opportunity to put his ideas into practice, there was sudden progress. Henry Bell had his little steam boat the *Comet* built, and began to operate her on the Clyde; and Matthew Murray of Leeds built a steam railway locomotive, and the following year machinery for a steam boat, both of them owing much to Trevithick's ideas. All three were successful in commercial service: but since the steam boats had greater and more widespread immediate consequences, they will be considered first.

Henry Bell (1767–1830) was born at Torphichen Mill near Linlithgow, West Lothian. His father and forefathers had been millers and millwrights for centuries, and in 1783 he too was apprenticed as a millwright. Subsequently he spent a year with Shaw & Hart, shipbuilders of Borrowstounness. Later he worked for eighteen months under John Rennie in London; this was a natural step to take, for Rennie, another Lowland Scot, had started his engineering career as a millwright and widened it to include designing and erecting steam engines. In these Bell was already interested. For the time being however he settled in Glasgow in 1790 as a builder.

Bell's own account of how his interest in steam boats originated and developed, as recorded by Edward Morris in *The Life of Henry Bell*, is unfortunately sullied by its having been told late in his life, when it seemed that there was some chance of a government pension or payment on the grounds that he originated steam navigation. Much the same, as already mentioned, applies to William Symington. Each was concerned to claim as much as possible for himself at the expense of the other – and both of them at the expense of Fulton.

According to Morris, Bell's interest in the possibility of steam navigation originated when he was serving with Shaw & Hart at Bo'ness, that is in 1786. This is two years before Symington's Dalswinton experiment, three before his trial for Miller on the Forth & Clyde Canal at Falkirk. That attracted enough attention and was near enough to Torphichen for it to be likely that Bell heard about it, indirectly if not directly – he may have been in London by then. What is a curious coincidence is that (according to A. I. Bowman, *Industrial Archaeology* spring 1981) George Hart, partner in Shaw & Hart, was the father of Alexander Hart who later built the first experimental *Charlotte Dundas* vessel in 1800–1. So if Bell had kept up with his former master he might well have heard what was going on. Symington claimed that Bell had observed the 1789 experiments, and was 'frequently seen to inspect' the *Charlotte Dundas*. Morris says that Bell in 1800 converted a small pleasure boat into a steam boat by installing engine, boiler and paddles, and attempted, unsuccessfully, to persuade the Admiralty to take up steam navigation.

Bell was also in touch with Robert Fulton – though how closely is a matter for conjecture. Bell claimed that Fulton visited him both before and after his visit to France, and

The year 1812 saw the entry into commercial service of both the steam locomotive and (in Europe) the steam boat. These are believed to be contemporary models. The model of a Blenkinsop & Murray rack locomotive (above) which is about 12½ ins. long overall, is thought to have been made by Murray himself in 1813 and is displayed in Leeds Industrial Museum. The wooden model of the hull of PS Comet (above right) is probably the original builder's model, dating from 1811, and is exhibited in Glasgow Museum of Transport.

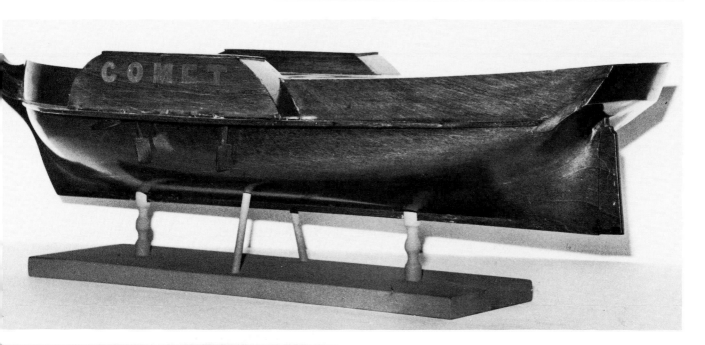

Henry Bell, as depicted in Morris's Life of Henry Bell *of 1844. The* Comet *appears in the distance.*

it was from him, writes Morris, that Fulton 'got the model of his steamboat'. Fulton, of course, was ready to pick the brains of anyone whose information might prove useful, but as we have seen there was no question of his getting the entire idea for the *Clermont* from Bell or any other single individual.

A greater claim is recorded by Joseph Mitchell in his *Reminiscences*. Mitchell and Alexander Easton, who have been mentioned on page 96, were good friends, both being protégés of Telford; Easton became, about 1807, resident engineer for construction of the western section of the Caledonian Canal. He was also related to Henry Bell, through Bell's mother, Margaret Easton; it may have been this connection which brought Bell and Mitchell together in 1825, after which they too became good friends. The story that Bell told Mitchell was that he had accompanied Fulton in visiting Symington to see his steam boat, that he had confided the ideas of his own steamship to Fulton, and that subsequently, at Fulton's request, Bell had gone to New York and taken a leading part in constructing Fulton's boat, after which he returned to Glasgow with the idea of starting a similar vessel on the Clyde. Mitchell was an old man by the time he wrote his reminiscences, but it seems likely that Bell was the one who exaggerated. According to H. W. Dickinson (*Robert Fulton*) on the other hand it was a letter from Fulton, after his success with the *Clermont*, that stirred Bell up into trying to emulate her.

The *Comet*

It is much to be regretted that Bell's claims were exaggerated, for his real achievement was solid and remarkable enough. It can be extracted from Bell's own *Observations on the Utility of applying Steam Engines to Vessels Etc* which is probably reliable, for it was published in 1813 before any incentive to exaggerate had arisen.

He says here that in 1809 he attempted to make a small model which was successful enough to convince him that an engine could be made to drive a vessel in all weathers. This he followed in 1810 with a small boat, 13 ft long by 5 ft beam, in which he tried many experiments and different machines. He does not specify the source of power for either of these boats; probably the full-size one was manually driven and he was experimenting with various types of paddles. In any event, his experiments were successful enough to be followed in 1812 by the *Comet*, 40 ft long by 10 ft 6 in. beam. *Comet* was the first steamer to enter commercial service in Europe.

Bell by this time was proprietor of the Baths at Helensburgh – a hotel and hydropathic establishment. Some sources say that he had built it in the course of his building business, and that it included a Boulton & Watt steam pump to pump water for the baths. The intended main purpose of the *Comet* was to transport visitors from Glasgow down the Clyde to Helensburgh, although in eventual practice, because there was no suitable landing place at Helensburgh, she went to Greenock on the opposite shore of the Firth of Clyde and Helensburgh passengers were ferried across.

Construction of the *Comet*'s wooden hull commenced in October 1811; she was built by shipbuilders John Wood & Co. of Port Glasgow. The engine was purchased from Glasgow engineer John Robertson – it had originally been intended for use as a stationary engine. Castings for it had been supplied by John Napier, from whose foundry Bell had often obtained castings for buildings, and it was to Napier that Bell went for a boiler for the *Comet*.

The work of producing both castings and boiler was supervised by Napier's son David Napier (1790–1869), who had examined *Charlotte Dundas* on her first visit to Glasgow, and later became a noted engineer and steamship owner in his own right. The malleable iron boiler for *Comet*, with its internal flue, something with which he was not then familiar, gave him considerable trouble, despite

being intended for the low pressures then usual. The engine had a vertical upright cylinder of $11\frac{1}{2}$ in. diameter and 16 in. stroke; power was transmitted through side rods, side levers and a connecting rod to a crankshaft. This drove, through gear wheels, two pairs of paddle wheels, mounted one ahead of the other, each wheel having only four floats. The steam plant was installed in the hull at Wood's yard. *Comet*'s accommodation, wrote Bell in 1813, consisted of, from the stern, a cockpit, a cabin elegantly furnished with sofas, a cabin containing the engine and machinery, and the steerage with beds and lockers. The deck above had seats all round; the funnel doubled as a mast, from which a single square sail was set. The *Comet* was launched on 24 July 1812.

At that period the usual time for a journey between

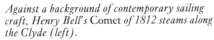

Against a background of contemporary sailing craft, Henry Bell's Comet *of 1812 steams along the Clyde (left).*

The engine of P.S. Comet *is preserved in the Science Museum. The cylinder is mounted above the crankshaft, but it is upright and drive is by side rods and side levers to the connecting rod. The large casting which forms the main frame of the engine incorporates the condenser and water tank; within them is the air pump, the upper part of which can be seen. The cylinder was an early replacement for the original, which was of similar diameter.*

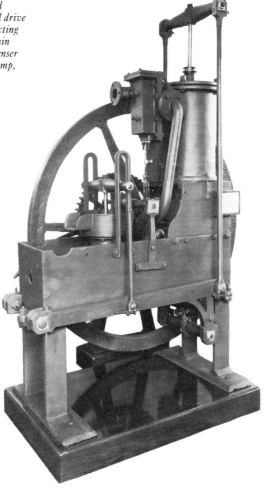

Helensburgh and Glasgow was five or six hours, whether by coach on the turnpike road or by 'fly boat', which here meant a small boat propelled by oars and sails, on the river. On trial, on 6 August 1812, *Comet* came up from Port Glasgow to Glasgow itself in $3\frac{1}{2}$ hours, and then went into service between Glasgow and Greenock, 26 miles, doing the journey usually in $4\frac{1}{2}$ hours. Even so, with her 3 hp engine, she was underpowered, as Bell acknowledged, and with a 5 hp engine would have been expected to take $3\frac{1}{2}$ hours only.

Bell, unfortunately, unlike Fulton and Livingston in the State of New York, had no monopoly of steam navigation in Scotland. As soon as he had shown that it was likely to be both practicable and profitable, others rushed to build steam boats and, since they usually had greater financial resources than Bell, their boats were larger and more powerful than the *Comet*. The first was laid down within a couple of months of *Comet*'s entering service.

Henry Bell had found that the *Comet*'s rear pair of paddle wheels were doing little work; they were removed. In an attempt to obtain more power, the cylinder of the engine was replaced by one of $12\frac{1}{2}$ in. diameter (the original $11\frac{1}{2}$ in. cylinder survives, in store, at Glasgow Museum of Transport), and to increase the boat's capacity her hull was lengthened by 20 ft. Nevertheless increasing competition on the Clyde, which will be described shortly, proved too strong and Bell moved *Comet* first, in 1816, to the Firth of Forth and then, about 1818, he used *Comet* to start a service between Glasgow and Fort William and offered shares in her to the public. His intention – perhaps influenced by his Easton connection – seems to have been to operate a service to Inverness via the Caledonian Canal so soon as it should be finished. In 1820 he started to operate another and larger steamer, the *Stirling Castle* of which he was part-owner, between Inverness and Fort Augustus on the eastern section of the canal which had been opened in 1818; a connecting coach conveyed through passengers between Fort Augustus and Fort William. From 1822, when the rest of the canal was opened, *Stirling Castle* was able to work between Inverness and Glasgow.

But not the *Comet*. Small and underpowered for such an exposed route, she had sadly been driven ashore and wrecked in December 1820. She was replaced by *Comet II*, though the extent to which Bell was now financially involved is not clear. The engine of the original *Comet* was fortunately salvaged, and after passing through various ownerships reached the Patent Office Museum, South Kensington, in 1862: John Robertson its builder, by then

aged 80, was persuaded to travel to London to set it up. It is now displayed in the Science Museum. Other relics associated with the *Comet* include what is believed to be an original builder's model of the hull, exhibited in Glasgow Museum of Transport, and documents and portraits relating to Henry Bell and John Robertson displayed in the McLean Museum & Art Gallery, Greenock.

To celebrate the *Comet*'s 150th anniversary, a full-size working replica was built in 1962, and fitted out and launched from the same site as the original, by then part of Lithgow's Yard, Port Glasgow. She was then operated under her own steam on the Firth of Clyde, and is now displayed at Shore Street, Port Glasgow, on land.

Steam Boats on the Clyde and Elsewhere

The first competition which Bell and the *Comet* had to face came in the form of PS *Elizabeth*. She was 58 ft long and, like the *Comet*, was built by Wood & Co., but to the order of John Thomson who had helped Bell with his experiments in 1811. James Cook, later described by David Napier as 'the oldest and most respectable engine-maker in Glasgow' provided a 10 hp engine and the vessel entered service in March 1813. Unlike the *Comet*, the schedule of which varied according to the tide, she was powerful enough to run to a fixed schedule irrespective of it.

The *Elizabeth* was followed into service by the *Clyde*, built by Wood & Co. in 1813 with a 14 hp engine by John Robertson. After that, steam boats came thick and fast. In 1818 there were said to be eighteen steam boats at work on the Clyde alone, some of them carrying passengers, some of them goods, and the number of travellers between Glasgow and Greenock had increased from 50–80 a day before 1812 to 400–600. Not only was the steam boat cruise down the Clyde proving attractive in its own right, but it was cheaper than land transport and as reliable. Some of the coaches between Glasgow and Greenock were withdrawn.

A typical Clyde steam boat of the period 1812–20 is depicted in Rees's Cyclopedia *(above right). The single-cylinder side-lever engine is positioned alongside the boiler; the fire tube of this makes three passes through it between firedoor and funnel, and the crankshaft penetrates through the boiler within a tube which extends across it. A continuous gangway, marked XXXX, extends all round the hull and protects the paddles.*

Most early steam boats had short lives, and none survive at the present day, but PS Industry, *which was built in 1814 to tow barges on the Clyde, lasted long enough to be photographed in, probably, the early 1860s (below right).*

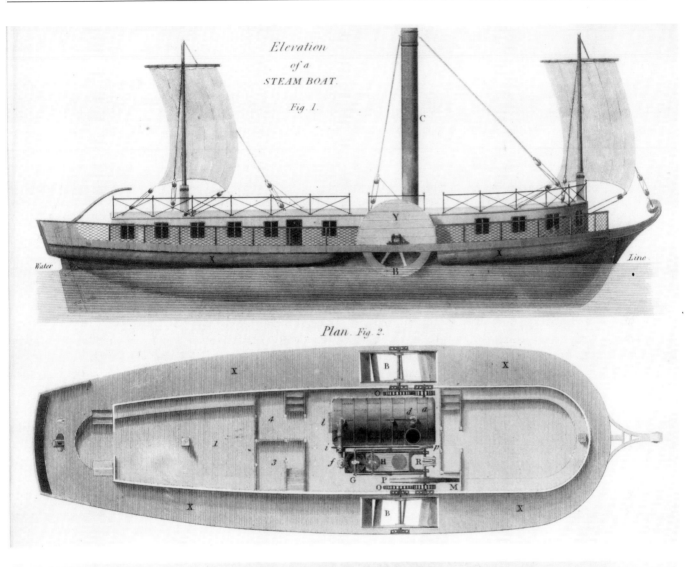

Elevation of a STEAM BOAT. Fig 1.

Plan. Fig 2.

During the same period, steam boats were spreading with comparable rapidity to other estuaries. PS *Elizabeth* was transferred to the Mersey in 1814 although, sadly, she does not seem to have been successful, being sold in 1816 and subsequently converted into a horse-drawn packet boat on, probably, the Mersey & Irwell Navigation. In 1814, also, steam boats were introduced on the Firth of Forth, and in 1814 or 1815 on the Firth of Tay. The first steam boats on the Thames started in 1815 and will be mentioned in detail below; the same year seems to have seen the first steam packets also on the Humber and the Trent, the forerunners of extensive services which later operated there. The Ellesmere & Chester Canal Co. put on a steam packet across the Mersey between Liverpool and Ellesmere Port, probably in connection with its horse-drawn passenger boats on the canal; and David Napier built the little steamer *Marian* which he took up to Loch Lomond the following year, the start of a tradition of paddle steamers on that loch which still persists at the time of writing. Further afield there were, by 1816–17, British-built steam boats plying on the Rhine, the Elbe and the Seine.

The Thames Estuary

The first steam boat on the Thames was the *Margery*, which had been built on the Clyde and launched in 1814; she ran on the Clyde for some months but in November of that year was sold to London owners. They took her through the Forth & Clyde Canal – the paddle wheels had to be removed so that she could pass through the locks – and then sailed her down the East Coast. She entered service between London and Gravesend in January 1815; but she proved to be unreliable, and at the end of the season was withdrawn. In March 1816 she left the Thames for the Seine, becoming en route the first steam boat to cross the English Channel.

The first to cross, but not the first to be seen there. In the spring of 1815 another Clyde steam boat was purchased by another London firm, and named the *Thames*; she was brought south by the West Coast, under steam and, when the wind was favourable, sail. *Thames* had been built by J. Wood & Co. with a 14 hp engine by James Cook; she was 79 ft long overall and 14 ft 6 in. beam, or 22 ft 6 in. extreme breadth of deck, which presumably includes the paddle boxes; and she was 'a capital seaworthy vessel' according to George Dodd who was in charge of her.

The voyage of 1,500 miles from the Clyde to the Thames took on an epic quality – fortunately a description of it survives in Dodd's book *An Historical and Explanatory Dissertation on Steam Engines and Packets.* . . . The *Thames* would have been driven ashore near Portpatrick had it not been for the power of the engine which enabled her to steam into the gale. She then called at Dublin and continued south. Off Wexford, Dodd quotes Isaac Weld, a passenger taken on at Dublin: 'The thick smoke which issued from our mast was observed . . . and it was concluded that the vessel was on fire . . . the pilots put to sea to fly to our assistance; and . . . it is impossible to describe the attitude of surprise, mingled with dissappointment, which they evinced in beholding us in very good condition, and which frustrated their hopes of right of salvage'.

From Wexford the *Thames* crossed to Milford Haven where, Dodd recorded, 'I ran around the Waterford Packet two or three times while she was on her course, and myself writing a letter for Dublin'. The manoeuvrability of steam boats was a revelation to those accustomed only to sailing whither the wind would blow them. At Portsmouth the *Thames* was inspected by senior naval officers who included three admirals and eighteen captains, and a few days after arrival in London in June Dodd was called before the House of Commons Select Committee on Holyhead Roads, chaired by Sir Henry Parnell. The committee's terms of reference covered communication between Dublin and London including the Irish Sea passage; and the committee itself was remarkably perceptive in interviewing so quickly one who had just navigated those waters in a steam boat, still a very new development.

Dodd's evidence – extracts from which are included in his book – was given with infectious enthusiasm, particularly when he was able to point out that in a calm, when another vessel could not proceed at all with the mails, a steam engine packet could carry them at from 7 to 9 knots. His enthusiasm affected the committee, which recommended steam-packets to the postmasters general; but the Post Office, for the time being, remained aloof. The *Thames*, however, went into service between Margate and London.

She was joined, probably early in 1816, by the *Richmond*, operating upstream between London and the town of her name; she was the first steam boat built specifically to ply on the Thames. She cost £1,800, of which £1,000 was for the engine; but the engine must have been good, for it came from the firm of H. Maudslay & Co.

Henry Maudslay (1771–1831) was the originator of precision engineering. A superb craftsman, he had set himself up in business with a small engineering workshop in 1797 – a workshop equipped in due course with tools of his own design such as screw-cutting lathes which were the forerunners of modern machine tools, a bench micrometer able to measure 0.0001 in., and taps and dies which, for the first time, had three cutting edges and were made to cut rather than squeeze a thread. With such equipment Maudslay was able to produce machinery which was both accurate and reliable and to him about 1800 came Marc Brunel, lately arrived from America with a set of drawings for machinery he had devised for manufacture of the blocks required by sailing ships. There was a big demand: in those days a 74-gun ship of the line required as many as 1,400 blocks. Maudslay first produced models, then the machinery itself, which was installed in Portsmouth Dockyard at the instance of Sir Samuel Bentham (of the steam bucket dredger). The Portsmouth block-making machinery was the first instance of mass production by machine tools.

Maudslay prospered, set up a larger engineering works in Lambeth and took partners. At Lambeth H. Maudslay & Co. built steam engines and other machinery for, for instance, minting coins and boring guns; and, in 1815, the 17 hp engine for the steam boat *Richmond*. It was the first of many marine engines built by the firm; later it styled itself Maudslay, Son & Field, and later still Maudslay, Sons & Field. Towards the end of his life, Maudslay took as personal assistant James Nasmyth, whose father Alexander had been present long before when Miller and Symington first steamed their little boat on Dalswinton Loch.

The *Richmond* and the *Thames* were soon joined by other steam boats. Dodd records nine in 1818; for some of them the Butterley Co., by now long-established as builders of machinery for steam dredgers, had supplied the engines. Dodd himself was in charge of five boats, one of which plied from London to Gravesend, two to Margate, and two to Richmond. Perhaps it was one of these which Miss Mitford, during her visit to Richmond made possible in 1820 by the newly-macadamised roads, noted 'walloping along with a regular mechanical combination of noise and motion, rumpling the quiet waters, and leaving a track of waves which vary most agreeably the level lake-like surface of the tranquil river'.

Matthew Murray and the *Experiment*

All the steam boats so far mentioned had low pressure condensing engines and followed the line of development which originated on the Clyde with the *Comet*. There was, however, another, though limited, line of development which had arisen independently out of Trevithick's work involving high pressure engines. It originated not long after the *Comet* and owed nothing to her.

About 1811 or 1812 John Wright, a Yarmouth Quaker, bought a captured French privateer, *L'Actif*, 62 ft long and propelled by oars and sails. Into her he and his brother attempted to install an engine driven by hydrogen. Having failed in this, they sent the boat under sail to the Humber and up the Aire & Calder Navigation to Leeds where she was fitted with a Trevithick-type high pressure engine and paddle wheels by Messrs Fenton, Murray & Wood.

The presiding genius of this firm was Matthew Murray (1765–1826). Murray was born on Tyneside, served an apprenticeship with, probably, a smith, and set out for Leeds to find his fortune. After several years working as a mechanic, during which he gained experience of steam engines, he formed a partnership with David Wood and James Fenton to establish a works which would make and repair engines and machinery. The works was set up on the south side of Leeds where an adjacent canal simplified despatch of heavy goods. Wood ran the works, Fenton looked after the money and the books and Murray designed steam engines for the works to build.

'This man makes very free with your patents, would it not be well to look sharply after him?' wrote John Rennie to James Watt; and though Watt's patent expired a few years later without action having been taken, relations between Boulton & Watt and Fenton Murray & Wood remained strained: they deteriorated even to the point at which Boulton, Watt & Co. surreptitiously purchased land adjacent to Fenton Murray & Wood's works to prevent its expansion. Murray's workmanship was good, however, and his prices low, and his firm prospered. In 1810 Murray commenced experimenting with steam locomotives, experiments which culminated in the successful production of his first in 1812: it will be mentioned below.

This was the firm to which Wright brought *L'Actif* in 1813. Fenton Murray & Wood made her boiler and engine, paying the Trevithick royalty. It seems unlikely that Trevithick personally had much to do with this application of his engine: he had sold his last share in the patent five years earlier. The engine was of 8 hp and the boat was tried out in public in Leeds in mid-June 1813. The following month she set off back to Norfolk. She was insured for the sea voyage on condition that sails only were used; but caught by a gale when she left the Humber, she was forced on shore. Wright then propped her up as the tide fell, rigged her paddles and raised steam and, when the tide rose again, steamed out to sea, preferring his ship to his insurance money. The ship reached Yarmouth safely, and renamed the *Experiment*, went into passenger service on the River Yare between Yarmouth and Norwich in the middle of August 1813, just over a year after the *Comet* entered service on the Clyde.

The *Experiment* performed well and passengers were forthcoming; Wright added another boat; the *Telegraph* also with a high pressure engine, the following year and later on moved the *Experiment*'s steam plant into a new hull – this boat was called the *Courier*. Another steam boat with a high pressure engine was built at Yarmouth for service in Holland. The *Telegraph* for a short time worked on trial on the Medway between Sheerness and Chatham, but found the currents too fast. She returned to Yarmouth.

On the Yare, Wright's steam boats worked well for several years: then, on Good Friday 4 April 1817, the *Telegraph* brought herself horrifically to public notice: just after she left the wharf at Norwich, the boiler exploded. Eight of the twenty-two passengers were killed, several others wounded. The accident attracted enough public concern for the House of Commons to appoint a select committee to consider 'means of preventing the mischief of explosion from happening on board steam boats . . .' From the report of this, and from contemporary newspaper reports, the cause of the accident can be established. It originated with the *Telegraph*'s visit to the Medway: on her return her boiler was found to be much encrusted with saline deposits, and one end damaged. A new end, made of cast iron, was fitted: the rest of the boiler was of wrought iron. The immediate cause was that the engineman had, almost certainly, loaded the safety valve, with a view to ensuring that the *Telegraph* was not beaten by a rival steamer which was put on that same day. It was the cast-iron boiler-end which gave way. The steam pressure is believed to have been more than 75 lb per sq. in. in a boiler originally intended for 40.

The select committee, in a report remarkably well-informed for its period, recommended regulations to ensure that all boilers for passenger boats were made of wrought iron or copper, tested by a skilful engineer and fitted with two safety valves, one of which should be inaccessible to the engineman. High pressure engines were cheaper than the usual low pressure ones; on the latter

the risk of explosion was less, but still present. The 1817 explosion and its aftermath were a setback to development of steam boat services, but only a temporary one. They provide, however, an opportunity to pause and consider what had been happening on rails.

Blenkinsop and Murray's Rack Locomotives

What had been happening was that the price of horse fodder had risen because of the Napoleonic Wars, and coal owners therefore had cause to consider ways of economising on waggonway transport. Among them was J. C. Brandling, on whose Middleton Waggonway, south of Leeds (mentioned on page 30) cast-iron edge rails began to replace wooden rails about 1807–8. Brandling is said to have seen Trevithick's *Catch me who can* running in 1808, and no doubt discussed it with his viewer, or manager, at Middleton Colliery, John Blenkinsop. The problem was – or so it was believed – that a locomotive light enough to run on cast iron rails without excessive breakage would be too light to haul, by adhesion, a worthwhile load. This Blenkinsop solved by his invention, patented in 1811, of what we now call a rack railway, in which a toothed wheel on the 'carriage', preferably driven by steam, would mesh with a continuous rack in the track.

For him, Murray designed and built a locomotive based very closely on *Catch me who can* – the royalty was paid to the patent owners. Instead of a single cylinder, however, two were used, both of them upright in the boiler, and with cranks at right angles. This must not only have made the locomotive run much more smoothly, but also have made it much easier to start. The crankshafts drove not the wheels but, through spur gears, a rack pinion; and the furnace was of the 'single pass' type with firedoor at one end of the boiler and chimney at the other. A supply of coal for fuel was carried on the locomotive.

While the locomotive was being built, one side of the waggonway track was being re-laid with rails incorporating a horizontal rack on the outside. The locomotive made its first public trial on 24 June 1812 with great success; it seems to have gone into service immediately and was joined in August by a second. They were named, respectively, *Prince Regent* and *Salamanca*. The Battle of Salamanca had taken place on 22 July: this was the period of great victories when de Quincey was glorying in the spectacle of laurel-garlanded mail coaches bearing the good news throughout the land. It was also the period which saw almost simultaneously, the first successful commercial use of both the steam railway locomotive and, in Britain, the steam boat, for *Comet* was launched on 24 July.

Murray's locomotives worked well on the Middleton Railway, as we must now start to call it, travelling at 10 mph when lightly loaded or at $3\frac{1}{2}$ mph with 30 coal waggons each weighing $3\frac{1}{2}$ tons. Other locomotives of the same type were built for Middleton, and similar lines were built near Wigan and at Kenton & Coxlodge collieries, Newcastle upon Tyne. These had short lives, but on the Middleton Railway the rack locomotives were used until 1835.

Of relics of the system, Leeds Industrial Museum has a length of the rack rail, and a model of one of the locomotives probably built by Murray himself. The National Railway Museum has a set of locomotive wheels, including a pair of rack pinions: these are believed to have come from Kenton & Coxlodge, where it is evident that both rails had cast-in racks. The route of the present-day preserved Middleton Railway follows, for the most part, later diversions from the original waggonway route and additions to it, except probably for a short distance at the present-day line's southern extremity. The original route can be traced along nearby streets, as shown in the illustration on this page.

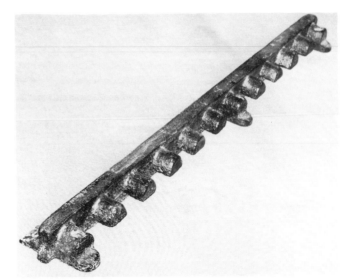

A length of rack rail (above) from the Middleton Railway, to Blenkinsop's patent of 1811, is preserved in Leeds Industrial Museum.

The original course of the Middleton Railway is marked by present-day Leeds streets (below). In the foreground is Old Run Road, marking the course of a gravity operated inclined plane: the photograph is taken at its foot and the line continued into the distance along the alignment of Moor Road. It was at this point, in 1812, that the first locomotives in commercial service collected laden coal waggons which had come down the incline and hauled them away to Leeds itself. The Engine Hotel on the left bears the date 1815, so it was part of the scene when Murray's locomotives were at work. While the author was taking this photograph in 1982, the horse-drawn cart trotted into view, as if to emphasise that, whatever might have happened here 170 years before, horse transport is not finished yet. OS grid ref. SE 306307.

Another attempt to solve the locomotive weight/rail breakage problem was made by William Chapman, who was mentioned on page 93. His concept for locomotive haulage on railways was to have a locomotive which would haul itself along a chain laid between the rails. The scheme was patented in 1812 and tried out on two lines in the North-East. The first locomotive to this principle was built by the Butterley Co. and though the system proved to be an expensive failure the locomotive had one feature of lasting interest: four of its six wheels were mounted on a swivelling bogie. A second locomotive, built in 1814, had eight wheels arranged on two bogies.

Wylam

The same rise in fodder prices which had prompted Brandling to introduce locomotives at Middleton prompted Christopher Blackett to think about them again at Wylam. His wooden waggonway had been re-laid as a plateway; he asked Trevithick to build him a locomotive but was refused. So in October 1812 he asked his viewer William Hedley (1779–1843) to undertake construction. Now Hedley had the idea that if all the wheels of a locomotive were coupled together by gears, then its weight alone would be sufficient for it to haul a train of loaded waggons: any tendency for one pair of wheels to slip would be resisted by the others. To confirm this he first had a model made, a frame with two pairs of wheels linked by spur gears and turned by handles – it survives in store at the Science Museum and is illustrated in *The Archaeology of Railways*. Experiments with this had results which were promising enough for him to have a full-size version built, propelled by men turning handles and loaded with iron weights to find out at what total weight it would cease to slip when attached to two, four or more coal waggons.

A locomotive was then built, probably using the test carriage as its frames, by Thomas Waters of Gateshead who was familiar with the 1805 locomotive and was assisted by Jonathan Foster, principal enginewright, and Timothy Hackworth, foreman smith. Timothy Hackworth (1786–1850) had a distinguished career ahead of him. This locomotive probably approximated fairly closely to Trevithick's early type, with a single cylinder and a flywheel, but with a single-pass fire tube as in Murray's locomotives. Its performance was erratic and it suffered from lack of steam.

A second locomotive was therefore built through the combined efforts of Hedley, Foster and Hackworth. The tube containing the fire was enlarged and made into a return tube (as in Trevithick's original locomotives) and two cylinders were fitted, positioned upright either side of one end of the boiler. This position enabled them to be as large as 9 in. diameter by 36 in. stroke. Drive was via overhead rocking beams and connecting rods to a crankshaft below the frames which drove the wheels through gears. This locomotive was much more satisfactory than the first: it could haul nine laden waggons at 4–5 mph. The date at which it went into service has been disputed down the years, but was reasoned by C. F. Dendy Marshall (*A History of Railway Locomotives down to the end of the year 1831*) to have been about March 1814.

In one respect however the locomotive was unsatisfactory: it damaged the track. To minimise this about 1815, it and two more like it were each mounted on two four-wheeled bogies similar to those devised by William Chapman. In this manner they ran until about 1830 when the line was re-laid as an edge railway and the locomotives were put back on to four wheels. They continued in service until the 1860s and two survived to be preserved: one is *Puffing Billy* in the Science Museum, the other is *Wylam Dilly* in the Royal Scottish Museum.

Those are the names by which these two locomotives have traditionally been known, 'dilly' being the term that

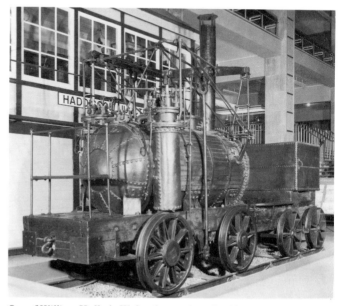

One of William Hedley's *Wylam* locomotives of c. 1814, Puffing Billy, *is preserved in the Science Museum. Flanged wheels, however, date from the 1830s; previously the locomotive ran on plate rails, with plain wheels.*

was used by Wylam colliers for coal waggons, so that *Puffing Billy* is probably a corruption of *Puffing Dilly*. However they carried no names when in use and it is not possible to identify them further (different names are sometimes quoted: W. W. Tomlinson for instance in his *The North Eastern Railway* gave the name *Old Duchess* to the Science Museum locomotive and *Puffing Billy* to the one in the Royal Scottish Museum). Doubt, too, has been cast on their dates of origin, following discovery of Blackett papers in Northumberland Record Office which suggest the original locomotives may have been replaced 1828–32; although Hedley wrote in 1836 that the original locomotives, built with four wheels and converted to eight, could still then be seen on four wheels 'at this day'.

George Stephenson

The uncertainty about the date of the first satisfactory Wylam locomotive arose from the anxiety of later historians, protagonists of Hedley and Hackworth, to establish that it was constructed before George Stephenson completed *his* first locomotive. The Wylam locomotive was first, but not by long: Stephenson's first locomotive was completed at Killingworth, Northumberland, in July 1814.

George Stephenson (1781–1848) has been well served by biographers from Smiles to Rolt and only the briefest resumé of his background is needed here. His father was fireman of a steam engine at Wylam Colliery, and George Stephenson was born at Wylam in a cottage beside the waggonway. It still stands, at OS grid reference NZ 126651, although the course of the waggonway itself, which was upgraded by stages into a public steam railway and then eventually closed down in the 1960s, is now a footpath.

The Stephenson family had moved away long before Hedley's locomotives were built, though George Stephenson visited Wylam and was an interested spectator of them at work. By then, his natural mechanical genius had overcome the handicap of minimal formal education – he was still illiterate at eighteen though he subsequently learned to read and write well – and he had risen to the position of chief enginewright at Killingworth Colliery. He was considered as, at this stage, a skilled craftsman – today he would be called a mechanical engineer – with responsibility for maintenance of the steam engines, pumps and other equipment, and for introducing new methods and new machines, both at Killingworth and other local col-

lieries in the same ownership. Those owners were no less than the formidable combination of coal-owning families – Wortley, Liddell and Bowes – that had been known in the North-East as the 'Grand Allies' since the 1730s at least. One of their early ventures had been construction of the Tanfield Waggonway mentioned in chapter two. By 1813 the chief partner was Sir Thomas Liddell, later Lord Ravensworth. By this date, indeed, the Grand Allies thought so well of Stephenson that they permitted him, provided that their own equipment was properly maintained, to work also for other colliery proprietors. During the next few years he became well known as the inventor of his safety lamp for mines, and as a builder of stationary engines for colliery work; and he introduced at Killingworth a system of underground tramroads worked by stationary engines and cable haulage.

Mining at Killingworth had commenced about 1802 and the Killingworth Waggonway, an extension of an earlier line, had been built as far as the colliery in 1806. During 1813 Sir Thomas Liddell instructed Stephenson to build a locomotive in the colliery workshops, and it was this that was completed, named *Blucher* and tried out for the first time on 25 July 1814 on part of the waggonway which was laid with cast-iron edge rails. The locomotive's layout probably followed that of Murray's locomotives – Stephenson had seen Murray's locomotive at Coxlodge – but its crankshafts, instead of driving a rack pinion, were connected by a train of gears to the wheels. These, of course, had flanges. George Stephenson was not the inventor of the locomotive, but he did, in *Blucher*, produce for the first time a locomotive driven by adhesion, with flanged wheels, and running on edge rails: the arrangement which soon afterwards became, as it still remains, the conventional one for locomotives. And *Blucher* was successful, able to ascend a gradient of 1 in 450 at 4 mph while hauling 8 loaded waggons with a total weight of 30 tons.

Though successful, *Blucher* was also clearly far from perfect. For a start there was a continual grinding of gears, as each alternately drove or was driven by its fellows according to the positions of the pistons in their strokes, and this suggested modification. *Blucher*, which probably only ran in her original form for about a year, was the start of a series of modifications and improvements in locomotive design over the next few years. Probably some of these were applied to new locomotives and some to old ones rebuilt – Stephenson later did not know exactly how many locomotives he built at Killingworth, although the complement of locomotives in use seems to have settled down at four. At any rate, in 1815, Stephenson with Ralph Dodd, viewer at the colliery, civil engineer and father of George Dodd, whose adventures on the Irish Sea in this year have been mentioned above, took out a patent for locomotive improvements.

These improvements included direct drive from connecting rods to crank pins on the wheels (as on *Catch me who can*, though the patentees were probably unaware of this), and coupling of the driving wheels together by an endless chain running over toothed wheels. Late in 1816 Stephenson took out another patent, jointly this time with William Losh, senior partner in a firm of ironfounders. Here they tackled the problem of improving locomotives' ride, from two angles. Firstly, their locomotives were to be carried on steam springs, cylinder-and-piston arrangements let into the bottom of the boiler. Presumably semi-elliptic springs of sufficient strength were not available; such springs were fitted to later Stephenson locomotives. Secondly, joints between rails were to be improved. At this period rails were still about one yard long butted up against one another in cast iron chairs on stone block sleepers. The track was no more than a continuous succession of joints, and if, or when, a sleeper block subsided slightly and tilted along the line of the track, the joint took on the form of a step. This problem Stephenson and Losh neatly solved by making the seating of the chair convex instead of flat and giving the rails scarfed ends, so that both continued to rest on the apex of the curved seating even when the chair was tilted. It was the first of several improvements to track that were an essential prerequisite to the general introduction of the steam locomotive.

In 1817, the year that general surveyor J. L. McAdam was starting to make marked improvements to the turnpike roads of Bristol, Stephenson for the first time supplied a locomotive to an outside customer. Indeed, it was the first for a public railway, the Kilmarnock & Troon. The Duke of Portland had been considering locomotives as early as 1813, for he obtained particulars of Blenkinsop's and Murray's locomotives and rack rail system; what the Kilmarnock & Troon in fact obtained was a locomotive to Losh's and Stephenson's patent. Its track was, and for the time being remained, a plateway: the locomotive was carried on six wheels, presumably to reduce the axle loading and minimise damage to the track. If so, it was evidently unsuccessful, for this locomotive does seem to have damaged the track excessively and did little if any useful work.

Nearer home, Stephenson's locomotives were more successful – indeed, in marked contrast to the rapid spread of steam boats after their first introduction, the North-East of England was the only place where any development work on steam locomotives was being carried out at this period, and Stephenson was the only engineer involved.

In 1818 Stephenson carried out a series of experiments to establish the resistance to traction of vehicles on railways. In these he was joined by Nicholas Wood, who had come to Killingworth in 1811 to learn the profession of viewer from Ralph Dodd, and in due course succeeded him. From these experiments Stephenson concluded, says Samuel Smiles, that so small a rise as 1 in 100 would diminish the useful effort of a locomotive by upwards of fifty per cent. On a locomotive-worked line, a suitably easy gradient would have to be obtained by earthworks and civil engineering features; where this could not be done economically, inclined planes with cable haulage could be used, worked either by stationary engines or by gravity.

Stephenson put these principles into practice when, in 1819 (or possibly 1820: authorities differ) he laid out for the first time an entirely new railway. This, the Hetton Colliery Railway, was the first railway to be built with the intention that no animal haulage should be used. It ran from the then new Hetton Colliery, Co. Durham, in a north-easterly direction for eight miles to staithes beside the River Wear at Sunderland. The first section of $1\frac{1}{2}$ miles was to be worked by locomotives; this was followed by inclined planes which ascended for $1\frac{1}{2}$ miles, worked by stationary engines, to a summit on Warden Law hill; these in turn were followed by $2\frac{1}{2}$ miles of gravity-operated inclined planes, a 2-mile section to be worked by locomotives, and a final gravity-operated plane. Stephenson had five locomotives, similar to the Killingworth locomotives, built for the Hetton line, which was completed in 1822.

The Hetton Colliery Railway remained a colliery line until its eventual closure in 1960. The author noted in 1980 that its course on either side of Warden Law was still clear (at, for instance, OS grid ref. NZ 365503). The winding engine from Warden Law was dismantled after closure and is held in store by Beamish North of England Open Air Museum. More remarkably, perhaps, Beamish has one of the original locomotives, much rebuilt, and this is on display. It was originally built in 1822 with chain coupling of the wheels, and steam springs; it was substantially rebuilt in 1859 and 1883 gaining coupling rods, laminated springs and other contemporary features, and remained in use until about 1912.

Before the Hetton railway was completed, other developments of great importance for steam railways were taking place. They included, notably, incorporation of the Stockton & Darlington Railway Company; but before considering them we will first consider how the rapid expansion in the use of steam boats and ships was continuing at the same period.

Steam Ships on Open Water

The earliest steam boat services had been introduced on sheltered rivers and estuaries, but confidence in the abilities of steam boats grew with experience of their operation. Attempts were soon made to establish regular steam boat services on open water such as the Irish Sea, for the demand at this time for an improved road between Holyhead and London was matched by the demand for an improved crossing between Dublin and Holyhead. Sailing packets, wrote Telford in his *Life*, were occasionally tossed

for several days on a stormy sea, and their passengers had to land at Holyhead on unprotected rocks.

Construction of improved packet stations at Howth and Holyhead – the work was started by Rennie in 1808 and continued after his death in 1821 by Telford – was contemporary with the development of steam boats, but the first attempt to introduce steam boats on to this route in the autumn of 1816 proved a failure. Probably the machinery of the two 80-ft long paddle steamers was inadequate. Although the manufacturer was James Cook who had engined the *Elizabeth* in 1812–13 and subsequent steam boats, he had succumbed to the temptation to include devices to lift the paddles during rough weather and strong beam winds; at any rate, the machinery was not robust enough to be reliable and the vessels were laid up.

About 1818 David Napier decided to attempt to build a sea-going steamer. He first took passage on board a Glasgow–Belfast sailing packet at a stormy time of year,

One of George Stephenson's Killingworth locomotives of c. 1817 has steam springs and driving wheels coupled by a chain.

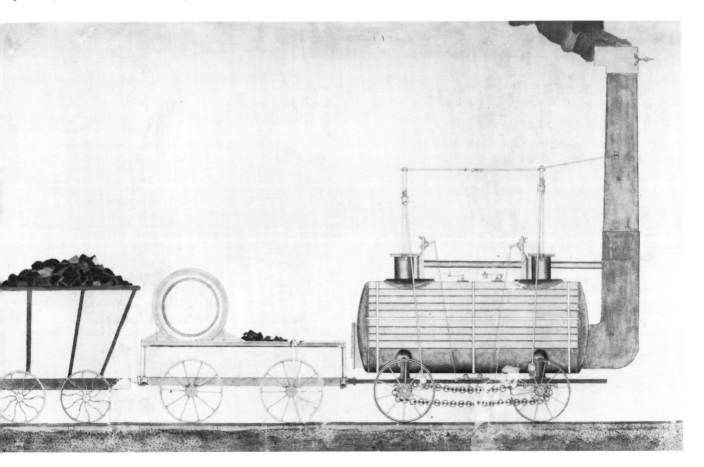

to see for himself how rough a sea he would have to contend with; then he carried out experiments on a mill dam adjoining his works, with a wooden model of the hull of the proposed vessel. From these he deduced that sharp bows were preferable to the blunt bows then usual.

The ship, the *Rob Roy*, was built the same year at Dumbarton with a 30 hp engine by Napier; her length overall was some 81 ft, and beam over the paddle boxes 27 ft. After a successful trial trip in a gale from the Clyde to Dublin and back, *Rob Roy* was put into service between Glasgow and Belfast carrying mails and passengers. She continued on this, the first successful steamship service on the open sea, for two years; then, in 1821 she was moved down to the Dover–Calais route where she inaugurated cross-channel steamer services. At this she was so successful that she was eventually purchased by the French government.

Meanwhile Napier had been having other equally successful ships built with his engines. PS *Talbot*, built by Wood & Co., went into service between Holyhead and Howth in 1819, on which route she was later joined by the *Ivanhoe*; PS *Robert Bruce* initiated a service between Glasgow, Greenock and Liverpool in 1819 or 20, and although she was burnt out in 1821, Napier had already added other ships to the route. Both of these routes were successes. The ships between Greenock and Liverpool were scheduled to take twenty-eight hours, which was quicker than the mail coach. Between Holyhead and Dublin, and Dover and Calais, the GPO itself put on steam

packets (two on each route with Boulton, Watt & Co. engines) in 1821, and a steamship service between London and Leith started the same year.

Now steamers were beginning to make ocean voyages too. The first to do so was PS *Savannah* which crossed the Atlantic from the USA to Britain in 1819. She was in effect a sailing vessel with auxiliary steam propulsion – most steamers at this period were rigged so as to go by sail or steam – and *Savannah*'s engine, with its single cylinder of 40 in. diameter and 60 in. stroke, was only used for parts of the voyage. It was to be some years before a crossing of the Atlantic would be made wholly under power: in the meantime ocean-going steamers, with their boilers hungry for coal, sailed when the wind was fair and steamed when it was not, and in this way travelled far and wide. The first east–west crossing of the Atlantic by a steamer was made in 1821 by PS *Rising Star*, with twin-cylinder engine by Maudslay, Son & Field. The same firm provided the engine for PS *Enterprise*, of 1824; she set out from Falmouth on 16 August 1825 and, voyaging via Capetown, reached Calcutta, 13,700 miles away, on 7 December. Of the 113 days taken for the voyage, she was under steam for 64.

Steamers and Coaches

So far as steamers were concerned, however, the main emphasis at this period continued to be on comparatively short voyages in comparatively sheltered waters. Here are three divers examples.

The first lake steamer in Ireland, the *Marchioness of Donegall*, was launched on to Lough Neagh in 1821, the forerunner of many steamer services on the large Irish lakes and the River Shannon.

In 1822 a steam ferry service was established across the Firth of Tay. The boats carried not only passengers but also carriages and cattle; they ran between masonry slipways sloped so that the boats could come alongside at all states of the tide, which had been designed by Thomas Telford. Telford was active in harbour improvements in general throughout the period of his other works in Scotland.

PS James Watt *entered service between London and Leith in 1821, one of the first steamers on the route. She was built by Wood & Co. (who had built the* Comet*) and had a 2-cylinder, 50 hp engine by Boulton, Watt & Co.*

About 1824, a steam tug started to haul boats through the 5,456-yd Standedge tunnel, by which the Huddersfield Canal passed beneath the Pennine ridge. Early canal tunnels had generally been built without towpaths: boats were propelled by legging, by boatmen, that is, who lay across the deck, or on the tarpaulins covering the cargo, and walked their feet against tunnel side or roof. The practice of providing steam tugs to tow horse-boats through long canal tunnels later became common, but otherwise on narrow canals lack of space on board boats for bulky low-pressure engines and paddle wheels prevented general adoption of steam power at this period, even though the arrival of a stern-wheel paddle steamer at Birmingham from London in 1826 is recorded. The Standedge tug hauled itself along a chain laid on the bed of the canal.

Actual relics of steam boats of this period are regrettably rare. Glasgow Museum of Transport, however, does have in store two side-lever marine steam engines, from the PS *Comet II* and the PS *Industry*. *Comet II* was the replacement for the original *Comet*, built in 1821. *Industry* had a remarkably long career, having been built in 1814 as a steam tug to tow barges on the Clyde. She was refitted in 1828 – from which refit the surviving engine dates – and lasted until 1862. Even then her career was brought to a premature end by a collision which damaged her beyond economic repair. By that date she was the oldest surviving steamer.

By the end of the 1820s, coastal steam boat services were extensive and well established, and nowhere more so than on the Clyde, and the West Coast of Scotland. Among the Western Isles, one of the most remote parts of Britain, they had already made steam transport familiar at a period when travel throughout most of England still meant horse-drawn vehicles. Or, as Lumsden & Son's *Steam-Boat Companion* (Third edition, 1831) puts it: 'The ease and rapidity with which travellers may be conveyed by steam-vessels cannot be more satisfactorily exemplifed than by stating, that a person may leave Glasgow, either by the Fort-William or Inverness boats, and be at Crinan, west end of the canal, the first night; where he can engage a boat to be in readiness, and next morning early may be in Jura; explore the island, and visit the singular caves on its western side; return at night to Crinan, and next day meet the boats from Inverary at the south-east end of the canal; thus visiting the wild . . . scenery of . . . the Highlands and be again at Glasgow, on the third day.' One could scarcely visit the Isle of Jura in comfort more quickly now.

An appendix to the same guide lists the steam boats 'employed in the trade of the Clyde'. Large ones called at Greenock, smaller ones came up to Glasgow itself, and their numbers were, by route:

To Liverpool	9 vessels
Dublin	2
Belfast	3
Campbeltown and Londonderry	2
Rothesay, Islay, Staffa and Iona	1
Rothesay, Inverary, Arran etc.	5
Dunoon and Rothesay	4
Greenock and Kilmun	2
Stranraer	1
Ayr	2
Campbeltown	1
Largs, Milport, Ardrossan, Arran	2
Helensburgh	8
Lochgilphead and Arrochar	1
Skye	1
Inverness	3
Greenock (boats for 'luggage': including *Industry*)	6
Greenock (towing boats)	3

It is an impressive list.

This period, when steam railways for passengers were as we shall see still a rarity, was the heyday of coastal steam boats, as it was of stage and mail coaches and indeed of passenger boats on canals. The *Steam-Boat Companion* gave details of passenger conveyance daily between Glasgow and Edinburgh: there were ten coaches throughout the day, including the mail at 10.30 pm, and two canal boats, each of which took far more passengers than a coach and travelled via the Forth & Clyde and Union Canals; passengers by the 8 am boat, however, had the option of travelling between Grangemouth and Leith by steam boat on the Firth of Forth. The latter arrangement had been instituted before the Union Canal was opened in 1822; there is more about this canal, and about passenger carriage on canals generally, in the next chapter.

When coastal steam boat services were introduced, coach services running parallel to the coast between the same places tended to lose traffic, for steam boat fares were cheaper than coach fares. Some coaches were taken off, and the turnpike trusts in consequence lost revenue. But the coach routes to and from the steam boats' ports of call found traffic increasing, and the turnpike trusts benefited

accordingly. A traveller from Glasgow to London might prefer the steamer as far as Liverpool, but from there onwards he travelled by coach. William Chaplin saw which way the wind was blowing: at the Swan with Two Necks travellers could get details not only of the coaches commencing there, but also of steam packets connecting with them. Chaplin's coach office also acted as a goods agent for the London–Leith steamers.

By combining fast coaches with steam boats, a traveller in a hurry could make good time. Nimrod stated that the subject of 'The Road' was suggested to him by a sentence in a letter from a personal friend: 'I was out hunting . . . on a *Monday*, near Brighton; and dined with my father in Merrion Square, Dublin, at six o'clock on the following *Wednesday* – distance 400 miles'. He had taken an afternoon coach from Brighton to London, caught the down Holyhead mail, and crossed the Irish Sea by steamer: the total journey time, evidently, was about 48 hours. Progress indeed, when not many years before the London–Holyhead mail coach timing alone had been nearly 45 hours, and the Irish Sea crossing, by sailing packet, had been known to take as much as 76 hours.

Iron Hulls

All the steam boats so far mentioned had wooden hulls. According to H. P. Spratt (*The Birth of the Steamboat*) iron hull construction dates from 1777 when a small pleasure boat was made of sheet iron on the banks of the River Foss in Yorkshire; ten years later an iron-hulled narrow boat was built experimentally in Shropshire. The Tavistock Canal had an iron boat in 1811, and in 1818 an iron-hulled passenger boat, the *Vulcan*, was built for the Forth & Clyde Canal.

The first steam boat with an iron hull was PS *Aaron Manby*, built in 1821–2. Her engine had two oscillating cylinders, and was designed by Manby himself; and her paddle wheels had blades which were feathered by a bevel-wheel mechanism patented by John Oldham. She was built at Manby's Horseley Ironworks, Tipton, Staffordshire, and taken in sections, presumably by canal, to London where she was assembled. Then, after trials, she left for France and the River Seine for which she had been intended, and where she worked for many years.

Manby's second iron steam boat was built during 1823–4 to the order of John Grantham. Grantham had been surveying the River Shannon under Rennie, and had

PS United Kingdom *(above), built in 1826, was considered the finest steam vessel of her time. She therefore exemplifies the stage that steamship development had reached in the year that the Menai Bridge was opened for horse-drawn coaches and the Liverpool & Manchester Railway was authorised. David Napier provided her 200 hp side-lever engines, and the hull was flared out so that gunwale enveloped the paddle wheels. United Kingdom was built for service between London and Leith; the voyage took from forty to fifty hours and was thus an alternative to the Edinburgh mail coach illustrated on page 109.*

The side-lever engine of 1828 from PS Industry *is now dismantled, held in store by Glasgow Museum of Transport. When this photograph was taken, probably in the 1920s, it was an open air display elsewhere in Glasgow.*

realised its potential for steam navigation – for the Shannon is not only long but connects a series of lakes far larger than any in England. Manby's connection with Ireland may have come through Oldham, who was engineer to the Bank of Ireland. This time the vessel, the *Marquis Wellesley*, was taken in sections to Liverpool for assembly, whence she left by sea for the Shannon. In 1825 she inaugurated the Shannon steam boat service, based on Killaloe at the south end of Lough Derg.

Other steamers were added; among them was the *Lady Lansdowne*, built in 1833 by William Laird of Birkenhead for Charles Wye Williams's Inland Steam Navigation Co. Williams, an old acquaintance of Oldham, had bought out Grantham. PS *Lady Lansdowne*, 133 ft long, was too large to pass through the locks of the canal which in those days bypassed rapids in the Shannon itself to provide a navigable link between Killaloe and the estuary at Limerick. She was therefore taken to Killaloe in sections and assembled there.

Many years later, in the 1860s after railways had been built and the steamer service had ceased, she was equally too large to leave again; nor yet, apparently, worth breaking up. Instead she was scuttled in shallow water close to the bank, almost opposite the dock where she had been assembled. Her wreck was found there in 1957 by Dr V.T.H. and Mrs D. R. Delany (authors of *The Canals of the South of Ireland*), and surveyed under water in 1967 by volunteer divers from Merseyside Sub-Aqua Club. Their survey, recorded in the Transactions of the Liverpool Nautical Research Society, Vol. X, confirmed the identity of the wreck, but reported, sadly, that boiler, engine and paddle wheels were all missing. The present author, visiting the scene in 1969 and no diver, found above water only the stem head rustily projecting.

In 1834 Laird built of iron for Wye Williams's company the PS *Garryowen*, almost certainly the first iron vessel to have watertight bulkheads, which had been designed by Wye Williams himself. Iron was coming slowly into use as a hull material: David Napier had built an iron-hulled steam boat on the Clyde for the first time in 1827.

A Steam Railway Network?

By 1820, protagonists of a national network of tramroads were active again, with the difference that now they thought they should be powered by steam locomotives. Thomas Gray, a native of Leeds, envisaged such a system

in his book *Observations on a General Iron Railway*, first published in 1820: motive power was to be provided by rack locomotives of the type developed by Blenkinsop and Murray. The book went into five editions before 1825. Among his recommendations was a railway between Liverpool and Manchester.

William James had come back into the transport scene through the medium of waterways. The Stratford-upon-Avon Canal, authorised in 1793 during the canal mania, had been built by stages, according to the finance available, from its junction with the Worcester & Birmingham Canal at King's Norton as far as a connection with the Warwick & Birmingham at Kingswood, 12½ miles, by 1802; and there construction had ceased. In 1813 James, who had been on the canal committee since 1808, took charge of the job of completing the remaining 13-mile section to Stratford. The same year he purchased the shares of the old-established Upper Avon Navigation from Evesham to Stratford. The canal was completed to a junction with it in 1816.

To extend the line of the canal, James in 1819–20 planned a tramroad to Moreton-in-Marsh, Gloucestershire; the plan developed rapidly into a much more grandiose scheme for the 'Central Junction Railway or Tram-Road' to extend also to Coventry, Cheltenham or London. The time was still not yet ripe for such ambitious ideas – at this stage James may have been thinking of horse traction. But the Stratford-Moreton proposal went ahead – James and other promoters started to seek finance and applied to Parliament for powers to build the line.

Stockton & Darlington Proposed

During the same period, there was a need for improved transport between the coalfield of south-west Durham and its markets at Darlington and Stockton, which had often been considered. As early as 1768 a route for a canal had been surveyed by Robert Whitworth and approved by James Brindley himself. It was not made, but the project was revived in 1810: the navigation of the Tees estuary up to Stockton had just been improved, and the possibility of constructing a canal – or possibly a horse railway – to the coalfield was considered. Throughout the ensuing decade there were arguments and counter-arguments, surveys and counter-surveys: the points at issue were whether the route should be through Darlington, or a more northerly one direct from Stockton to the coalfield, and whether it should be a canal, a railway, or a combination of the two. What eventually emerged was a line surveyed by George Overton, who had engineered the Penydarren Tramroad and other lines in South Wales, from Stockton via Darlington to collieries a little to the south-west of Bishop Auckland: and for this the Stockton & Darlington Railway Company was incorporated by Act of Parliament which received the royal assent on 19 April 1821. The Stratford & Moreton got its Act six weeks later.

What Overton intended the S & DR to be was a horse-drawn plateway of the South Wales type. But on the same day that the S & DR Act was getting the royal assent in London, George Stephenson and Nicholas Wood called on Edward Pease in Darlington. Pease was one of the principal promoters of the railway, and they probably called at his invitation. Stephenson's ideas on railways were clearly more advanced than Overton's and the upshot was that George Stephenson was invited to re-survey the line, and in due course became the railway's engineer. That meant it would be an edge railway, with steam locomotives as well as horses.

The development of malleable iron rails greatly enhanced the practicability of this. Edge rails of malleable iron had been tried at Walbottle Colliery, Northumberland, as early as 1805, but they were too narrow, wore grooves in the wheels, and were replaced by wider rails of cast iron. Between 1808 and 1812, however, malleable iron rails of $1\frac{1}{2}$ in. square cross-section were laid on the Tindale Fell Railway, near Brampton, Cumbria, and wore well. An example is preserved in the Science Museum. George Stephenson became aware of the Tindale Fell rails in 1818, and so malleable iron rails were laid on a new 3-mile long waggonway between Bedlington Glebe Colliery, Northumberland, and Bedlington Ironworks. Stephenson had become a partner in the colliery; the rails were made at the ironworks where manager John Birkinshaw had thought of, and in 1820 patented, the idea of making them of wedge-shaped cross-section, to combine a wide tread with maximum depth, for strength, and minimum weight of iron. These rails were made by passing heated bars of iron between profiled rollers, and could therefore be much longer than cast iron rails so fewer joints were needed. They were free, too, from cast iron's brittleness. Their potential for providing a strong and stable track for locomotives was obvious.

William James saw them, and enthused. He came to Killingworth, too, probably on 28 May 1821, to see Stephenson's latest locomotive undergo its trials. He enthused about that, also, and about Stephenson himself: and departed for the South. In July he was in Liverpool, explaining the advantages of locomotives to Joseph Sandars, corn merchant. Together they then promoted the idea of a tramroad, or railway, from Liverpool to Manchester. James made a preliminary survey the same summer.

He also returned to Killingworth, and became very friendly with George Stephenson, telling him of his plans for Liverpool and Manchester. At this stage in the development of railways, James's national breadth of vision complemented Stephenson's grasp of essential mechanical detail. In September 1821 Stephenson and Losh granted him a fourth share in their locomotive patent, to relate to locomotives made, sold or used south of a line from Liverpool to Hull.

Previously, in July 1821, James had also brought the advantages of malleable iron rails and steam locomotives to the notice of Stratford & Moreton directors. They were not immediately convinced, and after further enquiries referred the matter to Thomas Telford for advice. He rejected both. The company, however, did eventually have its line laid with malleable iron rails, but stuck to horses as motive power. Paradoxically, the engineer under whom the line was built was J. U. Rastrick, whose foundry had built *Catch-me-who-can* for Trevithick, and many stationary engines to his patent.

George and Robert Stephenson

George Stephenson recommended malleable iron rails to the Stockton & Darlington company despite his financial interest in cast iron rails through the Stephenson & Losh patent. The company decided in October 1821 that most of the line should be laid with malleable iron, the rest with cast iron. Meanwhile Stephenson was re-surveying Overton's route as instructed; in this work he was assisted by his son Robert. On Robert Stephenson (1803–1859) George Stephenson had lavished the education he himself had lacked.

When construction of the Stockton & Darlington Railway commenced in May 1822, however, Robert Stephenson was not there. He had been seconded to help William James, as one of a survey party with which James was making a detailed survey of the Liverpool–Manchester route. Sandars, the same summer, organised a provisional committee, mostly of Liverpool men, for the railway: one of the first to join was John Moss, Liverpool merchant and banker, at the start of an important career in railway promotion. By the autumn, James's survey party had completed its work in the field and Robert Stephenson was sent by his father to complete his education by six months at Edinburgh University during the winter of 1822–3. The father was coming to depend more and more on the son for access to the theoretical knowledge which he himself had been denied.

The Stockton & Darlington Railway Company obtained an Act of Parliament in 1823 which authorised deviations Stephenson had recommended from Overton's route. It also empowered the company to 'make and erect . . . locomotive or moveable engines . . . and to use and employ the same . . . upon the said railways'.

To manufacture locomotives – since at this period Fenton, Murray & Wood were no longer doing so – George and Robert Stephenson joined with Edward Pease and Michael Longridge (owner of Bedlington Ironworks) as a partnership to set up locomotive works of their own. This, called Robert Stephenson & Co., was established in June 1823; the works were at Forth Street, Newcastle, and Robert Stephenson was to be managing partner. The firm at first undertook other engineering work as well as locomotive construction.

Meanwhile, the Liverpool & Manchester provisional committee was anxiously awaiting from James the results of his survey, for it intended to promote a bill in Parliament. But James now delayed producing them. Until now he had been, in today's terms, a high-flyer: and it is the high-flyer who suffers the most spectacular crash. Of exactly what happened in James's case it is difficult, at this distance of time, to be certain. He had undoubtedly been overworking – at this period he was concerned in many other proposals for railways. Some were sensible, such as a line to fill a gap in the waterways map between the Rivers Stort and Cam; some were wild, such as a trunk line to link London with Rochester, Brighton and Portsmouth. His enthusiasm for railway projects had run away with him and he neglected his other business affairs. At the conclusion of his Liverpool–Manchester survey his health broke down. He had also become involved in a family quarrel of quite exceptional viciousness which resulted in his being declared bankrupt and imprisoned, for a while, for debt. James's fortunes never fully recovered. His children were convinced he was a victim of conspiracy.

The Liverpool & Manchester committee lost patience

and in May 1824 appointed George Stephenson – whom James had originally recommended as engineer – in his place. At the same time it decided to form a company to apply for an Act of Parliament. George Stephenson was to re-survey the Liverpool & Manchester Railway: but he was not to have the assistance of his son, for, like Trevithick before him, Robert Stephenson had set off for South America in June 1824 on a mining venture. His father and the other partners in Robert Stephenson & Co. thought he was going for a year: in fact, he had signed on with the mining company for three.

This extraordinary action puzzled historians for years until L. T. C. Rolt in *George and Robert Stephenson* convincingly interpreted it. George Stephenson had educated his son to fill in the gaps in his own knowledge which must be filled if he was to succeed as steam railway engineer and promoter. Robert, as he grew to manhood, inevitably reacted. During the Liverpool & Manchester survey Robert developed a warm friendship with William James and a great admiration for him: there was, so far as George was concerned, a serious risk that Robert would be deflected into working for William James and be lost to his father. The Edinburgh University period, and the establishment of the locomotive works in Robert's name, served not only their direct purpose but also kept Robert away from William James and under his father's thumb.

For Robert Stephenson, this was too much. When first approached by the mining company he turned them down, and asked William James for a job. James refused him, telling him to stay with his father. Robert Stephenson's reaction was to wish a plague on both their houses and set off for South America.

Whether or not George Stephenson conspired against William James, he certainly benefited greatly from his disappearance from the scene, even though he did lose the assistance of his son for three years and his performance during this period suffered accordingly.

George Stephenson made his survey of the L & MR, despite strong opposition by landowners, during the autumn of 1824, and in February 1825 the company approached Parliament for an Act. It based its case on the inadequacy of waterway communication, on the expense and unreliability of transport by the Mersey estuary and the Mersey & Irwell Navigation or the Bridgewater Canal. This was only partly justified. The real problem was rapidly increasing trade between Liverpool and Manchester. In 1787, for instance, when there were no power looms in Manchester, only 8 bags of cotton had been imported from America through Liverpool. In 1824 there were 30,000 power looms and 410,000 bags of cotton imported, and the increase continued. The bill for the L & MR generated strong and righteous opposition from the waterway undertakings. Landowners too were strongly opposed. Opposition from coach proprietors and turnpike trusts seems to have been (when considered with the benefit of hindsight) conspicuous by its absence. A point of interest, brought out in newspaper comment on proposed use of locomotives, was the smoke nuisance caused in Liverpool by steam boats.

In the House of Commons, William Huskisson, a member for Liverpool and President of the Board of Trade, made an important and persuasive speech in favour of the railway. But Stephenson, under cross-examination in committee about the proposed line of the railway, received a trouncing. His survey was shown to be inadequate and inaccurate. For instance, where the line was to cross over the Mersey & Irwell Navigation by a bridge, headroom of 16 ft 6 in. was required: but the plans showed the rail level only 10 ft above the water and 3 ft *below* maximum flood level. On 1 June the Liverpool & Manchester Railway Bill was defeated. The promoters took this as the loss of a battle rather than a war.

Opening of the Stockton & Darlington Railway

In the meantime the Stockton & Darlington Railway was fast approaching completion. Two locomotives had been ordered from Robert Stephenson & Co. During George Stephenson's absence surveying the L & MR, Timothy Hackworth from Wylam was engaged to take charge of the locomotive works. He subsequently returned temporarily to Wylam, then came to the Stockton & Darlington Railway in the summer of 1825 'particularly to have the superintendence' as the railway's books recorded 'of the permanent and locomotive engines'. *Locomotion*, the first of the 'locomotive engines' was delivered during September 1825 – the latest development of Stephenson's colliery locomotives, her wheels were coupled by rods instead of a chain.

The 'permanent engines' were installed to power two pairs of inclined planes at the western end of the line. The Stockton & Darlington Railway was, by contemporary standards, a long one: 26 miles, when completed. It com-

menced at Witton Park Colliery west of Bishop Auckland, climbed over a ridge at Etherley by the first pair of inclines, and then ran relatively level across the valley of the River Gaunless (horses provided the motive power here) to the second pair of inclined planes over the ridge at Brusselton. At the foot of Brusselton east incline lay Shildon, whence the line ran on gentler gradients for 20 miles or so via Darlington to a quay beside the River Tees at Stockton. On this 20-mile stretch both horses and locomotives were to be used.

There was a long tradition of ceremonial openings of both canals and waggonways, and the S & DR company complied fully with tradition. The line was opened on 27 September 1825 (one may note, by way of comparison, that at this time Telford was completing the Menai Bridge) and the opening was well-publicised in advance. Some 40–50,000 people assembled along the lineside to see the opening procession. Early in the morning twelve loaded waggons of coal were brought from Phoenix Pit (a mile short of Witton Park but that section was still incomplete) to Shildon by horses and cable haulage. There they were attached to a train consisting of *Locomotion*, driven by George Stephenson, the company's single passenger coach, and 21 waggons fitted with seats and in due course crammed with passengers.

This processed down the line, preceded by a man on horseback with a flag, and followed by a further 24 waggons drawn by horses. *Locomotion* drew her crowded train, among the lineside crowds, to Darlington and onwards to Stockton, at speeds of between 4 and 15 mph. The day culminated with a banquet in Stockton Town Hall at which no less than 23 toasts were drunk. Despite a couple of minor accidents, and an unscheduled halt early on while some oakum which was blocking *Locomotion*'s boiler feed pump was removed, the day was a great success. After the Liverpool & Manchester débâcle, George Stephenson must have needed one.

Built during a period of rapid technical development, the S & DR was both the long-familiar colliery waggonway or tramroad at the peak of its development, and the first of a new generation of public steam railways. In its equipment and mode of operation it showed its transitional nature. It was powered by stationary engines, by gravity and by horses as well as by locomotives. The company did some carrying itself, but preferred, in the early years, to contract it out. Locomotives – *Locomotion* was soon followed by others – were found to be a cheaper form of motive power than horses, but also less reliable. *Locomotion*, for instance, broke a wheel, and later her boiler exploded. A constant problem was the inability of the locomotives to make sufficient steam continuously over a journey as long as 20 miles. The problem was not solved until Hackworth, drawing no doubt on his Wylam experience, built the *Royal George* at Shildon in 1827 with a return-flue fire tube in a large boiler. From then on matters improved; Hackworth continued to design and develop locomotives of his own type, distinct from those later developed by the Stephensons but suited for the S & DR's heavy goods traffic, until the 1840s.

The manner in which the S & DR at first carried passengers was also symptomatic of transition – in this case, from road to rail. The passenger coaches were horse-drawn, although rails made them so free-running that they could be drawn by a single horse instead of the two or four needed on road, and the usual taxes on road coaches were paid. Two hours were at first allowed for the $11\frac{1}{2}$ miles from Darlington to Stockton: a schedule much slower than those of the best of contemporary road coaches. It was in the same year that the S & DR was opened that the first of the fast day coaches out of London, the Shrewsbury *Wonder*, was put on. The S & DR coach schedule was later

OPENING OF STOCKTON AND DAR

reduced to 1 hr 10 mins excluding stops.

The layout of the early S & DR coaches was a combination of rail and road practice. The wheels, frames and, notably, brakes resembled those of rail waggons, but the body was similar to that of a stage coach except that the rear boot was replaced by a second driver's box: the vehicle was double-ended and did not need to be turned round at each end of its journey. As with goods and mineral traffic, the company did operate a coach itself, but soon showed a preference for coaches operated by proprietors, who based themselves in the usual way on inns adjacent to the route.

The line itself was single, with sidings at quarter-mile intervals. Empty waggons gave way to loaded ones and both to passenger coaches. When two coaches met, the first past the half-way point between sidings had priority.

John Dobbin's painting of the opening of the Stockton & Darlington Railway is famous, but immensely detailed and worthy of close examination not only for the train (which is crossing the River Skerne in an area since built up) but also for the road vehicles, which include a stage coach and a stage waggon, and the people. The child in the left foreground appears to have as a toy a steam boat on wheels. The road is the Darlington–Durham turnpike. The original painting, some 4 ft 4 in. wide, is displayed in Darlington Museum, Tubwell Row, Darlington.

The main line here (above) is British Rail's East Coast main line, looking north near Darlington at OS grid ref. NZ 296152. Bearing left is the Bishop Auckland branch, following the course of the Croft branch of the Stockton & Darlington Railway built about 1827. The S & DR's main line of 1825 ran across the middle distance, for many years crossing the later main line on the level at right angles at approximately the position of the rear of the train. The building on the right was originally a locomotive shed of the Great North of England Railway, a main line company mentioned in chapter eight.

Traces of the S & DR

Horse-drawn traffic on the S & DR lasted until 1856; it had ceased much earlier, however (in 1833) on the main line east of Shildon, and this part of the railway eventually became incorporated into the steam railway network which subsequently grew up around it. Much of it remains in use, forming parts of the British Rail lines from Darlington to Stockton and Darlington to Bishop Auckland. Notably, the principal engineering work on this part of the line, the bridge over the River Skerne which appears in the illustration on page 141; is carrying trains to this day (OS grid ref. NZ 292156) although industrial surroundings now make it difficult to approach.

Nearby is North Road station – original S & DR work, but dating from the 1840s. Most of it now forms Darlington Railway Museum in which the most noted exhibit is *Locomotion* herself. The working replica built for the 150th anniversary celebrations in 1975 is housed not far away at Beamish North of England Open Air Museum. The National Railway Museum has a Stockton & Darlington Railway chaldron waggon – in design it conforms with the traditional coal waggon of the North-East, derived from the waggons of waggonways, with sides splayed outwards and bottom discharge at a staithe. Waggons of this type remained in industrial use until the 1950s or possibly later and many are preserved. The replica *Locomotion* is often coupled to a rake of them at Beamish.

At Shildon the house close to the line in which Timothy Hackworth lived has been restored as a museum devoted to the man and his achievements. British Rail Engineering Ltd's Shildon Works, builders of railway rolling stock and at the time of writing threatened with closure, occupy the site at the foot of Brusselton east inclined plane chosen for the works of the Stockton & Darlington Railway because it was here that locomotive traction commenced and ceased.

From Shildon westwards the original line has long been disused – deviation lines without inclined planes were built

The westernmost, horse-powered part of
Stephenson's Stockton & Darlington Railway
crossed the Hummer Beck at OS grid ref. NZ
194261 by this bridge (above), now long
disused. Its date of building, 1823, is carved on
the keystone the far side of the arch.

Locomotion, *built for the opening of the
Stockton & Darlington Railway in 1825, has
been preserved since the 1850s and is now
exhibited in Darlington Railway Museum. She
is in most respects a typical Stephenson
locomotive of her period, but coupling of wheels
by rods rather than chains was an innovation.*

– relics of the early days are common and the Shildon Rail Trail was laid out about 1975 as a footpath approximating to the course of the line. Highlights are stone block sleepers which survive on Brusselton west incline (OS grid ref. NZ 212256) and the little stone bridge which carried the line over the Hummer Beck at OS grid reference NZ 194261 and bears the date 1823 carved on one of its keystones. The ironwork of the bridge by which the line crossed the River Gaunless (an early use of iron for such a purpose) has gone but, re-erected, it now forms a prominent outdoor exhibit at the National Railway Museum. I have, in *The Archaeology of Railways*, described other traces of the S & DR.

The Railway Boom of 1824–6

Though they were the most important, the Stockton & Darlington and the Liverpool & Manchester were far from being the only railways under consideration at this period.

On the contrary, the boom years of 1824–6 which saw the formation of many new turnpike trusts also encouraged proposals for railways. According to Robert Young (*Timothy Hackworth and the Locomotive*) during 1824 and 1825 some 60 railways were projected. Their proposers were still thinking mostly in terms of horse haulage and goods transport.

There were some grand schemes among them. The London Northern Railroad Company, launched in December 1824 with a capital of £2,500,000 was to connect London with Birmingham, Derby, Nottingham, Hull and Manchester. Even J. L. McAdam found himself laying out a route for a 'London & Bristol Rail-Road'. A Leeds & Hull Railway Company was formed, to be part of a larger scheme for a line from Liverpool to Hull, from West Coast to East. Further north, a railway from Carlisle to Newcastle was proposed, a revival of a canal scheme, and a company was formed in 1825.

George Stephenson and his partners in Robert Stephenson & Co. formed another firm, George Stephenson & Son, at the end of 1824 to survey and construct railways, and went so far as to decide which of their staff should be allocated to which of the principal lines. But the boom soon collapsed, and its main result was to encourage canal companies to make belated improvements to their canals, as I shall describe in the next chapter. Nevertheless, some 17 railway Acts were passed during 1824–6. All of them were for comparatively short lines; most of them were for edge railways rather than plateways; and most of them were built. Many, still, were connected with canals. The Monkland & Kirkintilloch, incorporated in 1824, was in effect a branch of the Forth & Clyde Canal. The Cromford & High Peak, incorporated in 1825, was to link the Peak Forest and Cromford Canals, climbing over the Peak District by a series of cable-worked inclines, although contemporary promoters of a London & Northern Railway, from London to Manchester, planned to incorporate it into their line. The Bolton & Leigh Railway (Act, 1825) was intended to link Bolton with the Bridgewater Canal's branch to Leigh which had been opened from Worsley in 1795. George Stephenson was its engineer. Other lines linked ports with hinterland: such were the Canterbury & Whitstable and the Nantlle (running inland from Caernarfon), both authorised in 1825, and the Dundee & Newtyle of 1826. All these were built. Though the lengths of individual lines were still short, the practice of building public railways was spreading far and wide.

The Act for the Liverpool & Manchester Railway

And what of the Liverpool & Manchester? After the loss of their Bill in 1825 the promoters had decided, not unnaturally, that they needed another engineer instead of Stephenson. Telford was invited to take on the job, but declined, to the disappointment of his staff, out of loyalty to the canal companies he had served so long. At this time, too, he must have found ample preoccupation in raising the chains for the Menai Bridge. The company then appointed the brothers George and John Rennie, sons of the elder John Rennie who had died in 1821; the Rennies in turn appointed Charles Blacker Vignoles as their chief surveyor. Vignoles promptly re-surveyed the line, relocating the proposed railway to reduce objections so far as possible. The eastern terminus was now to be in Salford, for instance, so that no bridge would be needed across the Mersey & Irwell Navigation. Greater engineering works, however, meant that the new route would be more expensive to build than the old.

Bradshaw, of the Bridgewater Trustees, improved and cheapened the canal's services to shippers and to occupiers of warehouses, but was not prepared to come to terms with the railway company, at least on terms that it would accept. Then the railway promoters made what proved to be their master stroke: they approached, through intermediaries, the second Marquis of Stafford himself and invited him to take shares in the railway company.

Stafford considered the proposition, and weighed the relative merits of canal and railway. He consulted Telford, with whom he may well have come into contact over the Highland Roads. He decided to subscribe to the Birmingham & Liverpool Junction Canal which, as we shall see in the next chapter, was being promoted at that time to counter proposals for a railway over the same route. This canal was to have a branch into the Shropshire industrial district where the Marquis of Stafford already had extensive mineral and canal interests inherited from his father. He consulted also Josias Jessop, son of William Jessop and engineer of the Cromford & High Peak Railway.

Between Liverpool and Manchester the Marquis of Stafford evidently decided that there was room for a railway as well as the waterways. William Huskisson, an old friend, was instrumental in persuading him. What emerged was that Stafford would subscribe for 1,000 shares of £100 each and have the right to appoint three of the company's directors. At one stroke the railway promoters had raised the extra £100,000 they needed for Vignoles's route and demolished the cornerstone of the opposition. The Liverpool & Manchester Railway Company got its Act of Parliament in May 1826. The Marquis of Stafford held one fifth of the capital: to that extent, the Liverpool & Manchester Railway was to be paid for out of the profits of the Bridgewater Canal.

Exceptionally heavy snow with severe drifting on the night of 25 December 1836 brought communications throughout most of England to a standstill. Here, with the up Birmingham mail stuck fast in the snow, the mail guard is following his instructions and setting off for London on horseback with mail bags, and blunderbuss. By this date construction of the London & Birmingham Railway was already far advanced.

In the mid-1970s, the BBC Nationwide programme ran a series called Stagecoach and for this three preserved mail coaches were horsed and driven for the benefit of film-makers and viewers. This is the Holyhead mail.

Mail coaches prepare to start at Chaplin's yard at the Swan with Two Necks (left). These are West of England mails and so will go not to the GPO but, by custom, to Piccadilly to load their letter bags brought thither by mail cart.

'*A trip up Loch Lomond*' *in 1825, in the steam boat* Marian *(above). David Napier, who had built the boiler for Henry Bell's* Comet, *made his first venture into steam-boat ownership with the* Marian *in 1816.*

Steam boats in a calm, c. 1817 (left): sailing craft are immobilised off Gravesend but steam boats demonstrate their ability to move in any direction irrespective of the wind—or lack of it. The nearer one is Dodd's Sons of Commerce.

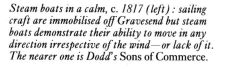

The London Engineer, *(bottom) built in 1818 to ply between London and Margate, had paddle wheels amidships in an airtight chamber where compressed air lowered the water level so that only the lowest blades were in the water. This scheme had been proposed by Trevithick as early as 1806.*

The Liverpool & Manchester Railway when new attracted the attention of numerous artists and engravers. These two aquatints, engraved from drawings by T. T. Bury and published by Rudolf Ackermann, are famous but nevertheless repay examination of their detail, and comparison with recent photographs of the same locations on pages 168 and 169. In 'Entrance of the Railway at Edge Hill' (above left) a locomotive is being attached to a train of carriages which has come by gravity down the tunnel on the right from Crown Street; one of the cables for cable haulage is seen running along the wall on the right (the engine house is behind the viewpoint). In the centre a double-track tunnel with cable haulage runs

down to the docks; the two chimneys are for the smoke from the haulage engine boilers. In 'Taking Water at Parkside (the station where Mr. Huskisson fell)' (above right) can be seen how early the familiar type of water crane originated.

To maintain a ruling gradient of 1 in 300 on the London & Birmingham Railway, which was built during the period 1833–8, extensive engineering works were needed. Here, (below) rocks are being blasted near Linslade, Bedfordshire.

Oxford Canal (left): a meeting point of the new line, completed in 1834, coming from the right and the old entering from the left and now retained as far as an overflow weir a short distance away. The cast iron bridge to carry the new towpath over the old line is typical. OS grid ref. SP 481779.

The original buildings of the Great Western Railway's Temple Meads terminus still stand in Bristol (centre). Passengers arriving to catch trains originally entered beneath the archway on the left; the main block contained the company's offices; a matching archway on the right, through which passengers who had arrived by train once emerged, has disappeared. OS grid ref. ST 595724. See also page 185.

The station at Hexham, Northumberland, was depicted from the north-east in 1836 by J. Blackmore and J. W. Carmichael in their Views on the Newcastle & Carlisle Railway. *Examination of the existing station building in 1982 suggested that it incorporated the original, extended.*

In the National Railway Museum (above), the Furness Railway's Bury locomotive **Old Coppernob** of 1846 is flanked by, right foreground, the London & Birmingham Railway's coach built in 1842 for Queen Adelaide, replica TPO of 1838, with mailbag-catching net, and black-and-yellow replica Liverpool & Manchester Railway coach of 1830.

By 1850, railway travel was a familiar experience to many people. This picture probably gives a good impression of what they saw despite the circular distortion. It may have been used on a music cover.

From December 1845 the London–Louth mail coach (below) was carried by rail between London and Peterborough: the Northampton & Peterborough Railway had been opened as a branch from the London & Birmingham. Here the up coach is being put on rail at Peterborough. See also page 192.

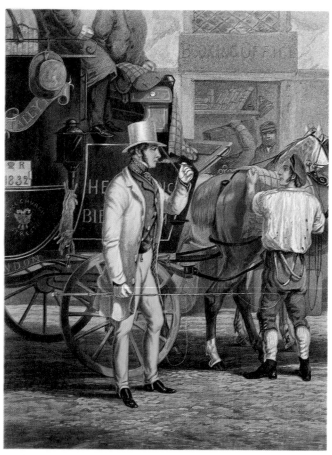

Drivers and guards of 1832 and 1852. 'Fores's Contrasts' illustrate the change that had taken place (above and next page). The drivers are ready to mount, one to his box seat, the other to the footplate; the guards appear to be attending to passengers' luggage—on the LNWR a luggage van has superseded the earlier practice of stowing luggage on carriage roofs. The stage coach stands outside a 'booking office'—railways inherited the term—and in the backgrounds of the guards' pictures are shown respective forms of motive power. Despite the date 1852, artist Henry Alken had died in 1851 and the prints were published posthumously, but the railway scenes must have been prepared after 1846 when the LNWR was formed. Alken was better known for sporting scenes.

Huddersfield station building—one of the finest railway buildings in Britain—was built by the Huddersfield & Manchester Railway & Canal Co. and opened in 1847. The local company was absorbed by the LNWR later the same year. The interior of the station is a contrast and is illustrated on page 197.

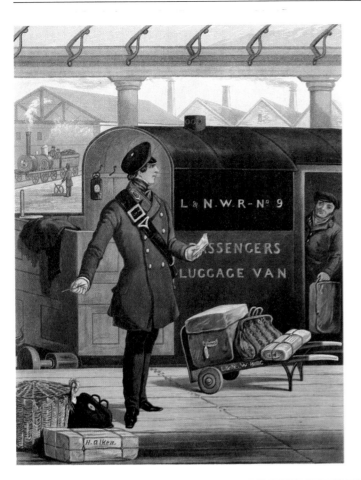

*Strood tunnel was built by the Thames &
Medway Canal Company and converted for
joint canal and railway use in 1845. Two years
later it was adapted for railway use exclusively.
At Higham (viewed from OS grid ref. TQ
715727) tracks emerging from the tunnel still
make a distinct S-bend to the south to gain their
original canal-bank alignment; the drainage
channel on the left marks the course of the
canal. See also page 198.*

'Carting Ice on the Surrey Canal' (above) : from this watercolour now held by the Waterways Museum can be seen exactly how London's railways and canals appeared on a frosty winter's day in, probably, the 1840s.

SL Dolly, built c. 1850, in action on Lake Windermere (below), provides a live link with transport in the middle of the last century.

CHAPTER SEVEN

Trunk Railways, Late Canals and Transatlantic Steamers

Canal Improvements

Telford's view of the railway proposals of the mid-1820s, as given in his *Life*, was this: 'a boundless rage for speculation had seized upon every object which ingenuity or invention could suggest; and as the price of iron was depressed, the iron-masters, to promote the consumption of that material, encouraged the construction of railways in sundry directions, the most important of which was a proposed line from Liverpool, through Birmingham, to London, all physical obstructions being forgotten or overlooked amid the splendour of their gigantic undertaking. Hereupon the canal proprietors became seriously alarmed. . . '.

Railways, it must be remembered, were at that date still primitive. Malleable iron rails were certainly a great step forward, but motive power still meant horses, cables with stationary engines, or locomotives which might, perhaps, lumber along at 10 mph. The effectiveness of rail competition against canals was by no means certain, and the immediate consequence of this minor mania of railway proposals was to produce a reaction in favour of improved canals. This meant, firstly, improvements to existing canals – by straightening out the most circuitous of the contour canals, for instance, and by duplicating features such as locks and tunnels where these were bottlenecks. Secondly, it meant construction of entirely new canals to produce direct routes where none already existed.

Into the design and construction of these canals was poured the accumulated expertise and confidence of sixty-five years of canal building; on them, canal engineers, most of them of Telford's school, did their finest work.

Each of these new canals was designed as an entity. Speed of conveyance now mattered, so obstructions to the free passage of boats were minimised. Locks of various depths were no longer placed at odd intervals along the line; instead, locks of uniform depth were grouped together in flights. Level pounds no longer meandered circuitously along the contours to avoid engineering works; instead, the canal took as direct a line as possible, by sweeping curve and lengthy straight along high embankments and through deep cuttings. Only exceptionally deep valleys were crossed by aqueducts, and extra high ground pierced by tunnels: but where tunnels were built, the obstruction they presented was minimised, for always there was a towpath, and in some instances one each side for traffic in either direction. Roads which crossed the line of the canal were taken not only over it on bridges but also, where the canal was on embankment, beneath it by small aqueducts or underbridges in the manner soon afterwards adopted for railways. Structures were uniform without being dull – fit for their purposes, elegant without being ornamented to excess. All these features can still be seen on canals dating from this period.

The forerunner of these late canals was the Edinburgh & Glasgow Union Canal. Incorporated, after many years of dispute over the best route, in 1817, the Union Canal as it is known was opened in 1822 from a junction with the Forth & Clyde at Falkirk, to Edinburgh. All the canal's eleven locks were concentrated in one flight, climbing away from the junction: above them, a single 30-mile-long pound led to Edinburgh. The locks were filled in in the 1930s but most of the rest of the canal is still in existence. Many of the features mentioned above can be seen on it and it is particularly notable for three great aqueducts – Avon, Almond and Slateford – of which the largest, the Avon aqueduct (OS grid ref. NS 967758) has 12 arches, is 810 ft long and has a maximum height of 86 ft. In *The Archaeology of Canals* I wrote more about the Union Canal.

The old-established Aire & Calder Navigation improved its line by building a new canal from the old line at Ferrybridge to the River Ouse at Goole, bypassing both the original river route and the later canal to Selby. The new canal was built between 1821 and 1826: when it was completed, fly boats for passengers and parcels were put on to connect at Goole with steam boats to and from Hull and at Ferrybridge with stage coaches.

The western end of the Trent & Mersey Canal provided at this time the only canal link between the Midlands and the North-West and, with increasing traffic, Brindley's long and narrow tunnel at Harecastle had become a bottleneck: boats could not pass in it and the passage took two hours. After years of procrastination the threat of railway competition encouraged the canal company in 1823 to obtain an Act for a new tunnel to duplicate the old. Telford was the engineer and the new tunnel, of larger bore than the old and with a towpath throughout, was opened alongside it in 1827. It is this tunnel at Harecastle that remains in use: the portals of the original tunnel can still be seen alongside those of the new, but it has suffered too much from colliery subsidence to be navigable, though it still provides a supply of water.

There had been for many years successive proposals for a canal to run from the Trent & Mersey, in the vicinity of the Potteries, along the western edge of the Pennines via Macclesfield to a junction with the Peak Forest Canal. Such a canal was promoted again in 1824, considered preferable to a railway, surveyed by Telford and authorised as the Macclesfield Canal by Act of Parliament in 1826. Leaving the T & M near the west end of Harecastle tunnel it would, when combined with the Peak Forest and Ashton Canals, provide a line to Manchester shorter by ten miles than that via the T & M and the Bridgewater, but with twenty more locks. The engineer under whom it was built was William Crossley.

The first canal company to take action directly as a result of the proposal for a Liverpool-Birmingham-London railway was the Birmingham Canal Navigations. The original line of the Birmingham Canal, from the Staffs & Worcs Canal to Birmingham, had been one of the earliest narrow canals, laid out by Brindley along the contours. Despite improvements by Smeaton, it was by the 1820s hopelessly inadequate for its traffic. Telford, called in in 1824, to survey further improvements, found it 'little better than a crooked ditch'. His improved canal was to be wide and run direct, leaving the old contour line as loops on either side and including a 70-ft-deep cutting to avoid the locks at Smethwick. The canal company started to carry out the work by stages.

However desirable, this was only a short distance improvement. What was needed was a better canal line than the Trent & Mersey could offer between the Midlands and the North-West. It should run, Telford recommended, from near Wolverhampton to Nantwich (whence there was already a canal to Ellesmere Port on the Mersey) with a branch to connect with the Shrewsbury Canal near Ketley and another from near Nantwich to the Trent & Mersey at Middlewich. This would reduce the distance from Birmingham to Liverpool and Manchester by 12 miles and avoid 'the delay of 320 feet of upward and downward lockage'. The Act for the main line of this canal, the Birmingham & Liverpool Junction, was passed, like that for the Liverpool & Manchester Railway, in May 1826. The proposal for a Birmingham–Liverpool railway lapsed for a few years and construction of the canal started with Telford as chief engineer and Alexander Easton as resident engineer under him. Acts for the branches – that to Middlewich was obtained by the Ellesmere & Chester Canal Co. – followed in 1827.

In that same year the first section of the improved Birmingham Canal line was opened. Although intended for narrow boats it is wide, flanked by dual towpaths, and with bridge arches so large that neither towpaths nor waterway are constricted. Approached as it is, up the cramped flight of locks at Farmer's Bridge, or through a short but gloomy tunnel from Gas Street Basin, the spacious scale of the Birmingham New Main Line is a revelation even now. Further improvements were made over many years.

With improvements to the Birmingham Canal under way, and the Birmingham & Liverpool Junction Canal under construction, attention was turned to the canal route from Birmingham to London. The problem lay between Birmingham and the start of the Grand Junction canal at Braunston: the shortest route was via Warwick but had seventy-seven locks; the alternative via Fazeley had only fifty-four but was longer. By following the ridge between the Avon and Trent valleys, Telford was able to survey a route for a canal which would have had only twenty locks. It was intended as a wide canal so that barges off the Grand Junction would be able to reach Birmingham and south Staffordshire.

The immediate effect of this proposal was to prompt the Oxford Canal Company – which stood to lose a lot

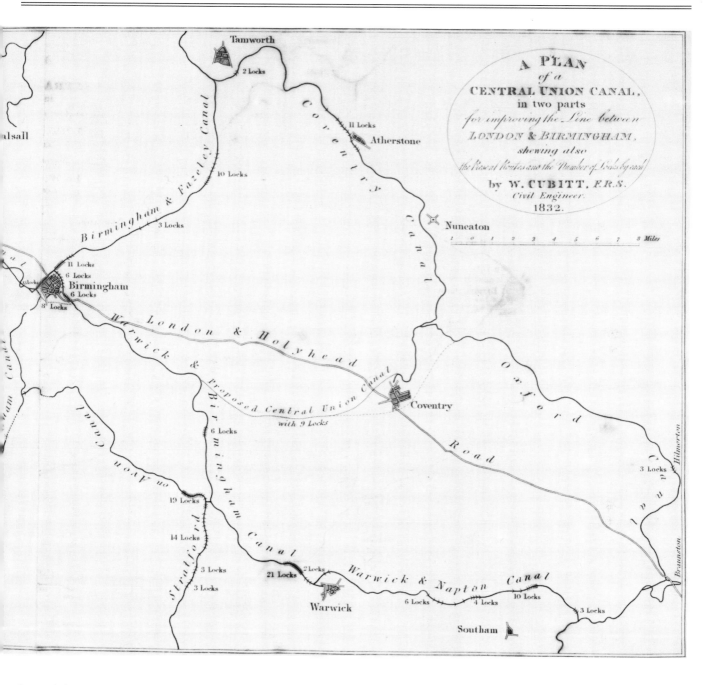

Proposals for an improved canal line between Birmingham and Braunstin were made several times during the late 1820s and early 1830s. This map of 1823 shows the proposed Central Union Canal in relation to other canals and the Holyhead Road.

of traffic – to do something about shortening the winding, contour-hugging line of the northern part of its own canal. Marc Brunel was consulted, and Charles Vignoles surveyed an improved line which reduced ninety-one miles of canal to seventy-seven. It was to be, mostly, new direct canal which the old contour line crossed and re-crossed at intervals. An Act was obtained in 1829 and work commenced.

The consequence of the Oxford Canal Co.'s action was that the Birmingham-Braunston proposal was altered so as to join the Oxford Canal near Coventry; but although bills were promoted in Parliament, the proposal was never to go beyond that stage.

It was competition from coaches on improved roads as much as the railway threat that first caused the managements of canals with passenger boats to consider making them faster. The Paisley Canal led the way in the early 1820s. From experiments with 'gig-shaped' boats it was discovered that if a light enough boat was towed fast enough it would rise up in the water and, as we would now say, plane. With long and relatively light boats which drew, laden, only $5\frac{1}{2}$ inches of water, the journey time for the 7 miles or so from Glasgow to Paisley was reduced from $1\frac{1}{2}$ hours to 45 minutes. In the 1830s such boats were copied elsewhere, but there are other developments to be considered before returning to them.

Swift passenger boats were pioneered by the Paisley Canal: here is one arriving at Paisley, the $7\frac{1}{2}$ mile journey from Glasgow having taken 45 minutes.

One of the Stratford & Moreton Railway's waggons (below) is preserved at Stratford, standing upon a length of original track on its original site close to the canal basin.

Railways Opened in the Late 1820s

The Stratford & Moreton Railway was completed and opened in 1826, a year after the Stockton & Darlington and several months after the Liverpool & Manchester had got its Act. William James was no longer involved: the line settled down to a long and uneventful career as a horse railway. The southern end was eventually converted for locomotive working; the northern end, much of which ran beside public roads, was not, and was last used in the early years of the present century. It has left notable remains – particularly a handsome brick viaduct by which it crossed the River Avon at Stratford (OS grid ref. SP 205548) and which is now used by a footpath and, close by, one of its

waggons, which stands on a short length of original track beside the Stratford Canal basin.

Another line opened in 1826 was the Monkland & Kirkintilloch: it ran down to the Forth & Clyde Canal which company built boats to carry its waggons without transhipment of coal. The Nantlle Railway was opened in 1828: part of it was still worked by horse haulage in the early 1960s. The Bolton & Leigh Railway was opened in 1828 also: its $7\frac{1}{2}$-mile length included two cable-operated inclined planes, but a locomotive supplied by Robert Stephenson & Co. and called *Lancashire Witch* was also used from the start, and indeed earlier, during construction. Her design, and its place in locomotive development, is mentioned below. With the Liverpool & Manchester Railway now being built a few miles to the south of Leigh, an Act was obtained on 14 May 1829 for a 2½-mile-long line to connect the two railways, called the Kenyon & Leigh Junction Railway. Another Act on the same day authorised a second branch from the L & MR, the Warrington & Newton Railway, which was to connect Warrington with the L & MR which passed a few miles to the north.

The Newcastle & Carlisle Railway Company, after a stiff Parliamentary fight, obtained an Act of Parliament in May 1829, though on this, at 63 miles the longest railway yet authorised, steam locomotives were expressly forbidden.

Construction of the Liverpool & Manchester Railway

Meanwhile the Liverpool & Manchester Railway was under construction. Following passage of its Act in May 1826, the directors of the company had to decide whom to appoint as engineer to supervise construction. The Rennie brothers reasonably expected to be appointed: but some of the directors still considered that George Stephenson, despite his abysmal record over his survey, had nevertheless got the experience of building railways and steam locomotives that they needed. By 3 July, the Rennies were out, and Stephenson was in, as principal engineer. Boardroom intrigues are nothing new.

C. B. Vignoles, who had surveyed the line under the Rennies, had already been asked to stake it out and had started work. By now, though, the engineering establishment and its representatives were quite unacceptable to self-educated George Stephenson: by the following February Vignoles, evidently finding his position impossible, had resigned. It was after this that he surveyed the Oxford Canal improvements. The railway that Vignoles and the Rennies had planned was built almost entirely under George Stephenson and his pupils from George Stephenson & Co.

It was a magnificent undertaking. At its western end, a tunnel 2,250 yards long was bored beneath Liverpool from the docks to Edge Hill. A little to the east, at Olive Mount, a rock cutting two miles long and up to 70 ft deep was needed; and further on, a viaduct carried the line over the Sankey valley and with it the Sankey Brook Navigation, mentioned earlier. This structure has nine arches of 50-ft span, brick with stone facings, and a height of about 70 ft allowed unobstructed headroom for sailing flats. This viaduct, destined to be the forerunner of many more railway viaducts, was at this period the largest of its kind built for a steam railway, although structures of similar scale were no novelty on canals, and to a lesser extent on roads.

The eastern part of the line was to run for 5½ miles across the peat bog called Chat Moss, so soft that it was impossible to walk upon without boards strapped to one's feet. Here, where many had doubted the possibility of making a railway at all, Stephenson built it upon a foundation of brushwood hurdles and branches of trees. He was, as mentioned earlier, following the usual method of the period for building a road across soft ground. It appears, for instance, in Telford's specification for Highland Roads.

By 1828 the railway company was negotiating with landowners with a view once again to crossing the Irwell and terminating the line in Manchester rather than Salford. This time it was successful, and was authorised to do so by an Act of Parliament the following spring.

The track was laid with malleable iron rails mounted on wooden cross-sleepers on some sections of the line – such as Chat Moss – and on stone blocks elsewhere. An example of L & MR track is included in the National Railway Museum's permanent way display. The gauge between the rails, here as on the Stockton & Darlington, was 4 ft 8 in.; waggonways in North-East England had always been of approximately this gauge. Later, half an inch was added to ease the passage of vehicles round curves, and so produced the standard gauge of 4 ft 8½ in.

Cable Haulage or Locomotives?

During 1828 controversy arose among the L & MR directors about the form of motive power to be used on the line. Locomotives had been intended originally, but had been played down to placate the opposition. Horses, locomotives and cable-haulage were now considered. That horses would be inadequate was soon decided, but the choice between locomotives and cable haulage was far more difficult. As yet no public railway was powered by locomotives alone, and the technique of operating inclined planes by cable haulage and stationary engines had been developed to power railways that were level or nearly so.

In 1821 coal-owner Benjamin Thompson had patented

The nine-arched viaduct which carried the Liverpool & Manchester Railway across the Sankey valley is shown in an engraving of 1831 (top) and a photograph of 1982. The OS grid ref. SJ 568947. The Sankey Brook Navigation, shown in the engraving, is now along this section filled in. A road viaduct of the same period is shown on page 107.

his system of 'reciprocal working'. Stationary engines were set up at intervals along a railway, and when a train of waggons was drawn along by cable towards one of these, it had attached to its rear the 'tail rope' from the previous engine, which was paid out from its winding drum, out-of-gear. When the waggons arrived at the engine to which they were being drawn, the tail rope was ready to become a 'head rope' to draw a train in the opposite direction. Several installations of increasing complexity were made on North-Eastern waggonways: and in 1826 the system was installed over five miles of the new Brunton & Shields Railroad, a colliery line in Northumberland running down to the Tyne near its mouth. Here the waggons were drawn at an average speed of 6 mph including stoppages for rope changes.

The locomotive, on the other hand, had not been developing so fast, nor indeed so fast as people's expectations of it. In 1825, at a time of intense speculation on railway proposals, Nicholas Wood, in his *A Practical Treatise on Railroads* . . ., counselled caution: although locomotives would be improved, he wrote, the idea that they would travel at twelve or more miles an hour was nonsense. During 1826 the Stockton & Darlington Railway was experiencing such problems with locomotives that it considered abandoning them in favour of horses.

As well as *Locomotion*, two other locomotives from this period survive. *Billy*, preserved by Tyne & Wear County Council Museums, came from Killingworth and was probably built about 1826. She has the vertical, in-line, within-the-boiler cylinders typical of early Stephenson locomotives. *Agenoria*, now in the National Railway Museum, was built in 1829 by Foster & Rastrick to the design of J. U. Rastrick. Here the layout of outside upright vertical cylinders and overhead beams harks back to the Wylam locomotives, though drive from the beams is direct to the rear pair of wheels and the front pair is mounted on springs.

George Stephenson, in any case, was by this date adept at laying out lines for cable haulage over considerable distances. One such was the Springwell Waggonway, completed in 1826 for Lord Ravensworth (as Sir Thomas Liddell had become) on the south side of the Tyne. A section of this, laid out for cable haulage, is preserved as the Bowes Railway, which name it had acquired over the years. The preserved section includes two complete inclined planes (neither of them very steep), the top part of another, the intervening sidings, and haulage arrangements. Power is now, as it was in the latter days of commercial use, electric: but demonstrations of cable haulage give a fascinating glimpse of railway operating practices of the 1820s, before locomotives had fully proved themselves.

Another line laid out mainly for cable haulage was the Canterbury & Whitstable Railway: George Stephenson had taken over as engineer from William James, and in turn deputed the position to Robert Stephenson. The latter had returned from America towards the end of 1827, and, maturer now, had immediately been reconciled with his father on, it seems, a basis of mutual respect.

Robert Stephenson's most important task on his return, however, was to take charge of Robert Stephenson & Co.'s locomotive works. Here he started to improve the design of locomotives. The firm had already built during 1827

– and one assumes George Stephenson largely responsible for the design – an improved locomotive for the Stockton & Darlington Railway, the *Experiment*. Her grate was formed of water tubes; her cylinders were set horizontally in the upper part of the rear of the boiler; and an arrangement of levers and a rocking shaft, mounted on the rear of the boiler, linked the piston rods with connecting rods which sloped downwards to crank pins on the leading pair of wheels. This must have made the footplate uncomfortable if not indeed dangerous (imagine bending down to fire such a locomotive, with the levers rocking to and fro past one's ears); and on the next locomotive built by the company, to the design of Robert Stephenson, the cylinders themselves were moved outside the boiler, sloping forwards and downwards like the connecting rods. The advantage of the layout, compared with vertical cylinders, was that all axles could be mounted on springs. This locomotive was the *Lancashire Witch*, which was ordered by the Liverpool & Manchester Railway but diverted to the Bolton & Leigh before delivery, which eventually took place during the summer of 1828. She had dual furnaces and fire tubes to increase her steaming capacity, and she was the first of a series of locomotives with sloping cylinders (but otherwise of various designs) built by Robert Stephenson & Co.; they included one ordered by Samuel Homfray for the Sirhowy Tramroad.

This was the background against which the L & MR directors had to decide how to power their railway. Split among themselves, they sent a delegation in October 1828 to inspect the Stockton & Darlington: it comprised director James Cropper, a strong proponent of cable haulage, and Henry Booth, treasurer and secretary of the company and proponent of locomotives. Henry Booth (1789–1869) was a Liverpool corn merchant with mechanical inclinations: he was a part owner of the steam boat *Cambria* which since 1821 had plied between Liverpool and North Wales, and by 1828 he was working with George Stephenson on locomotive development. The report by Cropper and Booth was, as might be expected, inconclusive, and the L & MR board then retained two independent engineering experts, J. U. Rastrick and James Walker, to advise them. These two, after familiarising themselves with the Liverpool & Manchester and Bolton & Leigh Railways made, early in 1829, a series of detailed inspections of the workings of the Middleton, Stockton & Darlington, Hetton, Brunton & Shields and Killingworth lines.

They came down, hesitantly but clearly, on the side of

stationary engines and the reciprocating system – if the L & MR was to be equipped to carry, from its opening day, the full amount of traffic anticipated. Only if it were possible to build up the traffic gradually and by degrees might locomotives be satisfactory. George Stephenson and his assistant Joseph Locke compiled a contrary report in favour of locomotives. Thomas Telford, too, recommended against cable haulage and in favour of locomotives: he had been called in to inspect the works on behalf of the Exchequer Bill Loan Commissioners, for the L & MR company, like many a canal company before it and many a railway company after, was finding itself short of money for construction and had requested a loan.

Rainhill

The way out of their dilemma, the directors decided, was to hold a prize competition – the idea originated with James Walker – for an improved locomotive, later modified to an 'improved moving power'. This competition became the famous Rainhill Trials, held early in October 1829 and won, as every schoolboy knows, by the *Rocket*.

The trials were held on a $1\frac{3}{4}$-mile section of the line, straight and level, at Rainhill near Liverpool; each locomotive entered was expected to haul a train of three times its own weight, making ten return trips up and down this section and then, after reloading with fuel and water, ten more. This was considered equivalent to a journey from Liverpool to Manchester and back. Locomotives were allowed $\frac{1}{8}$ mile at the start of the course to accelerate, and the same distance at the end to slow down; the intervening $1\frac{1}{2}$ miles had to be covered at not less than 10 mph. The judges were J. U. Rastrick, Nicholas Wood and John Kennedy. Kennedy was a Manchester inventor and manufacturer of textile machinery, and a supporter of the railway since 1822. The prize was £500.

Ten locomotives were said by the contemporary *Mechanics Magazine* to have been in preparation for the trials; five eventually appeared at Rainhill; and two of these can be discounted: Burstall's *Perseverance* which proved unable to achieve more than 5 mph, and Brandreth's *Cycloped*, which was powered by a horse working a sort of treadmill. This left three serious competitors: *Rocket*, *Sans Pareil* and *Novelty*.

Rocket was entered by a partnership comprising Henry Booth, George Stephenson, and Robert Stephenson. The arrangement of the boiler was Booth's idea. Typically,

locomotive boilers of the period contained a single fire tube, 12 in. diameter made from $\frac{1}{2}$-in.-thick iron: Booth realised that far more steam would be produced if the heating surface could be increased by passing hot gases from the fire through the boiler in a multitude of copper tubes 2 in. or so in diameter. He mentioned this idea to George Stephenson, who agreed; and Robert Stephenson was also admitted as a partner in the venture of building a locomotive with a boiler of this type for the competition. The *Rocket* was built, with some difficulty, by Robert Stephenson & Co.; the construction of her boiler meant that a water-jacketed firebox had to be provided at its rear; *Rocket* had the inclined cylinders of the time, driving her front pair of wheels, which were not coupled to the rear pair. She was tried out first on the Killingworth Railway and one may imagine Robert Stephenson's cautious glee at first discovering the capabilities of the locomotive he had built: for during the Rainhill Trials she alone of the entrants was to do all that was asked of her and more, proving not only reliable but fast, reaching on occasion speeds as high as 30 mph.

Sans Pareil was entered by Timothy Hackworth, who had designed and assembled her at Shildon: the boiler was supplied by Bedlington Ironworks, the cylinders by Robert Stephenson & Co. The layout of the locomotive was developed from Hackworth's *Royal George*: there was a return fire tube, and the cylinders were vertical and inverted, driving direct to one pair of wheels coupled to the other. Exhaust steam provided a strong blast up the chimney to draw the fire.

This locomotive proved to be over the stipulated weight, but was allowed to compete. On trial she ran well for two hours, but then a boiler feed pump failed. Probably also one of the cylinder castings was defective and allowed steam to blow through. *Sans Pareil* was unable to complete the trials.

Novelty was entered by John Ericsson and John Braithwaite; she was partly financed by C. B. Vignoles and at the start of the trials she was the popular favourite, and she owed nothing to the Stephensons' line of development.

John Ericsson (1803–1889) was a Swede: as a very young man he had helped survey the Göta Canal for which Telford was the engineer. He subsequently joined the Swedish army where great skill in draughtsmanship caused him to be employed on map making. In 1826 he was given leave of absence to go to England to seek his fortune in engineering, but he overstayed his leave and became, tech-

The Liverpool & Manchester Railway Co. announces a prize competition for an improved locomotive in the Liverpool Mercury of 1 May 1829.

Novelty and Rocket are depicted in an engraving of 1830 (below) complete with a cross-section of Novelty's boiler and one of many contemporary attempts to make a steam road carriage.

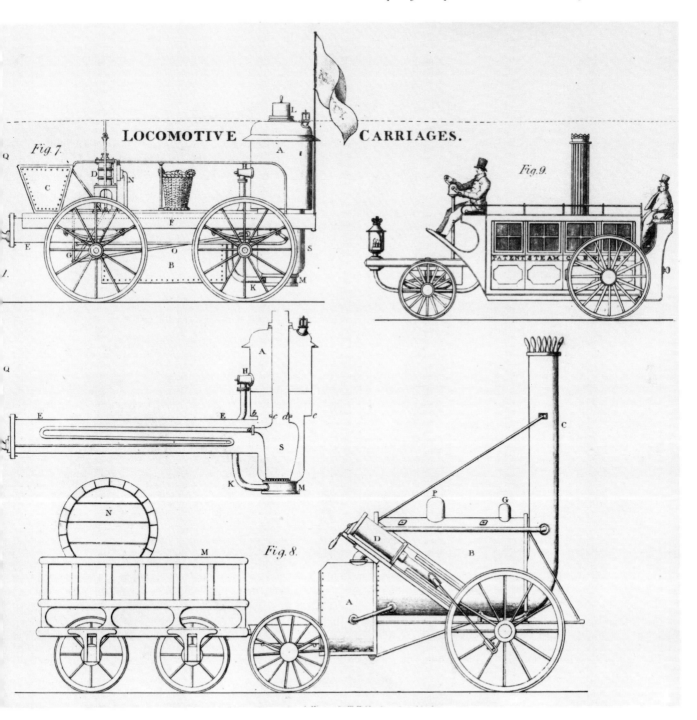

Two Rainhill entrants are preserved in the Science Museum. Sans Pareil *(above) is little altered, apart from her cylinders and wheels which are replacements fitted in 1837.* Rocket *(above right), after Rainhill, gained a front buffer beam and a cylindrical smokebox, and her cylinders were lowered to a position almost horizontal.*

nically, a deserter. By the intervention of the Crown Prince of Sweden, however, he was restored to the service and commissioned Captain in 1827: he resigned the same day but used the title to the end of his life. In 1827 he became junior partner in the firm of Braithwaite & Ericsson.

John Braithwaite (1797–1870) had inherited with his brother an engineering establishment in New Road, London, in 1818, but the brother had died in 1823. After becoming a partner Ericsson worked on developing bellows or centrifugal blowers for steamship furnaces and, in 1828, designed – and the firm built – the first practical steam fire engine (to use the term in its modern sense of an appliance to extinguish fires). It was technically satisfactory, but to firemen of the time the old ways were best. The fire engine, however, provided the basis of the design for *Novelty*.

Novelty's boiler had two principal components: one of them was vertical, cylindrical and included the firebox; the other branched from it horizontally and was cylindrical but of much smaller diameter. This component extended for most of the length of the locomotive. It contained a

single fire tube of even smaller diameter which doubled back on itself twice and so ran the length of this part of the boiler three times before emerging as a small chimney. Mechanically-worked bellows produced a draught for the fire. The piston rods from two inverted vertical cylinders were linked via bell cranks to horizontal connecting rods which drove a cranked axle and enabled all wheels to be sprung. *Novelty* was not so powerful as *Rocket*, but she was lighter in weight, rode better and was slightly faster. She had, however, been completed in only seven weeks and was untried: failures resulting from this prevented her from completing the trials. Even without such teething troubles, however, it is improbable that the bellows arrangement would have enabled her to steam well enough for continuous running.

In the circumstances the company very probably awarded the prize to the entrants of *Rocket*: and the multi-tubular boiler has been ever since the conventional locomotive boiler (it was, however, being invented independently but simultaneously in France by Marc Seguin).

Two of the Rainhill Trials entrants, *Rocket* and *Sans*

Pareil, are preserved in the Science Museum. Neither is in original condition, though *Sans Pareil* is not far removed from it. *Rocket* was altered to bring her into line with later locomotives developed from her: lower cylinders, almost horizontal, made her ride better, and an opening smoke box in front of the boiler barrel, with the chimney mounted upon it, improved access to the tubes for cleaning. The wheels and one cylinder from *Novelty* also survive, the property of the Science Museum; they were incorporated many years ago into a full-size non-working replica of the locomotive which was loaned in 1980 to the North Western Museum of Science & Industry (now the Greater Manchester Museum of Science & Industry).

Full-size working replicas of all three locomotives were built during 1979–80 for the 150th anniversary celebrations of the L & MR. The home of the replica *Rocket* is the National Railway Museum, though she is much in demand for temporary operation elsewhere. The replica *Sans Pareil* is at the Timothy Hackworth Museum, Shildon, and the replica *Novelty* has gone to the Swedish Railway Museum.

From *Rocket*'s performance at Rainhill it was quite clear that locomotives would be very much preferable to cable haulage for the Liverpool & Manchester Railway. Two other things were clear, too: that trains of passenger coaches could be hauled by such a locomotive at a speed much faster than anything road coaches or steam boats could offer; and that an extensive network of long-distance railways powered by such locomotives was not only feasible, but desirable. Such railways would prove superior to other means of long-distance passenger transport – horse-drawn coaches on turnpike roads, canal boats and steam boats on rivers and along the coast. This was immediately clear to some people, although others, understandably, took time to absorb so revolutionary a notion.

Road Steam Carriages

There was however another line of development which was equally overtaken; although, equally, this was not immediately acceptable to many at the time, for during the 1820s it had seemed as promising if not more so than the development of steam locomotives. This was the development of steam-driven road carriages.

After Trevithick there had been a lull in attempts to build steam road vehicles: then, early in the 1820s, there was an outburst of interest, helped along in practical terms by development of laminated elliptic and semi-elliptic springs and the improvement of road surfaces. At this period George Stephenson alone was developing the steam locomotive for colliery waggonways at a steady plod, and it was the steam carriage pioneers over the next few years who showed the greater degree of inventiveness in attempting to meet their greater need for lightweight compact engines and fast-steaming boilers.

There were at least two builders of steam road vehicles working about 1819–21, but the main activity of this era owes its origin to, as much as anyone, Goldsworthy Gurney, who first became interested in them in 1822.

Goldsworthy Gurney (1793–1875) was a Cornishman; as a child he knew Richard Trevithick and witnessed some of his road steam carriage experiments. He grew up to be doctor, surgeon and man of science, moving to London in 1820. Here, having formed the opinion two years later that steam could satisfactorily propel a carriage, he designed and built a series of steam carriages from 1825 onwards, taking out patents in 1825 and 1827. The 1825 patent included a water-tube boiler – that is to say, steam was generated from water contained in a great many small diameter tubes which linked larger drums and were exposed to the heat of the furnace. The tubes provided a large heating surface: four years later Booth and the Stephensons hit on the converse of Gurney's arrangement with their multitubular fire-tube boiler.

About 1825 Gurney developed a passion for steam carriages in much the same way that William James had earlier developed a passion for railways. Unable to find anyone to build carriages for him, he gave up his other occupations, turned engineer and established a steam carriage manufactory. His intention was to grant licences to others to operate steam carriages, built by him to his patents, over long-distance routes: this intent, coupled with trial runs of the carriages, gained him considerable publicity.

Other people too were by now working on steam carriages. Some of them made an extended series of trials, such as W. H. James, son of William James, from 1823 onwards, and Walter Hancock who started work about 1827. Elsewhere engineers who were, or were to be, prominent in other fields were at this time attracted to steam carriages and built one-off examples. Such were David Napier and James Nasmyth, both of whom independently built and operated steam carriages in 1827.

Gurney's 1827 patent steam coach incorporated a boiler contained in what to external appearances was its rear boot;

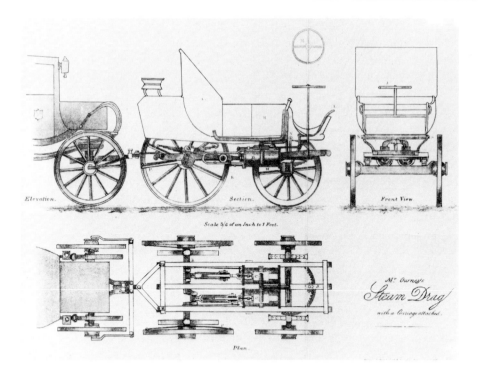

Unique survivor of the steam road-coach era (above): the frames and engine of a Gurney steam drag of c. 1830 are preserved in Glasgow Museum of Transport. The layout of horizontal cylinders driving a cranked axle originated with steam road vehicles and was later adapted to locomotives.

A steam drag built by Goldsworthy Gurney (left) for Sir Charles Dance c. 1830, with frames and engine of the type shown above.

pistons in two horizontal cylinders beneath the coach body drove a cranked rear axle. This and other improvements in engine layout which were being made by steam carriage designers were an important influence on Robert Stephenson when on his return from America he set out upon the road of improving locomotive design. In Gurney's case, there seems to have been an element of customer resistance to a design which placed the outside seats of the coach on top of the boiler and the inside ones immediately forward of it. During the winter of 1828–9 Gurney built a smaller vehicle, of the same general mechanical layout, as a steam 'drag' to tow an ordinary coach.

In July 1829 the steam drag, with a barouche in tow, made an impressive trial run to Bath and back; between Reading and Melksham it averaged 6 mph including stops, and these included halts every four miles or so to fill up with water by means of buckets passed from hand to hand. On return it was demonstrated at Hounslow barracks to the Prime Minister, the Duke of Wellington (who rode in the barouche) and to the military authorities. It ran at speeds up to 17 mph.

By the summer of 1829, therefore, Gurney's development of a steam road carriage had reached a highly promising stage. But this was also the summer in which the directors of the Liverpool & Manchester Railway Company had offered their prize of £500 for an improved

locomotive, modestly defined in their conditions as one to tow three times its own weight at 10 mph. Yet this offer prompted production of two locomotives able to reach 30 mph or so and one at least of them able to run continuously and reliably hauling loads much greater than that stipulated at speeds much faster.

Gurney's work on steam road carriages had been suddenly and unexpectedly overtaken by the development of the railway locomotive: yet he retained the apparent advantage in that his steam carriages would run on existing roads, but locomotives would need new and specially built tracks.

In parenthesis one may regret that there was no Gurney entrant at Rainhill. Gurney's steam drag could certainly have provided the basis of a locomotive to meet the L & MR's conditions, and its development period had been long enough for there to be a reasonable chance of completing the trials satisfactorily.

What a Gurney drag could do on rails was eventually demonstrated early in 1830, when South Wales ironmaster William Crawshay junior persuaded Gurney to allow one to be tried out on one of his family's tramroads at Hirwaun. The only modification made to it seems to have been to fit cast-iron plateway wheels. The drag, which probably weighed some 34 cwt, showed itself able to haul a total weight of 21½ tons over a 3-mile length of plateway in 18 minutes, or greater weights at slower speeds. This and another Gurney drag subsequently went into regular service on Crawshay's tramroads for a few years; probably they operated over the Hirwaun–Abernant tramroad which, as mentioned on page 53, has left an extensive run of stone blocks, illustrated in *The Archaeology of Railways*.

Gurney's true ambitions, however, lay upon the turnpike roads. In February 1831 one of his licensees, Sir Charles Dance, inaugurated a public passenger service, with Gurney drags towing coaches, between Cheltenham and Gloucester, intended as a preliminary towards a Birmingham–Bristol service. By this time the Liverpool & Manchester Railway was already open and carrying passengers in crowds; but Liverpool is far away from Gloucester and Dance's service was, at least at first, successful too. The coaches ran the 9-mile journey in 50 minutes, four times a day, and were reliable. The stage coach fare for the journey came down from 4s to 1s.

In March 1831 a similar drag was sent to Scotland, probably with the intention of starting an Edinburgh–Glasgow service; it was damaged in transit by sea, however, but managed a trial trip between Glasgow and Paisley. Then, while awaiting repairs, it was tampered with by unqualified and unauthorised persons, and the boiler exploded.

The chassis of this drag is preserved in Glasgow Museum of Transport – the only substantial relic surviving from this whole era of steam road carriages. What remains are, principally, the wooden frames with cylinders mounted between them, the drive to the rear axle, the valve gear and part of the steering gear. The arrangement of horizontal cylinders between the frames driving on to a cranked axle seems, with the benefit of hindsight, commonsense and obvious. It was familiar in a great many steam railway locomotives, such as, indeed, North British Railway 4-4-0 *Glen Douglas* of 1913, alongside which the Gurney drag chassis is displayed. It requires a considerable and conscious mental effort to appreciate that in the drag chassis we have the only example of the pioneer work which evolved this layout and incorporated it into road vehicles *before* it was adopted for locomotives. It is uncertain, however, whether this particular drag was built soon before or soon after the first such locomotives had appeared.

That 75-per-cent-reduction in stage coach fares which Dance's Cheltenham–Gloucester steam coach service brought about may have been good news for travellers, but it was extremely bad news for everyone with a vested interest in horse-drawn coaches: and that meant not only coach proprietors and their employees, and many innkeepers, but also farmers and landowners who provided horses and, more important, their feed. It was from the latter class that many turnpike trustees were drawn. Turnpike trustees and surveyors had in any case a legitimate concern that heavy vehicles running at, by the standards of the time, high speeds would damage their roads. The publicity attending Gurney's work encouraged belief that steam coach services were about to become widespread.

So Dance's service met strong opposition, and it came to a premature end in June 1831 when a considerable length of road, though in good condition, was obstructed by heaps of stones up to 18 inches deep. In attempting to cross these, a drag broke its crank axle. Simultaneously many turnpike renewal Acts which were being rushed through Parliament included powers to impose prohibitive tolls on carriages propelled by machinery. Gurney was influential enough to secure the setting up of a House of Commons Committee to investigate, and both Sir James McAdam and Thomas Telford agreed in evidence before it that horses' hoofs caused greater wear on road surfaces than carriage wheels. The committee's report confirmed that steam road carriages were safe and advantageous, but that the tolls on some roads, if allowed to remain, would prohibit their use.

Unfortunately no legislation followed (how little some things change!). Gurney turned away from steam carriages to (among other things) seeking a cure for cholera, developing bright lights for lighthouses and ventilating the Houses of Parliament. He was knighted in 1863.

Others continued in attempts to develop steam road carriages for some years. Walter Hancock successfully commenced a service between London and nearby Stratford in February 1831, pre-dating Gurney and Dance's Cheltenham–Gloucester service. A series of improved vehicles followed over several years, and various services were operated, most of them in or about London and none of them long-lived, although Hancock's main problems seem to have been financial. John Scott Russell had four steam coaches built in 1834 to operate a service between Glasgow and Paisley (and so in competition with swift canal boats as well as stage coaches). One of these broke a wheel, as a result of meeting a mass of loose road material and rubbish on the road: in the ensuing accident the boiler exploded and four passengers were killed. The obstruction had been placed there by order of the turnpike trustees. The resulting legal action between Russell's company and

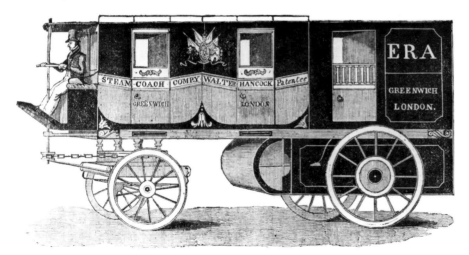

Walter Hancock's steam carriages ran successfully in and around London for several years in the 1830s.

the trustees were settled out of court, but an interdict was placed upon continued operation of the steam coaches.

Of the many others who attempted to build and operate steam carriages during the period 1820–40, none was more successful than those mentioned; by the end of the period, steam railways were a proven success and interest in steam road vehicles lapsed for several decades.

Steam on Road, Railway or Canal?

To Telford – who was taken down the Holyhead Road in 1831 by one of Dance's Gurney drags, and approved – and to others like him, construction of trunk railways for steam locomotives seemed an unnecessary duplication of the existing, and now highly-developed, networks of turnpike roads and canals. Yet on roads, steam coaches were in obvious and dangerous opposition to horse-drawn coaches and so aroused the immediate wrath of vested interests. And also of the man in the street – one may get a glimmer of insight into this by considering the opposition at the present time to introduction of juggernaut lorries of ever-increasing size (and these at least do not have boilers to explode).

Railways, at any rate until after Rainhill, did not appear to present a threat to the coaching interest, and when that threat was realised, it was too late to do much about it. Railway proposals could still be, and were, vociferously opposed in Parliament, but once authorised a railway company presented a very much more formidable opponent to turnpike trusts and coach proprietors than did the individual steam coach promoter. There was little the opposition could do about them: only railways, as things turned out, could offer the freedom from opposition inter-

ference and obstruction which the steam vehicle, carriage or locomotive, needed to develop to total success.

The relationship between canals, on the other hand, and steam railways became a complex one and is dealt with in the next chapter; but in any case canal companies could prohibit or restrict the use of steam boats on grounds of bank damage. Besides, it was only the widest artificial waterways – such as the Caledonian Canal – that could safely accommodate vessels with side paddle wheels. By the time a form of propulsion – the screw propeller – had been successfully developed that was compatible with the restricted dimensions of most canal structures, it was (as we shall see shortly) already, just, too late. The railway idea had become established. So it was not in the form of steam tugs or boats on existing canals that steam came to be the power for a national transport network but, once again, in the form of locomotives on specially built railways. Any general adoption of steam power to canals was delayed for many years.

Railways in 1829 and 1830

While the Liverpool & Manchester Railway was approaching completion, promoters of other railways were active. C. B. Vignoles was busy laying out the St Helens & Runcorn Gap Railway, which would cross over the L & MR, and the Wigan Branch Railway, which was to branch from it. Elsewhere the Stephensons were working on the Leicester & Swannington Railway, intended to link Leicester with those coal mines to the north-west, which the Forest Line of the Leicester Navigation had failed to do effectively. It got its Act in May 1830; so did the Leeds & Selby Railway, intended as part of a Leeds–Hull line but for the time being to connect with steam boats on the

River Ouse at Selby. It had been laid out by James Walker, who had originated the idea of Rainhill.

The same period saw two railways opened – the first part of the Cromford & High Peak, with steep cable-worked inclines, and horse-haulage on the relatively level sections; and the whole of the Canterbury & Whitstable, with much less steep inclined planes and, to work a short near-level section, the Robert Stephenson & Co. locomotive *Invicta*. On this locomotive the cylinders, though still steeply inclined, were placed towards the front, and the connecting rods drove the rear pair of wheels, which were coupled by rods to the front wheels. The Canterbury & Whitstable offered a passenger service from its opening on 3 May 1830, so *Invicta* became the first locomotive regularly to haul passenger trains. This locomotive is now preserved in Canterbury; the line was eventually converted wholly to locomotive traction, and closed in 1952.

Invicta as built formed part of Robert Stephenson's process of rapid development of locomotive design: she was contemporary with four locomotives for the Liverpool & Manchester which were similar to *Rocket* but had their cylinders low down and an increased number of tubes. Then in July 1830 Robert Stephenson & Co. built *Northumbrian* for the L & MR, and in this locomotive the boiler attained the definitive form for locomotive boilers, with the firebox at the rear made integral with the barrel, and with the chimney mounted on a smokebox at the front. With such locomotives the Liverpool & Manchester Railway was equipped for public traffic.

Opening of the Liverpool & Manchester Railway

During 1829 the Liverpool & Manchester company negotiated unsuccessfully with the New Quay Company, carriers on the Mersey & Irwell Navigation, with a view to their acting as carriers on the railway. It also considered contracting out the passenger carrying to H. C. Lacy, a Manchester coach proprietor who was also a subscriber to the railway company, but eventually decided against doing so.

The company itself was therefore the passenger carrier when it opened its line to passenger traffic on 15 September 1830.

The line was opened ceremonially by the Prime Minister, the Duke of Wellington, conveyed in an ornamented carriage and fresh from his ride behind Gurney's steam drag: whatever may have been his policies elsewhere, he

was evidently no reactionary in means of transport. The train conveying him and other VIPs was to traverse the line from west to east; mid-way, at Parkside, it was to take water while a procession of other trains overtook it in review. Here, celebration was suddenly replaced by tragedy. Passengers were requested not to alight, but many did so, among them William Huskisson, long-term friend of the railway, its supporter in Parliament and its successful advocate with the Marquis of Stafford. The duke beckoned to him. Politicians had been hoping – possibly scheming – for a reconciliation between the two prominent Tories, who had differed. Then, as Huskisson answered the duke's call, he was run down by *Rocket*, and terribly injured.

In conveying the injured man to Eccles, to which point physicians were brought from Manchester, George Stephenson drove *Northumbrian* at the unprecedented *average* speed of 36 mph for the 15 miles; but in vain, for Huskisson died the same evening. The tragic events of that day have often been told, and one need not dwell on them – except to remark that somewhere among the crowd at Liverpool was William James.

Despite the opening day's tragedy, public passenger trains commenced the next day with one round trip from Liverpool: a full service of three passenger trains each way daily commenced the day after – or, as *The Railway Companion* of 1833 put it, 'six carriages commenced running regularly upon the road', for familiar terminology was only slowly superseded. The actual coaches that were used for first-class passengers comprised, in effect, three road-coach bodies mounted on a railway-wagon underframe with sprung axles; the guard sat outside, high up, on a seat mounted on the end of the roof, a position no doubt approximating to that to which he was accustomed. Coaches for second-class passengers were open above the waist but, unlike outside passengers on a stage coach, they did have the benefit of a roof over their heads. Those who were wealthy enough to travel post in their own carriages could still in effect do so on the L & MR, by travelling in their own carriages upon carriage trucks. The appearance of the Liverpool & Manchester Railway's first passenger trains and their coaches is familiar from the many contemporary engravings, and from the full-size replicas of the coaches which were built for the centenary celebrations in 1930 and now form part of the NRM collection.

The L & MR's passenger trains proved immensely popular. Their speed – the journey of 31 miles took $1\frac{1}{2}$–2

These illustrations of the route of the Liverpool
& Manchester Railway in the 1980s may be
compared with colour illustrations of it when
new on page 147. Chatsworth Street cutting
(left) is still recognisable as 'the entrance of the
railway' at OS grid ref. SJ 367898, although
it was widened slightly on the left in Victorian
times and what was originally a blind entrance
was opened out into an additional tunnel.
Foundations of the Moorish Arch engine house
appear in the foreground.

At Parkside (right) the line is still a main line
at OS grid ref. SJ 605955; a memorial to
Huskisson, alongside the track, occupies the
position of the water tanks.

hours – seemed phenomenal. 'Surely Daedalus is come amongst us again' commented Nimrod. They were also cheap: the first class fare from end to end was 7s, second class 4s. Both were later reduced. Prior to the opening of the railway, coaches between Liverpool and Manchester took 4½ hours and charged about 10s inside and about 5s 6d outside. By early December the railway had carried more than 50,000 passengers: but fourteen of the twenty-six road coaches previously operating between Liverpool and Manchester had been withdrawn. In November 1830 it was announced that the mails between Liverpool and Manchester would be transferred to the railway. By 1832 there was but one road coach between Liverpool and Manchester, and that chiefly for parcels.

The instant and considerable success of the Liverpool & Manchester Railway as a passenger carrier was one of history's most unexpected developments. This railway, which had been built for freight traffic (and strongly opposed by existing freight transport undertakings, but not by carriers of passengers) did not even attempt to carry freight until nearly three months after its opening for passenger traffic. The first freight train ran on 4 December 1830, when it inaugurated a regular freight service. In 1831 the railway carried 77,000 tons of freight, and in 1833, 113,000 tons. In view of the railway's catastrophic effect on competing stage coaches, it is interesting to compare these figures with those for Liverpool–Manchester freight traffic routed via the Bridgewater Canal: in 1831, nearly 92,000 tons, in 1833, 106,000 tons. To achieve this, however, the canal had had to cut its rates: so receipts were down, and profits, too.

At Liverpool, trains of passenger coaches started from Crown Street station, then descended a cable-worked incline through a tunnel to an 'engine station' in Chatsworth Street cutting, Edge Hill. Goods waggons from the docks were drawn upwards by cable through the long tunnel beneath Liverpool to the same point. Engine houses to work both inclines were disguised as an architectural feature, the Moorish Arch, which spanned the tracks: George Stephenson, the protagonist of the locomotive, had here provided the L & MR with an advanced cable-haulage installation. Today, most of the tracks in the cutting have been lifted, and excavations, by the North Western Society for Industrial Archaeology & History, and the Edge Hill Railway Trust Ltd, have revealed both the foundations of the Moorish Arch (which was demolished late in the nineteenth century) and other trenches and pits provided for the cable haulage apparatus.

At this point, locomotives were attached to trains to haul them to Manchester. A little to the east, today's passenger trains, which start from the slightly later station of Lime Street, join the original route. They still pass through the depths of Olive Mount cutting, widened during the Victorian era, cross over the Sankey Viaduct (though the Sankey Brook Navigation beneath is now filled in), pass the site of Parkside Station with its monument to Huskisson, and traverse the wastes of Chat Moss, still remarkably wild. Then, in the suburbs of Manchester they diverge from the original route to go to Manchester Victoria.

As opened, the line crossed the Irwell and terminated at Manchester, Liverpool Road, not far from the Bridgewater Canal basin. At its Manchester terminus the com-

pany had provided itself with, for passengers, a 'coach office' derived from stage coach practice, and, for freight, a warehouse similar to those built on canals, even to the extent that its entrances, like those of a canal warehouse, lay at right angles to the main track. Wagons entered it via turntables.

Fortunately both buildings survive through the happy chance that although passenger trains were diverted away from Liverpool Road in the 1840s, it remained in use for freight until 1975. Their historic importance is now recognised, largely through the efforts of the Liverpool Road Station Society; the coach office and adjoining buildings were undergoing extensive restoration during 1982, and the location now houses the Greater Manchester Museum of Science & Industry.

The delay in commencing a freight service over the L & MR was caused partly by pre-occupation with carriage of passengers, partly by waiting for the delivery of Robert Stephenson's latest locomotive, the *Planet*, delivered early in October 1830.

In *Planet* the steam locomotive achieved what became its conventional layout. The integral multitubular boiler and firebox of *Northumbrian* was allied with the arrangement of horizontal cylinders between the frames driving on to a cranked axle which had been pioneered by Gurney. The cranked axle part of the arrangement had already been used in a locomotive by Braithwaite and Ericsson in *Novelty*. In *Planet* the cylinders were placed beneath the smokebox, where they were kept warm; later on, locomotives would have them outside the frames with the connecting rods driving crank pins on the wheels.

Almost simultaneously with the construction of *Planet*, two other engineers were adapting Gurney's layout to locomotives. One was Timothy Hackworth, who incorporated it into the *Globe*, a passenger locomotive for the Stockton & Darlington Railway which was built by Robert Stephenson & Co. The other was Edward Bury, Liverpool sawmill proprietor turned locomotive builder, who used it in the *Liverpool*. This was put on the Liverpool & Manchester Railway for trials late in October 1830, but does not seem to have worked satisfactorily until rebuilt with a multitubular boiler the following year. It is from *Planet*, however, that the conventional British steam locomotive is descended. Robert Stephenson's design development continued: the original *Planet*, with only the rear pair of

The Planet *of 1830 had a multi-tubular boiler with smokebox and integral firebox, and horizontal cylinders between the frames. Robert Stephenson had achieved the definitive layout for the steam locomotive.*

wheels driven, was a 2-2-0, but a 0-4-0 version with both pairs of wheels coupled together appeared on the L & MR early in 1831. Later that year a locomotive of this type was one of several locomotives exported at this period to the USA. This particular example, the Camden & Amboy Railroad's *John Bull*, survived to be preserved in the Smithsonian Institution, Washington DC: and in 1980, anticipating her 150th anniversary, she was restored to working order and operated under her own steam.

From these four-wheeled locomotives Robert Stephenson in due course developed a larger, six-wheeled type called *Patentee*, with wheel arrangement either 2-2-2 or 0-4-2 for passenger or goods traffic respectively. One of two locomotives of the latter type built by Todd, Kitson & Laird of Leeds for the L & MR during 1837–8 was named *Lion*. Today, as the oldest workable locomotive in Britain, she is well known from her appearances in the 150th anniversary celebrations of the L & MR in 1980. She is now owned by Merseyside County Museums and the story of her survival and restoration has been much written about elsewhere, not least in the museums' own publication *Lion*.

Trunk Lines Authorised

The Liverpool & Manchester trunk railway quickly sprouted branches: the Kenyon & Leigh Junction Railway, opened on 1 January 1831, connecting it with the Bolton & Leigh, and the Warrington & Newton opened during the following summer. Far more important than these, though, was the fact that its evident promise and success brought about a resurgence of interest in the promotion of other trunk lines, which had lain fallow since the boom of the mid-1820s.

On the Liverpool–Birmingham–London route, the Liverpool to Birmingham proposal had been revived by John Moss in 1829 and surveyed over its northern half by Joseph Locke, and over its southern half by J. U. Rastrick, both working under the general direction of George Stephenson. Separate bills for the two sections were defeated in Parliament in 1830, but the promoters picked up the pieces and went forward with the line as a single entity. It was now called the Grand Junction Railway and was to run from Warrington (which was accessible after 1831 by rail from both Liverpool and Manchester) to Stafford, Wolverhampton and Birmingham. The opposition was bought off, and a new bill started a fairly uneventful passage through Parliament.

Further south, the Stephensons reported in 1830 on rival routes proposed for the London & Birmingham Railway; Robert Stephenson then made a detailed survey, which was followed by a bitter Parliamentary battle. The route chosen closely followed both the Holyhead Road and the Grand Junction Canal: coaching interests were at last ranged with canals in opposition to the railway.

Meanwhile two other important trunk lines were being promoted. Early in 1831 a railway from London to Southampton was proposed, and surveyed by Francis Giles; and late in 1832 the proposal for a railway from Bristol to London was revived. A committee was formed the following year which advertised for an engineer to survey the route.

The man it got was Isambard Kingdom Brunel.

I. K. Brunel (1806–1859), probably the greatest and best-known of all British engineers, was partly of French descent, the son of Marc Brunel. He was educated in Britain and France, apprenticed in France to a noted maker of scientific instruments, and spent much time on his return to England in Henry Maudslay's works. He, for a time, assisted his father in boring a tunnel beneath the Thames, a project which, like Trevithick's earlier venture, proved extremely perilous. He then set himself up as a civil engineer. In November 1830 he examined Telford's improvements to the Birmingham Canal; in December 1831 he travelled on the Liverpool & Manchester Railway. In Bristol, early in 1833, he was working on improvements to the docks. He was appointed engineer to the Bristol–London railway in March at the age of 27; and he energetically set about surveying it. The following August a name for the railway was decided: Great Western Railway.

The London & Birmingham and Grand Junction Railways both eventually got their Acts of Parliament on the same day: 6 May 1833. Robert Stephenson was appointed engineer-in-chief of the London & Birmingham and under him construction commenced. He had, following Stephenson principles, made it as nearly level as possible, with a ruling gradient of 1 in 300. This meant that, as several ridges lay across the route, extensive engineering works were needed – notably, deep cuttings at Tring and Blisworth and, above all, Kilsby Tunnel, about 2,400 yards long.

On the Grand Junction the problems were not so much physical as personal. Rastrick in any event played little if any part after the Act was obtained; between George Stephenson and Joseph Locke, originally the former's devoted pupil, a long-smouldering row broke out with the result that, by autumn 1835, Locke was engineer-in-chief and Stephenson had resigned.

During this period, the London & Southampton had obtained its Act in July 1834, and construction had commenced under Giles; a Bill for the Great Western was defeated in 1834 but an Act was eventually obtained in August 1835. Having laid out a railway that was easily graded (for the most part) and magnificently aligned Brunel then, as is well known, persuaded his directors that it should be built in equally grand style to a broad gauge of 7 ft $0\frac{1}{4}$ in.

While these trunk lines radiating from London were taking shape, railway promoters were also active in the provinces. In 1836 came a series of Acts of Parliament for five railways which, adjoining end to end, were intended to link Gloucester with Birmingham, Derby, York, Darlington and Newcastle upon Tyne. Also incorporated the same year were the Midland Counties Railway, to provide a route from London to the North-East by linking the London & Birmingham at Rugby with the northern lines at Derby, and the Manchester & Leeds to provide a cross-pennine link. A more southerly link across the Pennines was to be provided by the Sheffield, Ashton-under-Lyne & Manchester Railway, which got its Act in 1837, supplanting a long-proposed scheme for a canal over the route.

The Glasgow & Garnkirk Railway, opened in 1831, was one of the first railways to be equipped with locomotives from the start, following the example of the Liverpool & Manchester.

Rail and Canal in the 1830s

While all these great schemes were in preparation, the improved canals which had been authorised during the mid-1820s were being completed and opened. So were the local railways which had been under construction; and Acts were obtained for others, a few of which were still to be horse-operated. The course of the principal events between the opening of the Liverpool & Manchester Railway in 1830 and the opening of the Grand Junction Railway in 1837 is best shown in tabular form, year by year, with notes of the motive power for railways and other points of importance.

1831

Birmingham Canal Navigations improvements continued throughout period

Kenyon & Leigh Junction Railway opened (locomotives)

Warrington & Newton Railway opened (locomotives)

Macclesfield Canal opened

Cromford & High Peak Railway opened throughout (horses, inclined planes)

Glasgow & Garnkirk Railway opened (locomotives)

Dundee & Newtyle Railway opened (locomotives, inclined planes)

Trent & Mersey Canal duplicates locks west of Harecastle

Manchester, Boulton & Bury Canal gets Act authorising conversion of canal into railway (but see below)

Act for Wigan & Preston Railway

Act for Dublin & Kingstown Railway (first in Ireland)

1832

Wigan Branch Railway opened (locomotives)

Leicester & Swannington Railway partly opened (locomotives)

Stanhope & Tyne Rail Road (sic) company formed; line to be built using the old system of way leaves

Act for Festiniog Railway

Act for Bodmin & Wadebridge Railway

Manchester, Bolton & Bury Canal Navigation & Railway gets Act for separate railway (partly opened 1838–9) and retains canal also

1833

Act for London & Birmingham Railway

Further proposals for improved London–Birmingham canal (which eventually fade out *c.* 1838)

Act for Grand Junction Railway

Leicester & Swannington Railway open throughout (locomotives and inclined planes)

Act for Coleorton Railway, to extend Leicester & Swannington, opened same year (horses)

Act for Whitby & Pickering Railway

St Helens & Runcorn Gap Railway opened (locomotives, horses, inclined planes)

Ellesmere & Chester Canal's Middlewich branch opened (ends E & C Canal's isolation from rest of canal system by linking it with Trent & Mersey)

1834

Act for London & Southampton Railway

Oxford Canal improved line completed

North Union Railway, incorporating Wigan Branch Railway and Wigan & Preston Railway, opened to Preston (locomotives)

Bodmin & Wadebridge Railway opened (locomotives)

Leeds & Selby Railway opened (locomotives)

Act for Hull & Selby Railway

Newcastle & Carlisle Railway partly opened (horses)

Acts for several short railways in North-East England

1835

Act for Great Western Railway

Act for London & Croydon Railway (branching from London & Greenwich)

Birmingham & Liverpool Junction Canal opened

Aire & Calder Navigation completes improvements on line up to Leeds

Newcastle & Carlisle Railway – on which locomotives were prohibited by authorising Act in 1829 – introduces locomotives, has an injunction served on it to prevent their use, and subsequently gets Act to authorise them

Whitby & Pickering Railway partly opened (horses)

Bristol & Gloucestershire Railway (authorised 1828) completed (horses and gravity)

1836

Acts for trunk railways:

    Birmingham & Gloucester Railway

    Birmingham & Derby Railway

    Midland Counties Railway, from Rugby to Derby and Nottingham (engineer, Charles Vignoles)

    North Midland Railway, from Derby to Leeds (engineer, George Stephenson)

    Manchester & Leeds Railway

    York & North Midland Railway

    Great North of England Railway, from York to Newcastle

    Bristol & Exeter Railway

    Cheltenham & Great Western Union Railway

Act for Taff Vale Railway

Act for Glasgow, Paisley, Kilmarnock & Ayr Railway

Act for London & Blackwall Railway (opened 1840 with reciprocating cable haulage)

London & Greenwich Railway partly opened (locomotives: opened throughout 1838, first steam railway in London)

Festiniog Railway opened (horses, gravity, inclined planes)

Durham & Sunderland Railway opened (cable traction, gravity)

Whitby & Pickering Railway open throughout (horses, inclined plane)

Newcastle & Carlisle Railway, further sections opened

with locomotives (eventually open throughout 1838)

Liverpool & Manchester Railway, new passenger terminus at Lime Street, Liverpool, opened with approach line from Edge Hill (inclined plane)

Croydon Canal sold to London & Croydon Railway, which uses route for railway (opened 1839: locomotives)

1837

Act for London & Brighton Railway (extending London & Croydon: engineer J. U. Rastrick)

Act for Sheffield, Ashton-under-Lyne & Manchester Railway

Act for Lancaster & Preston Junction Railway

Further improvements to Holyhead Road at this period under engineer J. B. MacNeill, particularly by laying two lines of stone blocks on hills to form a continuous smooth track for carriage wheels

Grand Junction Railway opened (locomotives)

London & Birmingham Railway partly opened (locomotives, and inclined plane out of Euston)

This list is not exhaustive, but it is comprehensive enough to indicate how transport routes were developing at this period.

The Last Canals

Of all the transport routes completed during this period, those which are most evocative of it are (in the author's opinion) the late trunk canals – the Macclesfield and the Birmingham & Liverpool Junction. Both were early faced with railway competition: the Macclesfield was competitive with the Cromford & High Peak Railway, opened the same year, and the promoters of the Grand Junction Railway were casting covetous eyes at the route of the B &

Belated turnpike road improvement: despite the construction of the London & Birmingham Railway nearby – or perhaps in an effort to counter it – further improvements were made to the Holyhead Road about 1836 under engineer J. B. MacNeill. They included long continuous pairs of lines of granite 'trams' or blocks, to help coaches up hills. A short piece of road of this type still exists beside the modern A5 in Northamptonshire (above) at OS grid ref. SP 657563. The construction is made clear by the engraving (below) in F. W. Simms's Public Works of Great Britain.

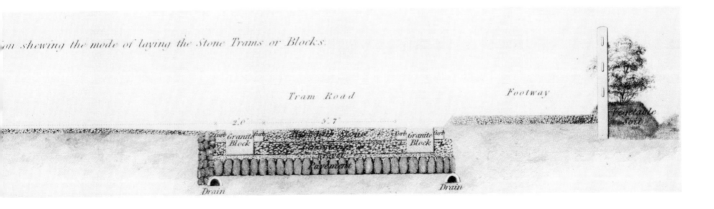

LJ Canal even while it was under construction. But both canals are still open for navigation, even though they are used today by pleasure craft rather than the trading boats for which they were built. In contrast with the twisting, winding courses of older canals, they lead the traveller by boat purposefully onward: features which might cause a moment's avoidable delay have been eliminated.

In 1833 Joseph Mitchell, taking time off from his Highland Roads responsibilities, journeyed south and looked up old friends whom he had known during construction of the Caledonian Canal. One of them, Alexander Fyfe, who had superintended the steam dredger used to deepen Loch Oich, was now locomotive superintendent of the Liverpool & Manchester Railway, opened three years before. Another, Alexander Easton, was resident engineer in charge of construction of the Birmingham & Liverpool Junction Canal, which was still being built.

Telford had retired and was writing his memoirs. Sadly, he did not live to see his last great canal completed, for he died in 1834; the canal was eventually completed the following year by William Cubitt, who had been deputising for Telford since early in 1833.

Many of the canal's cuttings and embankments gave trouble, for the ground was unstable, but the biggest problem was the great embankment at Shelmore, a mile long and sixty feet high. The marl from which it was at first attempted to build it constantly slipped and, despite the efforts of the navvies, completion was delayed for three years. Shelmore embankment (OS grid ref. SJ 796220) remains perhaps the greatest single engineering feature of these canals, though it is the first among many. Locks concentrated in flights are a feature of both canals – twelve locks at Bosley (OS grid ref. SJ 904663) on the Macclesfield, and fifteen at Audlem (OS grid ref. SJ 659425) on the Birmingham & Liverpool Junction – or as it is more commonly called today from the system of which it later formed part, the Shropshire Union Main Line. So are iron-trough aqueducts over main roads, as at Congleton (OS grid ref. SJ 866622) on the Macclesfield Canal and at Nantwich (OS grid ref. SJ 642526) and Stretton (OS grid ref. SJ 873107) on the B & LJ.

The improved Oxford Canal – between Hawkesbury Junction (north of Coventry), Braunston and Napton – for much of the distance resembles other new canals of the period: broad, and straight or gently curved. Every few miles, however, there comes a length where the bends are sharp and the course is winding – a section of the old canal

Locks on the Birmingham & Liverpool Junction Canal were grouped in flights: the most extensive is at Audlem (above) at OS grid ref. SJ 659423, where the even downward slope is maintained by means of a cutting. The design for the locks on this canal was included in the Atlas *to Telford's* Life *(right).*

retained and incorporated into the new. Where they part company the new towpath is, in many places, carried over the old canal (of which parts were kept as short branches to serve village wharves and so on) by an elegant cast-iron bridge. These were made, according to their cast-in inscriptions, by Horseley Iron Works – the same firm, presumably, which had earlier pioneered construction of iron steam boats with the *Aaron Manby*. One is illustrated on page 148. At Newbold, the tunnel on the new lines wide with dual towpaths (OS grid ref. SP 487774). The towpath elsewhere is single, so presumably it was thought that the entanglement in the dark of the tow-lines – and horses – of passing boats was a hindrance worth avoiding.

Duplicated facilities elsewhere dating from this period and still to be seen are the duplicated locks of the Trent & Mersey Canal as it descends from Harecastle into the Cheshire Plain, and the Grand Junction at Stoke Bruerne.

Relics of Railways of the Early 1830s

One of the most conspicuous features which distinguished railways laid out in the late 1820s and early 1830s from those built later was their continuing use of inclined planes. Where these were not too steep they were often later simply used by locomotives, and the cables were removed. The approach to Liverpool Lime Street is an example, which is now incorporated into a modernised main line; another was Hopton incline on the Cromford & High Peak Railway (OS grid ref. SK 253546), of which part was as steep as

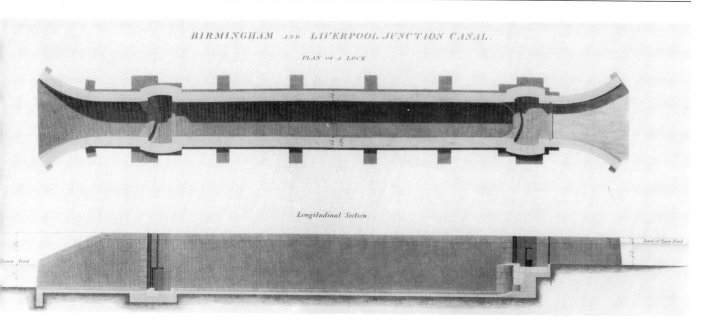

1 in 14 and was one of the steepest inclines used by locomotives. It is now without rails since the line was closed in 1967.

Elsewhere easily graded (and often circuitous) diversionary routes were built and the inclines closed, though their traces remain. There are examples on the Dundee & Newtyle at Newtyle (OS grid ref. NO 302412) and elsewhere, on the Stanhope & Tyne at Waskerley (OS grid ref. NZ 053455) and on the Whitby & Pickering at Goathland (OS grid ref. NZ 833015). Courses of the later routes, also now closed, can be seen near the first two of these; at Goathland the deviation line is in use as part of the North Yorkshire Moors Railway. The case of the Festiniog Railway was slightly different: originally, it surmounted a ridge by a pair of inclines, rather as did the Stockton & Darlington at Brusselton and Etherley, but this was a temporary expedient and even in horse railway days a tunnel was bored to eliminate the need for the inclines. Their courses can be seen at OS grid references SH 679428 and 677433.

Some cable-worked inclines remained in use as long as the railways of which they were part. Such were Swannington incline on the Leicester & Swannington, the course of which can be seen at OS grid reference SK 418162 (other parts of this railway remain in use for freight) and the steep inclines at the eastern end of the Cromford & High Peak. At the head of one of these, Middleton (OS grid ref. SK 275552), the engine house is preserved, complete with the winding engine built by Butterley Ironworks in 1829, and is opened to the public from

time to time. The winding engine from Swannington incline is preserved in the National Railway Museum, and so is the engine from the Stanhope & Tyne's Weatherhill incline. The course of the incline which this engine worked can be seen at OS grid reference NY 997422 high among the eastern foothills of the Pennines.

Of buildings peculiar to the period, warehouses for canal/rail interchange survive at both ends of the Cromford & High Peak Railway – at Whaley Bridge (OS grid ref. SK 012816) and Cromford Goods (OS grid ref. SK 314559). A curious cottage survives (derelict in 1982)

Looking down the course of the Stanhope & Tyne Rail Road's inclined plane at Waskerley, Co. Durham. In the foreground is a pile of stone sleeper blocks.

beside the course of the Leicester & Swannington Railway at Bagworth (OS grid ref. SK 445095): with its bow front it resembles a turnpike toll house, and may well have been intended as a toll house for the railway.

The original station building of the Leeds & Selby Railway's Selby terminus (opened 1834) still stands in the present-day goods yard (OS grid ref. SE 619323). This must be the earliest surviving example of the 'train shed' which was soon to become a familiar feature of large stations. In this instance the building is of wood and is still in use as a store, rail-connected. It stands close to the River Ouse, for here passengers from Leeds transferred to steam boats on the river for the onward journey to Hull. There are still wooden jetties and moorings along the bank, but of their date it is impossible to be certain.

The station buildings at Edge Hill, Liverpool, date from the opening of the Lime Street line in 1836 and are still in use: they were handsomely restored by British Rail about 1979. Hexham station on the Newcastle & Carlisle Railway was opened in 1836 also, and here again the original building (incorporating the present-day waiting room) is still in use, though obscured by additions in the same style made later, though probably not very much later. Similar station buildings, probably of about the same date, still stand at other stations on the line – Corbridge, Riding Mill, Stocksfield, Wylam – but are no longer in use for their original purpose.

From the Bodmin & Wadebridge Railway came three four-wheeled coaches preserved by the National Railway Museum; their under-frames are believed to date from the 1830s, though their bodies are probably of later construction.

Swift Passenger Boats

To meet the threat of rail competition, canal companies had an alternative to improving their lines: they could improve the performance of the boats that used them. The Forth & Clyde tackled the problem during the period 1828–32 in two ways: by introduction, firstly, of steam boats, and secondly of swift horse-drawn passenger boats. The first steam boat to go into regular service there, the *Cyclops*, in 1830, was a horse drawn boat reconstructed with a steam engine and stern paddle wheel in accordance with plans obtained from New Orleans. She was followed by at least three others which plied, for passengers and goods, between Glasgow and Edinburgh and ports on the

Forth: but bank damage was excessive and all had been discontinued by 1839.

Meanwhile the canal company was having greater success in following the Paisley Canal's example in using light, swift passenger boats drawn by two horses. In 1831 they had reduced the time taken for the 24½-mile journey from Glasgow to Lock 16 (Falkirk) from six hours to three.

The Aire & Calder Navigation was acting similarly. The first of many steam tugs was introduced in 1831; and there were steam and fast horse-drawn passenger boats operating a year or two later. These latter do not seem to have long outlived the opening of the Leeds & Selby Railway in 1834, but the steam tugs were a continuing success. The banks of the canal to Goole were protected against their wash.

Other canals used horse-drawn swift passenger boats. The Lancaster Canal, faced with the threat of construction of a railway parallel, put on the first of three passenger boats based on those of the Paisley Canal, in 1833: they covered the 30 lock-free miles from Preston to Lancaster in 3 hours. The same year another 'Scotch Boat' was brought south by a consortium of canal companies, ran speed trials on the Oxford Canal's new line, and was then purchased by the Kennet & Avon Canal Co.: she went into service between Bath and Bradford-on-Avon. There were extensive turnpike road improvements in progress in the district at this period, and Brunel was surveying the GWR as well.

The Grand Canal in Ireland, which had earlier made its own experiments with fast boats, accelerated its daytime passenger boat services in 1834 by introducing 'Scotch Boats'. This line of development seems to have been taken to the extreme on the Shannon Navigation's Limerick-Killaloe canal. Charles Wye Williams had probably seen trials of the Forth & Clyde boats and appreciated that swift boats needed to be long in relation to their beam. The

Brunel's paddle steamer Great Western *passes Portishead outward bound on her maiden voyage, from Bristol to New York, April 1838.*

maximum length of boat to pass through the canal locks, however, was 74 ft 9 in.; Williams designed a boat 80 ft long with bow and stern which hinged upwards when passing through locks. One may reasonably see in this a continuation of the line of thought which produced the watertight bulkhead. According to an article by J. F. Petree (*Transactions of the Liverpool Nautical Research Society* Vol X) this boat was highly successful.

Development did not stop there, however. Ruth Delany (*The Grand Canal of Ireland*) notes a series of experiments with a boat designed by Mr Watson, manager of the Shannon Navigation Company, in which Williams was involved. The boat parted in the middle, and the two halves passed through locks side by side. A scale drawing, apparently original, of a vessel answering to this description is held by the Waterways Museum, Stoke Bruerne: 'Plan of a Canal Passage Boat planned and built under the Directions of William Watson Esq 1840', it depicts a hull of two interlocking halves; the overall length is 117 ft and beam about 6 ft 6 in. There is accommodation for first and second class passengers, two luggage compartments and a bar. Narrower than a narrow boat, but more than half as long again, this vessel must indeed have been a striking sight in operation.

PS *Great Western*

That is a byway in marine development into which, however fascinating, we must not be deflected to excess, for other developments of far greater importance were taking place.

The story is famous of how, at a meeting of the directors of the Great Western Railway Company in October 1835, only about two months after the company had got its Act, someone expressed misgivings about the enormous length of the line they planned to build: to which Brunel made his well-known response that they should make it longer – they should have a steam boat to go from Bristol to New York and call it the *Great Western*.

To the student only of railway history, that reply seems the classic out-of-context remark. Yet in truth Brunel's background was, as we have seen, closer to marine engineering than railways. Furthermore, he was aware of a principle of which many were not. Despite a successful west-to-east crossing of the Atlantic in 1833 by the Canadian PS *Royal William* under steam all the way, except when the boilers had to be shut down to clear them

of salt, there was a strong body of opinion that held that no ship would ever be able to steam all the way from Britain to the USA because it could never carry enough coal: if the size of the hull were, say, doubled, to increase the coal capacity then, it was thought, double the power would be used to propel it, requiring yet more coal, and so on. To Brunel, however, it was clear that resistance to ships passing through the water did not increase in direct proportion to their tonnage, but rather that while tonnnage was related to the cube of dimensions, resistance was related to their square. Therefore a big steam ship was not merely practicable but desirable.

The GWR directors were convinced, or at any rate sufficient of them were to form the Great Western Steamship Company. The PS *Great Western*, 236 ft long overall and 58 ft beam over the paddle boxes, was built to Brunel's design, launched in July 1837 and engined by Maudslay, Sons & Field. She had two of the largest engines they had built, each with a cylinder of $73\frac{1}{2}$ in. diameter by 84 in. stroke, providing a total nominal horse power of 450, and indicated horse power of 750. She was ready for her maiden voyage by April 1838, which was two months before the opening of even the first section of her parent railway.

Establishment of the GWSS Co. as a Bristol venture had, however, provoked immediate responses from shipowners in Liverpool and London, who were anxious not to be beaten in starting a steamship service across the Atlantic. One of the backers of the Transatlantic Steamship Company, formed in Liverpool, was C. W. Williams and, pending completion of a large vessel, the new company chartered a much smaller one, *Royal William* (but not the vessel of the same name mentioned above) from Williams's City of Dublin Steam Packet Company. In London the British & American Steam Navigation Company was formed and, equally pending construction of a large vessel, to be named the *British Queen*, chartered the *Sirius* which, like the *Royal William*, was intended only for the Irish Sea service.

Sirius, not much more than half the size of the *Great Western* (their gross registered tonnages were 703 tons and some 1,320 tons respectively), was ready first. She set out from Cork on 4 April; *Great Western* left Bristol, a day's steaming farther away from New York, on 8 April. Despite bad weather and head winds, *Sirius* arrived off New York on 22 April and docked on the 23rd: later the same day the *Great Western* arrived. *Sirius* was down to her last 15 tons of coal, but *Great Western* had 200 tons to spare: the

The SS Archimedes, *built in 1838 to demonstrate Francis Pettit Smith's patent screw propeller, is here shown in a strong breeze off the North Foreland. The working of the screw propeller is unaffected, and the artist makes the point by depicting also a paddle steamer which, as she heels over, has one paddle wheel lifted almost out of the water.*

former's voyage was heroic, but the latter's was the substantial achievement. *Royal William* eventually arrived from Liverpool, after a crossing lasting nearly 19 days, on 24 July. *Sirius* made one more crossing to New York, and *Royal William* two more, before delivery of larger ships enabled them to return to the Irish Sea. *Great Western*, however, settled down to make more than sixty crossings in eight years.

Brunel plans the *Great Britain*

In 1838 with the *Great Western* operating successfully, Brunel and the GWSS Co. started to plan a sister ship. Originally intended as a wooden ship of the same size, her design evolved rapidly through several stages and it was for an iron-hulled ship, to be as large as 3,270 tons gross, that the keel was laid in July 1839. Her name was to be *Great Britain*. Because her size was unprecedented she was built not on a slipway but in a dry dock made for the purpose at Bristol, and construction was undertaken by the company itself, as was construction of the engines.

This meant that it needed to install machine tools at the dry dock, and for them James Nasmyth was approached. By now he was a partner in Nasmyth Wilson & Co. of Patricroft, near Manchester: the firm's location had been chosen for its transport facilities, because not only was it bounded along one side by the Bridgewater Canal, but on another – a sign of changing priorities – by the Liverpool & Manchester Railway. It is well known how Francis Humphrys, the GWSS Co. engineer, in despair because no existing tools could manufacture a 30 in.

diameter paddle shaft he needed, wrote to Nasmyth for advice: at which Nasmyth immediately designed the steam hammer, and within half an hour of receiving Humphrys's letter had the details worked out on paper.

Although the steam hammer became one of the most important tools of Victorian engineers, the paddle shaft which had prompted its invention was never needed. For completion of the *Great Britain*'s paddle engines – construction had already started – was pre-empted by the arrival in Bristol in May 1840 of the SS *Archimedes* which was demonstrating the advantages of the recently-invented screw propeller. It was as a screw steamer that the *Great Britain* was eventually completed.

That, however, was not to be until late in 1844, and to follow her story through at this stage would be to jump too far ahead. What must be done first is to trace the development of the screw propeller.

The Screw Propeller

The concept of the screw propeller was old, antedating even the use of steam power. Many had considered it, including some famous names – Watt, Fitch, Fulton for example. As early as 1804 in the USA, Col. John Stevens had successfully operated a small steam boat driven by a pair of screw propellers of about 18 in. diameter. But when steam boats went into commercial service it was, as we have seen, with paddle wheels.

Inventors continued to be fascinated by screw propellers, but it was far from simple to establish suitable combinations of their many variables. These included

Captain John Ericsson, 1803–1889, was the designer of the locomotive Novelty which participated in the Rainhill Trials, and also one of two successful inventors of a screw propeller for boats and ships.

The Robert F. Stockton was built of iron by Laird of Birkenhead in 1838, and fitted with Ericsson's propeller and two-cylinder engine. She was sailed across the Atlantic in 1839 to be used as a canal tug in the USA.

dimensions, number of turns and threads or blades, pitch, blade angle and blade shape, the number of propellers and its – or their – position on the hull; and once these had been established, power had to be transmitted from engine to propeller, and thrust from propeller to hull. Several patents were taken out during the 1830s: the breakthrough came from two of them taken out almost simultaneously in 1836. One of them was taken out, in May, by Francis Pettit Smith; the other, in July, by John Ericsson.

Ericsson we have met before, at Rainhill. Pettit Smith was a farmer whose hobby was making model boats. The original part of his invention was not so much the shape of the propeller as its position, forward of the rudder. This made a vessel fitted with Pettit Smith's propeller easy to steer, and at the same time it was simple to transmit power to it. In 1836 Smith had a steam boat built and fitted with a screw propeller in this position; the boat was small, rather less than 32 ft long, and named *Francis Smith*. She was tried out first on the Paddington branch of the Grand Junction Canal and then on the North Kent coast. Drive was through bevel gears and the propeller, which was made of wood, had two complete turns; during trials half of it broke off and the speed of the boat increased.

The performance of the *Francis Smith* was so promising that The Ship Propeller Co. was formed to promote the use of Smith's screw propeller. It was to the order of this company that the SS *Archimedes* was built in 1838. She was 125 ft long overall, rigged for sailing (as was still usual with steam ships at this period), in her case as a three-masted topsail schooner; and she was fitted with an engine constructed by the Rennie brothers which drove the pro-

peller through gears. Her first propeller had a single thread, making one complete turn; this was later replaced experimentally by other propellers which were double-threaded, each thread making half a turn, and it was discovered that a short segment of a screw gave best results. The *Archimedes* was a success and it was during the course of a demonstration voyage round the coast of Britain that she came to Bristol and aroused the interest of Brunel. The consequences are described on page 200.

Ericsson's Propeller

During his first ten years in England, Capt. John Ericsson had taken out thirty patents for inventions. After Rainhill he experimented with various methods of making the locomotive *Novelty* steam better, and built two locomotives, called *King William IV* and *Queen Adelaide*, of an improved version. In them the draught for the fire was intended to be produced by a fan above it: they were failures.

He also experimented with a rotary steam engine in conjunction with William Laird, the Birkenhead shipbuilder, and F. B. Ogden, the United States consul in Liverpool. Ogden had been a pioneer of steamship operation in the USA – as early as 1815 he had obtained two engines from Fenton, Murray & Wood for use in steam boats on the River Mississippi.

It was impracticable to adapt side paddle wheels to canal narrow boats which had to pass through locks 7 ft wide, and it may have been this which first drew Ericsson's attention to propulsion of boats from the stern. By 1833 he was carrying out experiments with various types of stern propellers, installed in a narrow boat at the request of canal carriers Robins & Mills, and in 1834 he experimented on the Regent's Canal with steam propulsion of a boat by means of movable shutters resembling Venetian blinds. His invention of a screw propeller seems to have been a continuation from these experiments.

Ericsson designed his screw propeller in 1835. In his own words, it consisted of 'a series of segments of a screw, attached to a thin broad hoop supported by arms so twisted as also to form part of the screw'. The arms radiated from a boss on the propeller shaft; in early applications at least there were two contra-rotating propellers mounted coaxially one astern of the other, with the forward propeller mounted on a tubular shaft through which the shaft to the rear propeller passed. Ericsson's propeller was mounted aft of the rudder.

In 1837 – and this appears to have been wholly original thinking – he designed a high-pressure steam engine to be coupled direct to the propeller shaft. Its two cylinders were placed at right angles to one another and at 45 degrees to the vertical centre line of the engine, one either side of it; their connecting rods drove a single, common crank pin and the crankshaft was in line with the propeller shaft to which it was coupled.

In association with F. B. Ogden, Ericsson then had an experimental vessel, 45 ft long, built on the Thames and launched in the spring of 1837: she was named the *Francis B. Ogden* and was fitted with screw propeller and engine to Ericsson's design. Her trials were extensive, effective and well-publicised; and though senior representatives of the Admiralty, when taken for a cruise, remained unimpressed, the trials did attract the attention of Robert F. Stockton, an American builder of canals then visiting England, who ordered a steam canal tug with an iron hull to be built by Laird of Birkenhead, and fitted with Ericsson's engine and propeller.

Before this vessel was completed, however, a screw propeller driven by a single cylinder engine was fitted to one of Robins Mills & Co.'s horse-drawn fly boats, by Ericsson in association with John Braithwaite. This, after a demonstration run on the Grand Junction Canal and the Thames, made a commercial voyage with eleven tons of goods from London to Manchester, and then gave further demonstrations in the Manchester area. The voyage was reported at length in the *Manchester Guardian* and this report was repeated in the *Mechanics' Magazine* (vol. xxix page 283),

complete with some acid comments on inaccuracies.

This boat was called *Novelty* and according to the *Guardian* the boiler had previously been used on one of the locomotives on the Liverpool & Manchester Railway. The *Mechanics' Magazine* pooh-poohs this notion, pointing out that the boiler, only 5 ft 10 in. long, was one invented by Capt. Ericsson. Nevertheless, Dendy Marshall's *Locomotives* states that the *Novelty* locomotive had been rebuilt in 1833 with a tubular boiler, so it is intriguing to speculate whether Braithwaite and Ericsson might have reused the original boiler, modified and shortened, in the canal boat which was given the same name. A more mundane explanation would be that the combination of vessel name and engineers might have given rise to such a rumour.

The tug being built at Birkenhead was launched in July 1838 and named *Robert F. Stockton* after her owner. After trials on the Mersey she was taken by sea down to the Thames, where she ran further trials in public, satisfactorily towing four coal lighters. Then, in April–May 1839, she was taken across the Atlantic under sail – at 70 ft length and 10 ft beam a remarkably small vessel to make the voyage. She did so successfully, however, and operated for many years, as intended, as a canal tug.

During 1839 another iron canal steamer, called the *Enterprise*, was built with an Ericsson propeller and entered service on the Ashby Canal that August as a passenger boat. This venture proved unprofitable, but she was subsequently used for several years to tow coal boats on the Trent & Mersey.

By 1839 Ericsson was working again with Braithwaite, constructing the Eastern Counties Railway. It evidently seemed to him, however, that the USA offered greater scope than Britain for his propeller and other inventions: in November 1839 he took passage to the USA aboard PS *Great Western*. Three years after his arrival, there were thirteen river steamers in the USA using his propeller, and he stayed there for the rest of a long and inventive life.

There was, however, at least one other application of Ericsson's propeller in England at this period. One was fitted to a 22-ft steam launch called the *Fire Fly* which was launched on to the Oxford Canal at Banbury in 1841. She was owned by H. Warriner, a pupil of Braithwaite & Milner – as Braithwaite's firm had become. It was run by his brother F. Braithwaite and partners. They provided the boiler, and Warriner personally built the engine, with two near-horizontal opposed oscillating cylinders. It is now to be seen in the Science Museum.

CHAPTER EIGHT

The Transport Revolution Completed

Opening of the First Trunk Railways

By the end of 1838 the issue of the transport revolution was no longer in doubt. On land there was long-distance communication by steam railway between London, Birmingham, Liverpool, Manchester and Preston. At sea there was regular transatlantic communication by PS *Great Western* between Bristol and New York. The formative years of steam transport – indeed, of mechanical transport – were over, and the next few years would see a continuing rapid expansion of the long-distance railway network on land and of steamer services at sea. For older methods of transport there lay ahead only overall decline, at a rate which would range from the gentle to the catastrophic.

The start of this phase was marked by completion of the Grand Junction Railway, the first long-distance railway to be based on the example of the Liverpool & Manchester, and its opening for passenger and parcel traffic on 4 July 1837. As on the L & MR, goods traffic started later, in February 1838.

Joseph Locke, aided by contractors such as Thomas Brassey, who had once worked on the Holyhead Road and became the first of the great railway contractors, and by innumerable navvies, had built a line some 78 miles long from Warrington to Birmingham; it passed beneath 100 bridges and 2 canal aqueducts and through 2 tunnels; and over 50 bridges and 5 viaducts. On the formation thus provided, Locke laid track composed of double-headed rails (that is, of dumb-bell cross-section) weighing 84 lb/yard – more than twice the weight of the original Liverpool & Manchester rails – carried in chairs which were mounted, on some sections of the line, on wooden sleepers, and on others, on stone blocks. The wooden sleepers were intended as a temporary expedient, but it was the stone blocks which were in due course replaced. Locke's GJR track was the prototype for the later, familiar, railway track with bullhead rails. Over it, Robert Stephenson & Co.'s newest 2-2-2 locomotives hauled trains of coaches based, like those of the L & MR, on road coach practice. Unlike road coaches, however, they covered the $97\frac{1}{4}$ miles from Birmingham to Liverpool or Manchester in $4\frac{1}{2}$ hours: an average speed, including stops, of 21.6 mph.

Although passenger trains between Birmingham and Wolverhampton now take a later route, much of the rest of the GJR remains in use as a main line. Between Stafford and Warrington it forms part of the West Coast route main line between London and Scotland. Included in this section are the railway's principal civil engineering works, the viaducts over the River Weaver at Vale Royal (OS grid ref. SJ 643706) and Dutton (OS grid ref. SJ 582764).

The Grand Junction Railway's Dutton Viaduct was its biggest engineering work, crossing the valley of the River Weaver, and with it the Weaver Navigation. The viaduct remains in use by the West Coast main line, but is otherwise difficult of access and little known. OS grid ref. SJ 582764.

The first section of the London & Birmingham Railway, from Euston to Boxmoor, was opened on 20 July 1837. Because this railway's engineering works were more extensive than those of the Grand Junction, it took longer to complete. By 9 April 1838 it was open from Euston to Denbigh Hall, north of Bletchley, and from Rugby to Birmingham; Chaplin & Horne's coaches filled the gap until Kilsby tunnel was finished and the line opened throughout on 17 September 1838.

Robert Stephenson had engineered the line, but locomotives were provided by Edward Bury who had built *Liverpool* as a rival to Stephenson's *Planet*. They were mostly 2-2-0s or 0-4-0s, with frames constructed from iron bars rather than plates and so appeared – but probably were not – less robust than Stephenson locomotives. The first mile or so out of Euston is inclined at 1 in 70 and was worked during the early years by cable haulage.

The route of the London & Birmingham Railway is still the basis of the present-day main line between London and Birmingham. Despite quadrupling of the track between Euston and Roade, many original structures remain in use. The most notable, of course, is Kilsby tunnel itself, the north-west portal of which (OS grid ref. SP 565714) can be seen from the A5. One important building which survives, though no longer in railway use, is the Ionic portico provided by architect Philip Hardwick as the entrance to the L & BR's terminus at Curzon Street, Birmingham (OS grid ref. SP 078870), the counterpart of his now-demolished Doric arch at Euston.

The London & Southampton Railway's engineer having got into difficulties, the line was finished by Joseph Locke. It was opened in stages between 1838 and 1840; it also changed its name, in 1839, to London & South Western Railway. Its route from London (the original terminus was at Nine Elms) to Southampton is still the main line, as is that of the Great Western from London to Bristol. Here again the first section was opened in 1838 but the difficulty of boring the $1\frac{3}{4}$-mile Box tunnel (west portal at OS grid ref. ST 829688) delayed complete opening of the line until 1841.

Brunel's civil engineering works were superb: but the locomotives he originally designed for the railway were, as is well known, hopelessly inadequate. The earliest reliable locomotive the GWR had was *North Star* which had been built by Robert Stephenson & Co. for the New Orleans Railway (5 ft 6 in. gauge) but left on the maker's hands, before it was snapped up by the GWR and its gauge

In early stations much use was made of turntables to transfer carriages and waggons from one track to another. This London & Birmingham Railway example (above) was unearthed at Euston during reconstruction of the station.

Broad gauge by night: an Illustrated London News *engraving of 1849 gives a vivid impression of a GWR mail train.*

The west portal of Box Tunnel (below): the tunnel, $1\frac{3}{4}$ miles long, was engineered by Brunel and the main line from London to Bristol still passes through it.

At Denbigh Hall, near Bletchley, the London & Birmingham Railway crossed the Holyhead Road (above); the line (below) is still the main line, here at OS grid ref. SP 863353. For several months during 1838, this was a temporary terminus: trains from Euston terminated here and passengers changed into stage coaches, until completion of Kilsby tunnel enabled the L & BR to be opened throughout.

In recent years the train shed of the original Bristol Temple Meads terminus has been used by BR as a car park (left), but in 1981 it was leased to the Brunel Engineering Centre Trust. How it appeared in the early days is shown in J. C. Bourne's lithograph.

widened. This locomotive was preserved after withdrawal but eventually was cut up in 1906; the replica now displayed in the Great Western Railway Museum, Swindon, was built about 1925 and incorporates many parts from the original locomotive.

A quite remarkable survival is the greater part of the original GWR terminus building at Bristol Temple Meads. The adjoining station now in use grew up some years later on the curve connecting the GWR with the Bristol & Exeter Railway – the original Bristol terminus of which was at right angles to that of the GWR. So the importance of the original GWR station was reduced, though trains still used it until 1965. Subsequently its tracks were removed and its train shed was used as a car park. Then in 1981 the original station buildings – offices and train shed – were leased by British Rail to the Brunel Engineering Centre Trust.

In contrast to the classical terminus buildings of the London & Birmingham Railway, Bristol Temple Meads is Gothic revival. The style was not merely applied to the road frontage, but was carried through to the baronial hall of a train shed with its mock-hammerbeam roof, and even to the interior decorations of the railway company's offices.

To ensure the building's preservation the trust's plans, though still in a state of flux at the time of writing, envisage its use as a national centre for civil engineering, both past and future, combined with sympathetic commercial developments, probably in the vaults, so that the scheme may pay its way. Probably part of the building will be open to the public by the time this is published.

The permanent way designed by Brunel for the broad gauge Great Western comprised, principally, bridge rails (of inverted U section) mounted on longitudinal timber baulks with cross ties at intervals. After some initial problems had been solved, this form of track proved sound and lasted as long as the broad gauge, that is until 1892. Rails redundant after gauge conversion were used for all sorts of purposes. They were used as posts for notices, and in fences, and are still a common sight. They were used in the locks of the Kennet Navigation (which had come to be owned by the GWR) to build frameworks to prevent boats settling on their sloping sides of turf, and as such can be seen in the illustration on page 35. More remarkably, redundant broad gauge track materials were used to construct stardard gauge sidings serving a quarry at Burlescombe, Devon; and from there, after many years of disuse, they were recovered in 1978 by members of the Great Western Society. The society is devoted to preservation of all things Great Western, and has used the materials to construct broad gauge track at its Didcot Railway Centre.

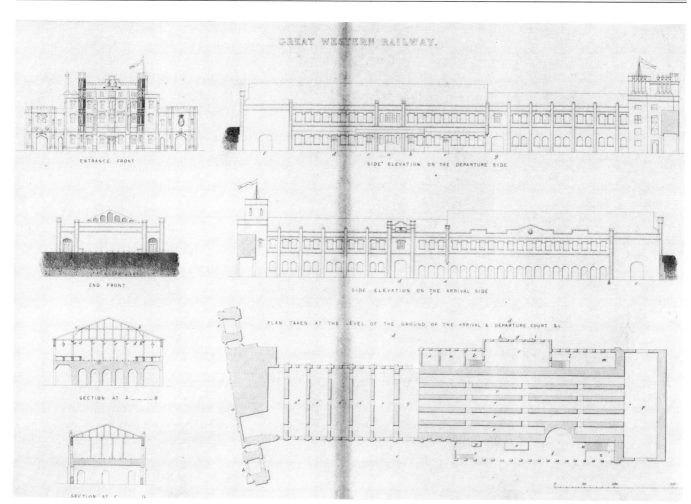

Details of the GWR's Temple Meads terminus in Bristol, as it was in the mid-1840s, were included by S. C. Brees in his fourth series of Railway Practice. The tracks approached on an embankment and in the station itself were at first floor level. The train shed covered the arrival and departure platforms and sidings between. In the track plan (below), the departure platform is shown at the top, and the booking office was beneath it with stairs up to the platform. To the left of the train shed the tracks continue into a carriage shed, and on the extreme left of the plan is the office building, flanked by archways through which passengers entered and left the station. See also page 148.

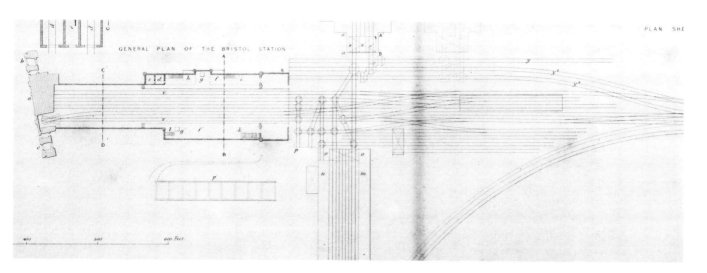

The Network Expands

By the time the Great Western main line was open through to Bristol, the Cheltenham & Great Western Union was open to Cirencester as a branch from Swindon, and the Bristol & Exeter continued the main line as far as Bridgwater. (It eventually reached Exeter in 1844). Elsewhere the railway system was rapidly expanding as other trunk lines authorised in 1836 were completed and opened.

The Birmingham & Derby, renamed the Birmingham & Derby Junction, had been opened in 1839 to Derby from Hampton in Arden on the London & Birmingham; its branch line direct into Birmingham was opened in 1842. The Midland Counties linked Rugby and the L & BR with Nottingham and Derby in 1840. The same year saw completion of the Birmingham & Gloucester, the North Midland (Derby-Leeds), the York & North Midland, the Hull & Selby, the Lancaster & Preston Junction and the Chester & Crewe Railways. All these formed part of the connected system: the last-mentioned line had made of Crewe a junction for the first time. Isolated, for the time being, in South Wales was the Taff Vale Railway (Merthyr-Cardiff), opened that year: the first steam railway, rather than tramroad, in that part of the world, it had been built, on Brunel's advice, to standard gauge; in its upper part it passed through the same valley as the Penydarren Tramroad. The first railway in Ireland, the Dublin & Kingstown, was completed the same year.

In 1841 expansion of the railway system continued apace. This year saw completion of the London & Brighton and Manchester & Leeds Railways, and the Great North of England from York as far as Darlington, where it linked the Stockton & Darlington into the main network. In 1842 there were completed the Edinburgh & Glasgow Railway, the Manchester & Birmingham Railway (which in fact ran from Manchester to Crewe) and the South Eastern Railway from Redhill, on the London & Brighton, as far as Ashford, Kent; it eventually got to Dover in 1844.

The Battle of the Gauges

By the end of 1844 there were some 2,236 route miles of public steam railways in operation, of which 2,013 were standard gauge and 223 broad gauge. The inconvenience of break of gauge, as it was called, first became apparent at Gloucester, where the broad gauge Bristol & Gloucester Railway, opened in 1844, met the standard gauge Birmingham & Gloucester. Passengers, goods, parcels,

livestock, all had to transfer or be transferred from trains on one gauge to trains on the other.

Given the will, the inconvenience could have been mitigated by some form of transferable container, such as were already in use on canals and tramroads, and were considered by Brunel; but the subject was already involved with railway company politics, as the standard gauge companies established in the Midlands strove to prevent the Great Western and its satellites getting powers to build lines into their territories, and vice versa.

In this way the gauge question rapidly became a matter of national politics too. The outcome was a Royal Commission which in 1845 examined witnesses and arranged trials of broad and standard gauge trains. During these the GWR locomotive *Ixion*, built by Fenton, Murray & Jackson (successors to Fenton, Murray & Wood who long before had built rack locomotives for the Middleton Railway), ran from Didcot to London with an 80-ton train at an average speed of 53.9 mph, and reached a maximum of 61 mph. This was far better than anything the standard gauge could match and, even though it was a special event, quite phenomenal compared with the Grand Junction's average speed of 21.6 mph eight years before, which had itself been double the speed of fast horse-drawn coaches.

Even so, the far greater extent of the standard gauge lines meant that they won the 'Battle of the Gauges': with the Gauge Act, 1846, the 4 ft $8\frac{1}{2}$ in. gauge become the obligatory standard gauge for new railways in Great Britain, unless they extended existing broad gauge lines.

The Railway Mania

By this date the opening in the early 1840s of the trunk railways authorised in the mid-1830s, and their successful operation, had attracted the attention of speculators. The most notable among such figures was George Hudson (1800–1871), small businessman who had contrived to become Lord Mayor of York, and chairman of the York & North Midland Railway Company, bringing to railway promotion the dubious practices of contemporary local politics. In 1844 he arranged for the North Midland, the Birmingham & Derby Junction and the Midland Counties Railways to amalgamate as the Midland Railway with himself as chairman. The Great North of England Railway had failed to build its authorised line north of Darlington, so Hudson promoted the Newcastle & Darlington Junction Railway: by means of running powers over some of the existing local railways south of the Tyne, trains from the South and the Midlands reached Gateshead in 1844; the following year, when the Birmingham & Gloucester and Bristol & Gloucester Railways were amalgamated into the Midland, the railways controlled by George Hudson, the 'Railway King', extended continuously from Gateshead to Bristol and to many places in between.

In 1845, railway speculation, fuelled by activities such as Hudons's, reached fever pitch. As there had previously been a Turnpike Mania and a Canal Mania, now there was the 'Railway Mania'. In November 1845 *The Times* reported that the capital invested in existing railways was £71 million, and another £67 million had been spent, or was to be spent, on lines under construction: but the cost of 620 schemes for new railways would come to some £563 million. This was, of course, a financial bubble, and in 1846 it burst. Many who had been, or thought themselves, rich, found themselves poor again. George Hudson, within a few years, was ruined: investigations into one after another of his companies revealed financial irregularities, and by the middle of 1849 he had resigned all his many railway company chairmanships.

In 1845, at the height of the Railway Mania, it was decreed that 30 November would be the closing date for reception, by the Board of Trade, of the plans etc of projected railways for which authorisation was being sought from Parliament. Since some 650 new railway companies were proposed, the scene outside the Board of Trade offices on that Sunday evening approached a riot. The Illustrated London News *depicted the railway room at the Board of Trade packed with rolls of plans for railways (above).*

A monument to the excesses of the Railway Mania is this viaduct over the River Wharfe at Tadcaster (OS grid ref. SE 484438). Intended for a direct railway from York to Leeds promoted by George Hudson and authorised in 1846, the viaduct has never been used for, after the fall of Hudson, the line was not completed.

The Late Forties

During the period of the railway mania, despite its excesses, its folly, its corruption, there were authorised nevertheless some lines which were soundly based, which were well built, and which came to form important components of the railway network. These railways included the Great Northern, from London direct to York, the Chester & Holyhead, the Trent Valley (Rugby to Stafford, forming a direct route from London to the North-West avoiding Birmingham), the Newcastle & Berwick, the Lancaster & Carlisle, the Caledonian from Carlisle to Glasgow and Edinburgh, several other lines in Scotland which were to form the basis of a railway network there, and many more.

Following the formation of the Midland Railway, the process of amalgamation of railway companies continued during 1845–6 with formation of the London & North Western Railway out of, initially, the London & Birmingham, Grand Junction, Liverpool & Manchester and Manchester & Birmingham companies. Such amalgamations of railway companies were to be a continuing practice.

The year 1848 was marked by the death of George Stephenson; but in the same year Queen Victoria, who had made her first railway journey in 1842, was able to travel

south by rail from Montrose to London. The West Coast route was complete from London to Glasgow, Edinburgh, and as far north as Montrose; it reached Aberdeen in 1850. The same year, with the opening of the Great Northern Railway, it was possible to travel by the East Coast route from London to Edinburgh and onwards to Aberdeen with the aid of ferries across the Firths of Forth and Tay; and the opening of the Britannia Tubular Bridge built by Robert Stephenson over the Menai Strait completed the rail route from London to Holyhead. In 1850 there were 6,084 miles of public railway open in Great Britain. The basic railway system was established, but for the next three-quarters a century the railway network would continue to expand, the pre-eminent means of land transport.

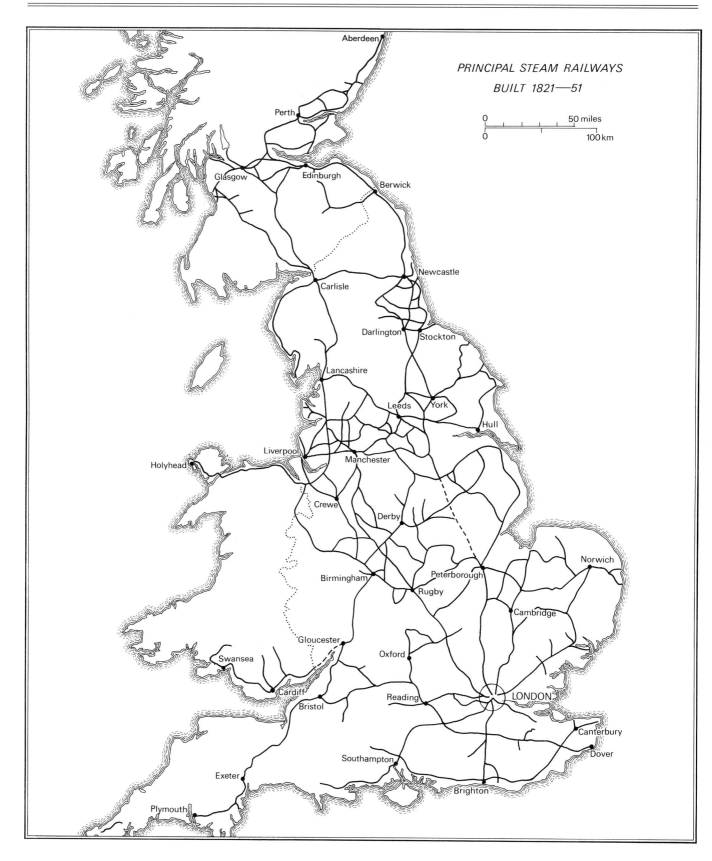

PRINCIPAL STEAM RAILWAYS
BUILT 1821—51

Immensely impressive and, from its wooded location, extraordinarily difficult to do justice to in a photograph, Ballochmyle viaduct (OS grid ref. NS 508254) incorporates the largest masonry span – 181 feet – in Britain. It was built in 1848 for an extension to the Glasgow, Paisley, Kilmarnock & Ayr Railway which shortly afterwards became part of the Glasgow & South Western Railway's route from Glasgow to Carlisle.

Plain but neat and well-proportioned, as befitted the main station of a line promoted largely by Quakers, Darlington North Road station was built in the 1840s by the Stockton & Darlington Railway to replace earlier makeshift passenger accommodation. Today, apart from one platform used by British Rail, it houses Darlington Railway Museum.

The Leeds & Thirsk Railway was opened in 1849. Its workshops in Leeds backed on to the Leeds & Liverpool Canal, and the surviving gateway on to the canal bank suggests that even at that date – or possibly later still – the railway company found it worthwhile to use the canal for transport of engineering materials. OS grid reference SE 289332.

Technicalities of the 1840s

The 1840s therefore were a period primarily of geographical expansion of the railway system rather than technical development of railway equipment. Many of the railway routes then completed remain the basis of the present-day railway network, though some of them have long since been bypassed. Successive schemes of modernisation and improvement on the one hand, and of closure and dismantling on the other, have destroyed many original features: but a lot remain, and some examples are illustrated. Others are mentioned in *The Archaeology of Railways*.

Probably the most important development of the period was not strictly a railway one at all: it was the introduction of the electric telegraph, first used on a railway by the Great Western in 1839. It enabled time interval working to be replaced by block signalling – trains no longer followed each other down a line at successive intervals of time, but instead the line was divided into sections, into each of which only one train was allowed and each section was considered to be blocked until an enquiry telegraphed from one end to the other confirmed it was clear. This contributed greatly to safety. The first line to be equipped with block signalling from the start was the Norwich & Yarmouth, opened in 1844. A telegraph instrument of 1845 from Norwich Trowse is preserved in the Science Museum.

On the track, fishplates to join the ends of the rails together were introduced in 1847, the invention of W. Bridges Adams of the equirotal phaeton. They superseded the earlier method of securing adjoining ends of two rails in a common chair. By this period, too, stone block sleepers were going out fast in favour of cross-sleepers of wood.

Coaches of the type used on the Liverpool & Manchester Railway came into use on the Stockton & Darlington and Leeds & Selby Railways about 1834, and two later S & DR examples, dating from the 1840s, are preserved, one

Columbine, preserved in the National Railway Museum, was built by the Grand Junction Railway at Crewe in 1845. The GJR had suffered much from breakages of locomotive crank axles, particularly on the sharp curves at Newton Junction where the original Warrington & Newton Railway joined the Liverpool & Manchester Railway. In this design cylinders were moved outside the main frames so that a stronger plain driving axle could be used. Many locomotives of this type were built.

in Darlington Railway Museum, the other in the NRM. By far the finest example of a coach surviving from this era, however, is a coach provided by the London & Birmingham Railway about 1842 for Queen Adelaide, and preserved in the National Railway Museum. Although its internal trimmings and external decorations are exceptionally elaborate, it is otherwise similar to first class coaches of its period, and is illustrated on page 149. It was last used in 1849.

In locomotives, to enable steam to be used expansively, link motion valve gears came into use during the 1840s. Locomotive designers were increasingly successful in their attempts to combine elegance with utility, to produce locomotives such as the Jenny Lind type of 1846. The Grand Junction Railway's *Columbine* of 1845 shows the same characteristic and is preserved in the NRM. Other preserved locomotives from this period show earlier trends still surviving. The Furness Railway's no. 3 *Old Coppernob* (now in the NRM) illustrated on page 149, was built to Edward Bury's design in 1846 but is basically similar to locomotives he had built ten years earlier for the London & Birmingham Railway. The Stockton & Darlington Railway's *Derwent* of 1845 has an even earlier origin: it is the culmination of the work commenced by Hackworth to produce a heavy goods locomotive for that railway. She is preserved in Darlington Railway Museum.

No broad gauge locomotives from this period survive – indeed the only original broad gauge locomotive remaining is the untypical vertical-boilered shunting locomotive *Tiny* of 1868 preserved at Buckfastleigh, Devon, by the Dart Valley Railway. This yawning gap among relics of mid-nineteenth century transport is happily to be filled, so far as it can be, by construction to the order of the Science Museum of a full-size working replica of the GWR

broad gauge locomotive *Iron Duke* of 1847. It is hoped that this will be completed during 1984.

The Post Office and the Railways

On 13 July 1837, nine days after the opening of the Grand Junction Railway, the Post Office received a memorial addressed to the Postmaster General by the inhabitants of Leek, Staffordshire. With the opening of the railway, they complained, the mail coach between London and Manchester via Leek had been discontinued. The London mail bags were being brought from the railway at Whitmore, seventeen miles away, by mail cart; and letters for Manchester and Nottingham were being taken by post-boy on horseback to Buxton to connect with a mail coach there. They had to be posted three hours earlier than previously and both the post-boy and the mail cart were less secure than the coach had been.

The document is now held by Post Office Archives, and is endorsed with a note – presumably written by contemporary Post Office staff for the benefit of the Postmaster General – to the effect that it was not from any wish of the Post Office that the mail coach via Leek had been discontinued. The contractors had given notice that, as they would no longer get passengers after the opening of the railway, they could not continue the mail coach. Like all mail coach contractors, they were dependent on passenger revenue to supplement the limited amount they received from the Post Office.

As a consequence of the opening of a railway, this sort of dislocation of mail services was probably not untypical. The London-Manchester mail coach had not in fact been totally discontinued, but had been diverted to run further away from the railway, through Bakewell and Buxton

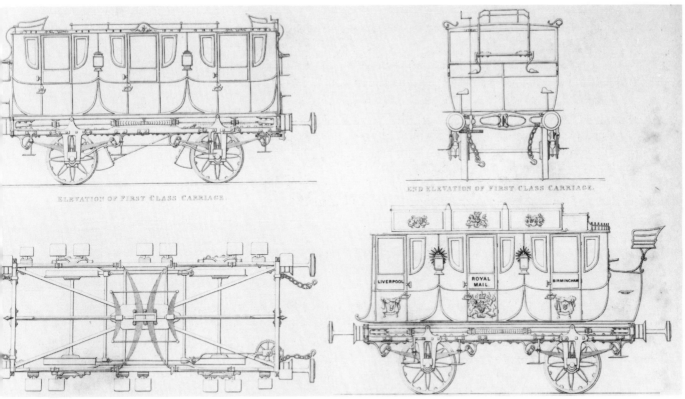

Grand Junction Railway carriages were depicted like this in F. Whishaw's The Railways of Great Britain & Ireland of 1840. Bottom right is a mail coach. The Royal arms are painted on it, as required by an Act of 1838 / *which obliged railways to carry mails. The mail guard has a raised external seat, as on a road coach, but the bags are carried in boxes on the roof.*

instead of Leek and Macclesfield. Four other mail coaches, however, had been taken off completely: London–Liverpool, Birmingham–Liverpool, Birmingham–Manchester and Knutsford–Manchester. Instead, the Grand Junction Railway provided 'mail coaches' on its trains. To places served by rail, they provided a much faster service: but to places on the former mail coach roads, and off the railway, the consequences were no doubt as inconvenient as they were for Leek. Indeed it is interesting to note that Leek, so far as I am aware, has never recovered its position on a main route between London and the North-West, and remains to this day, if I may say so without disparagement to its inhabitants, something of a backwater.

So far as railway passengers were concerned, a GJR mail coach was in effect a superior first class, with four passengers per compartment instead of six. In one of the compartments the seats could be converted into a bed (accommodation of this type was already provided by private road carriages such as the Dormeuse introduced in the early 1820s, and in this as in much else the early railway carriage builders no doubt followed contemporary

road coach practice). The mail bags were carried in a large box on the roof, guarded by a Post Office mail guard seated, as he had been on a road coach, high up on an external seat. In this position on trains, however, it was found that mail guards' eyes suffered much from wind and sparks: provision of spectacles for them was approved by the Postmaster General.

As the railway network spread, so carriage of mails was transferred to trains. By 1841 there were twenty Post Office mail guards on railway routes. On the roads, mail coaches connected with trains, to serve areas where railways had not yet been built. In 1846 for instance the up mail coach was still departing from Glasgow in all its splendour: but it ran only as far as Lancaster, and from there to London the train was used.

In some instances coaches were carried complete by rail over the first part of their journey from London, to finish it by road in due course. With the opening of the London & South Western Railway, for instance, the *Quicksilver* mail coach was carried by train from London to Basingstoke, and continued thence by road.

The Travelling Post Office

Under the mail coach system, letters had been sorted at successive forwarding offices: at the sorting office at Birmingham, for instance, letters for Scotland were sorted and forwarded to the next sorting office at Lancaster; at Lancaster they were sorted and sent forward to Carlisle, and so on; at each forwarding office, mail coaches were delayed while letters were being sorted. Diversion of mails on to the railway was doubly advantageous for it meant that a vehicle could be provided that would be large enough and stable enough for letters to be sorted en route: the first such travelling post office, a converted horse box, was introduced experimentally on the Grand Junction Railway as early as January 1838. In June of that year it was decided to make the arrangement permanent, and the first TPO railway coaches were built and fitted out internally with pigeon holes and so on. Within a fortnight of the opening throughout of the London & Birmingham Railway, a TPO service was introduced, on 1 October 1838, between London and Preston, and TPOs in due course became (and remain) a familiar feature on British railways.

Another development was contemporary with the introduction of TPOs. Even in the days of mail coaches on the roads it had been the practice, when a mail coach passed a village post office at which it did not stop, for the guard to drop its mail bag off, and to catch the outgoing bag from the end of a pole on which it was held out to him by the postmaster. With the first experimental TPO attempts were made to transfer this practice to rail, but it meant that the train had to slow down to 8–10 mph and even so it was frought with danger.

Nathaniel Worsdell, the GJR's carriage builder under whose supervision the first TPO was fitted up, invented an apparatus to exchange mail bags mechanically between train and lineside, patented it and then attempted to sell the patent to the Post Office. He had been too clever: the Post Office was far too wily an institution to accept, and while negotiations continued, one of its own clerks, John Ramsay, designed an iron frame covered with netting, to be fixed to the side of a TPO to catch mail bags, and

On a timebill (right) for the Louth mail coach someone has inked in the improved schedule expected from carrying the coach by rail between Euston and Peterborough from December 1845 (see page 149). The down coach was due at Louth at 9.12 am instead of 11.56 am. Several years earlier (far right) the GPO had already adapted usual mail coach timebill format for the Euston–Preston travelling post office.

A travelling post office (left) between London and Preston was introduced shortly after the London & Birmingham Railway was completed in 1838. The interior is shown above.

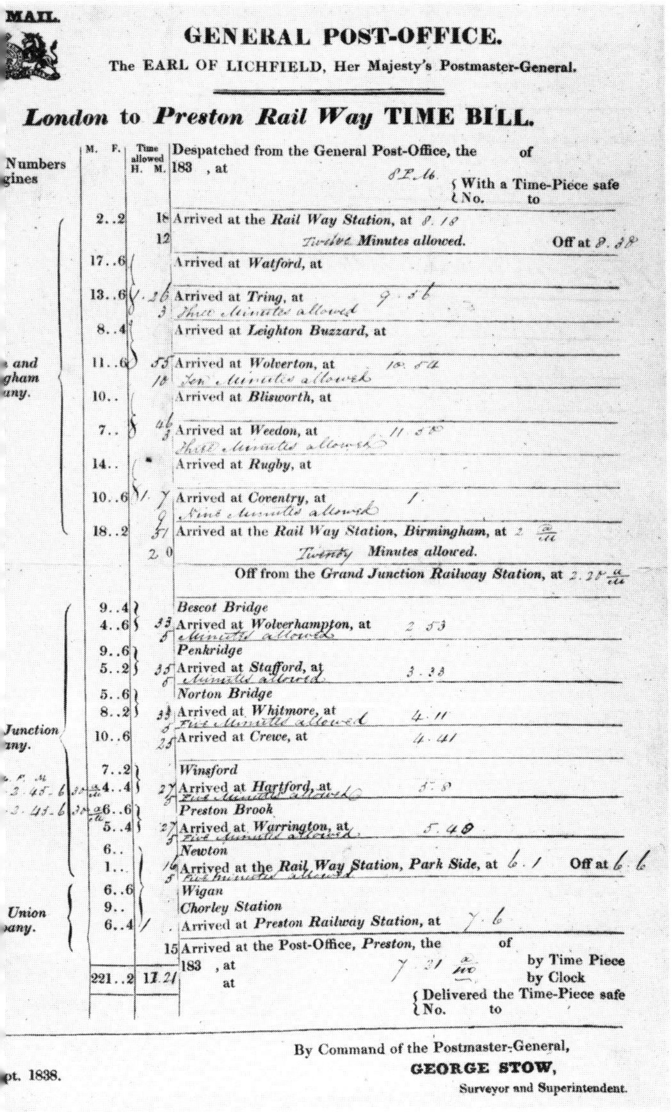

MAIL.

GENERAL POST-OFFICE.

The EARL OF LICHFIELD, Her Majesty's Postmaster-General.

London to Preston Rail Way TIME BILL.

M. F.	Time allowed H. M.	
		Despatched from the General Post-Office, the of 183 , at 8 P.M. With a Time-Piece safe No. to
2..2	18	Arrived at the *Rail Way Station*, at 8.18
	12	Twelve Minutes allowed. Off at 8.38
17..6		Arrived at *Watford*, at
13..6	1.26	Arrived at *Tring*, at 9.56
	3	Three Minutes allowed
8..4		Arrived at *Leighton Buzzard*, at
11..6	55	Arrived at *Wolverton*, at 10.54
	10	Ten Minutes allowed
10..		Arrived at *Blisworth*, at
7..	46	Arrived at *Weedon*, at 11.58
	3	Three Minutes allowed
14..		Arrived at *Rugby*, at
10..6	1.7	Arrived at *Coventry*, at 1.
	9	Nine Minutes allowed
18..2	51	Arrived at the *Rail Way Station, Birmingham*, at 2
	20	Twenty Minutes allowed.
		Off from the *Grand Junction Railway Station*, at 2.20
9..4		*Bescot Bridge*
4..6	33	Arrived at *Wolverhampton*, at 2.53
	5	Minutes allowed
9..6		*Penkridge*
5..2	35	Arrived at *Stafford*, at 3.33
	5	Minutes allowed
5..6		*Norton Bridge*
8..2	33	Arrived at *Whitmore*, at 4.11
	5	Five Minutes allowed
10..6	25	Arrived at *Crewe*, at 4.41
7..2		*Winsford*
4..4	27	Arrived at *Hartford*, at 5.8
	5	Five Minutes allowed
6..6		*Preston Brook*
5..4	27	Arrived at *Warrington*, at 5.40
	5	Five Minutes allowed
6..		*Newton*
1..	16	Arrived at the *Rail Way Station, Park Side*, at 6.1 Off at 6.6
	5	Five Minutes allowed
6..6		*Wigan*
9..		*Chorley Station*
6..4		Arrived at *Preston Railway Station*, at 7.6
	15	Arrived at the Post-Office, *Preston*, the of 183 , at 7.21 by Time Piece at by Clock
221..2	11.21	Delivered the Time-Piece safe No. to

By Command of the Postmaster-General,
GEORGE STOW,
Surveyor and Superintendent.

pt. 1838.

another apparatus to drop a bag from the TPO at a point where boards had been positioned to prevent its rolling under the wheels.

On 30 May 1838, two days after Worsdell's offer had been finally turned down, Ramsay's apparatus was tried out experimentally at Boxmoor on the still-incomplete London & Birmingham Railway. It was successful, and became standard equipment for TPOs; Ramsay got a payment of £500 from the Post Office on condition that he took out no patent!

This was the origin of the mail bag exchange apparatus which became a common sight on British railways and continued in use until the early 1970s. The Great Western Society at Didcot has preserved a comparatively recent example, and operates it from time to time. A replica of an 1838 travelling post office was built by the London, Midland & Scottish Railway in 1938 for the centenary of the service and is preserved by the National Railway Museum.

Rapid expansion of the railway system during the 1840s meant correspondingly rapid contraction of the mail coach system on the roads. The last horse-drawn mail coach to serve London was that to Norwich via Newmarket; it ceased in 1846. In the provinces, along routes not yet paralleled by railways, there were still mail coaches in the 1850s between, for instance, Plymouth and Falmouth, Cheltenham and Aberystwyth, and Derby and Manchester, and in the 1870s between Wick and Thurso. In 1907 M. M'Iver, 'Posting Master and Mail Coach Contractor' was still advertising, in Baddeley & Ward's guidebooks, details of the 'old-established coach service' which left Achnasheen station, Highland Railway, on the arrival of the South Mail, for Loch Maree and Gairloch; but to it he had also added a 'public motor service'. No railway was ever built on this route, and today it is operated by Post Office minibus: the wheel has come full circle.

Stage Coaches and Railways

With the carriage of mails, then, there was some continuity through the change from coach to train, despite transitional problems such as those of the inhabitants of Leek, and the average 40 minutes late arrival daily of the mail train at Newcastle upon Tyne recorded between June 1853 and March 1854. With stage coaches it was different. 'There rises my *arch* enemy' John Kershaw coachman of the Hitchin–London coach would remark, pointing with his whip at the Great Northern Railway's Welwyn Viaduct as it took shape. Coach proprietor B. W. Horne had earlier put it differently but equally succinctly to the 1838 House of Commons Select Committee on Communications by Railroads. The following exchange took place:

The chairman: 'As the railroad system expands, you calculate upon the probability of a great diminution of the business of coach proprietors?'

Horne: 'Annihilation is the best word to apply to it.'

He was right. Innumerable stage coaches were taken off the road as soon as a competing railway was opened – Kershaw's Hitchin coach was one among the many. A proprietor who did attempt to stem the tide was Edward Sherman. The *Red Rover* London–Manchester coach had been taken off on the opening of the Grand Junction Railway. Three months later it was put back on again: perhaps it was hoped that a through service, without the inconvenience of changing from road to rail in Birmingham, would attract sufficient passengers despite its comparative slowness. It did not; and the coach was soon taken off again. Sherman was more prudent when the London & Birmingham Railway was completed: the Shrewsbury *Wonder* was carried by rail between Birmingham and London.

William Chaplin, whose coaching business had an annual turnover of £$\frac{1}{2}$ million, was even more prudent. Not only did Chaplin & Horne supply the coaches to fill the gap in the London & Birmingham Railway until it was completed, they also acted as goods delivery agents in London for the Grand Junction Railway. Then Chaplin sold out all his coaching interests, and with the proceeds invested in the London & South Western Railway. He was chairman by 1843 and held the position for many years.

As chairman of the LSWR Chaplin may well have re-encountered former employees once again in his employment, for many stage coach guards found new employment on the railways. Railways inherited from coaching the practice of appointing a guard to take charge of a train, and coach guards provided the only reservoir of men with even remotely relevant experience. One task which was new to them was that of applying the brakes when necessary. As on a road coach, the railway guard initially rode high up on an outside seat, and passengers' luggage was carried on the roof of the coach in which they travelled. Later, as speeds increased, guards and luggage, and also the mails, were moved down into purpose-built vans. 'Guard' and 'coach' were not the only coaching terms

which made the transition to railway use – there were others, such as 'up' and 'down' for coaches, or trains, travelling respectively up to London or down to the country.

Coachmen were less fortunate than guards: railways had little use for their skills, A few were lucky, finding that their skills were still appreciated in gentlemen's service, or usable as drivers of omnibuses. Some became innkeepers: yet with the rapid diminution in long-distance road traffic the innkeeper's business was declining too. Not only were there fewer travellers wanting refreshment or accommodation, but there was a declining demand for post horses.

There came, eventually, in the 1860s a revival of interest in coaching, rather as a later age discovered railway preservation. It led to the establishment of several public coaches on routes radiating from London, on which people might once again savour the past means of travel, and to the expansion of clubs for those who enjoyed driving four-in-hand as a sport. Such clubs had originated early in the 1800s. It is from this revival period that many surviving coaches date, to confuse the unwary who may think they are admiring actual relics of the era of long-distance coaching. As a sport, driving continues to be popular.

Carriers of goods by road found themselves in a different position from proprietors of coaches, a consequence of the long-established principle that a highway should be open to all comers. Established carriers were admitted to a share in railway goods traffic, using either their own or the railway companies' vehicles, though the extent to which they might do so varied greatly from line to line. At one extreme was the Liverpool & Manchester Railway, which carried all goods on its own account and excluded carriers; at the other was the neighbouring Bolton & Leigh Railway which, with the Kenyon & Leigh Junction, was worked by carrier John Hargreaves who even provided the locomotives. In between came concerns such as the London & Birmingham, which let carriers use the railway for long-distance carriage of goods which they collected and delivered by road. Controversy went on for years over the extent to which steam railways should either admit carriers, to avoid monopoly and keep rates down, or should not admit them, so that all trains and vehicles should be under the control of the railway company in the interest of safety. Safety was, perhaps, the respectable face of monopoly; but in the end safety, by and large, won. Nevertheless the 'private owner' wagon became a feature of railways in Britain, and to this day provides a reminder that public railways were originally thought of as highways open to all.

What happened to Turnpike Trusts

The decline of long distance traffic on roads parallel to railways was to a limited extent compensated for by an increase in short distance traffic on roads to and from railway stations. So while grand improvement schemes for long distance roads, such as that prepared by Telford for the Great North Road, were quietly forgotten, coachbuilding and design of private coaches continued to evolve throughout the Victorian era, though in terms of refinement of craftsmanship rather than technical innovation. For public use, omnibuses, introduced in 1829, became popular in towns; Hansom cabs originated about 1836.

For many turnpike roads, however, railways meant extreme competition. Between London and Birmingham, for instance, the Holyhead Road turnpike trusts' income was reduced by half following completion of the London & Birmingham Railway. The consequence of such an effect, multiplied across the country, was that trusts could no longer afford to maintain their roads and had to call on parishes – whose parishioners were already paying tolls – for financial aid. Reform in general was slow in coming but, after the mid-1870s, Parliament ceased to renew Turnpike Acts as a matter of course and the trusts therefore were gradually extinguished. Their roads reverted to parishes, or to combinations of parishes called highway districts; in 1888 the Local Government Act set up county councils with responsibility for main road maintenance, and in 1895 the last turnpike trust was dissolved.

Something of how turnpike roads appeared during the height of the steam railway era can be gathered from *Lark Rise to Candleford* in which Flora Thompson described her 1880s childhood in Oxfordshire. There was hardly any traffic on the turnpike road then, and people said too much money was being spent on repairs: she was often taken for a walk for a mile along the turnpike road and back without seeing anything on wheels; except, perhaps, one of the first penny-farthing bicycles, a harbinger, had she but known, of road revival to come.

Canals and Railways

Canal passenger boats were no more able to compete with steam railways than were stage coaches. Generally – as on the Paisley Canal for instance – they were withdrawn soon after a parallel railway was opened. A few canals managed for a time to run passenger boats in connection with trains on adjoining railways, until directly-competing railways were opened. Such canals included the Lancaster Canal with its swift boats, and the Ashton and Peak Forest Canals. Horse-drawn passenger boats on the Bridgewater Canal seem to have lasted as long as anywhere – the *Duchess-Countess* was still carrying passengers and parcels in 1913.

With canal-borne freight traffic, however, things were different. Canal companies did not find that freight deserted them immediately a railway was opened. They often retained it, or even increased it, but only by means of extensive toll reductions. Goods carried on the Grand Junction Canal, for instance, amounted in 1838 to 948,481 tons and had risen in 1858 to 1,142,450 tons; but receipts for the same years fell from £152,657 to £67,634. Maintenance of canal traffic was assisted by the Canal Carriers Act of 1845 which enabled canal companies to act as carriers as well as providing the routes. Several companies took advantage of it to set up carrying departments; they included the Grand Junction and the Leeds & Liverpool.

So although the construction of steam railways was a threat to canals, canals themselves represented substantial competition for railways.

Four main trends emerged:

Purchase of canals by railway companies and their conversion into railways;

Purchase of canals by railway companies and their continued existence as canals;

Establishment of canal/railway companies with powers to operate both forms of transport;

Continued independence of some canal companies.

Canals Converted

Physical conversion of canals into railways was much talked of but little practised – rather like conversion of railways into roads in our own time. Conversion of the Croydon Canal has already been mentioned; West Croydon station is on the site of the canal basin. The Paisley Canal was eventually purchased by the Glasgow & South Western Railway Co. in 1869; it was closed in 1881 and a railway built along its course. This involved reuse of Telford's Blackhall aqueduct, over the White Cart Water, as a railway bridge (OS grid ref. NS 494634), though the most obvious reminder of the railway's previous existence was the station called 'Paisley Canal'. This, along with the line itself, was closed to passengers while this book was being written; a journey along it a few months before closure provided the curious experience of travelling along a contour railway: plenty of sharp curves but few earthworks and apparently no gradients at all.

Railway-owned Canals

A great many canals were eventually purchased or leased by railway companies. The railway companies' motives were, in their initial stages, to buy off opposition to their bills for railway construction, and subsequently to eliminate a competitor for traffic. Amalgamation of a canal company with a railway company required the sanction of Parliament, and was likely to be strongly opposed by carriers, who had seen tolls come down, and now saw them likely to rise again; and by other canal companies, particularly where it seemed that a link in a chain of canals forming a continuous route might be broken.

Although canals, when acquired by railway companies, came complete with obligations for their continued maintenance, there was much that railway companies could, and did, do to discourage canal traffic and stifle competition, by misuse of canal company powers which they inherited. For instance, tolls could be raised to the legal limit; stoppages for 'repairs' made as long as possible instead of as brief as possible, use of locks by night prohibited. The record of the Great Western Railway in connection with the Kennet & Avon and Stratford Canals was particularly bad. The Regulation of Railways Act, 1873, eventually imposed on railway companies a general obligation to maintain their canals and keep them open. Even so, there was no requirement and little incentive for railway companies to do anything to improve their canals or keep them up to date.

Only where a canal extended beyond its owning railway, into territory served by other railways, was there an incentive for a railway company to exploit its canal, in the interest of inter-railway competition. The main line of the Trent & Mersey Canal, owned by the North Staffordshire Railway, was the most notable instance; the Manchester, Sheffield & Lincolnshire Railway (later the Great Central) also acted in this way with its Ashton, Peak Forest and Macclesfield Canals.

The network of the Birmingham Canal Navigations was a special case. In 1845, at the beginning of the railway mania, it moved over 4 million tons of goods: it served all the Staffordshire ironworks, it had 1,500 works located on its banks, and 700 steam engines depended on it for

a supply of water. No railway could provide such a service. Yet the Staffordshire ironmasters did want a railway in their district, and the London & Birmingham Railway was anxious to extend to the north-west, relations with the Grand Junction Railway at the time being strained. The upshot was an agreement by which the BCN company would sell to the L & B Railway the land needed to build a railway from Birmingham to Wolverhampton, generally beside the canal, and the railway company would guarantee a four per cent dividend by the canal company. Control of the canal was to stay with the canal company, unless the railway company was actually called upon to make good its guarantee, in which event control would pass to the railway company.

By the time this had been approved by Act of Parliament, railway circumstances had changed: the London & Birmingham had amalgamated with the Grand Junction to form the London & North Western Railway; but the agreement went ahead and the canalside railway was built – today it is the main line between Birmingham and Wolverhampton. The railway company's dividend guarantee was not called upon until the late 1860s and in the meantime, since canals rather than railways still met the local transport needs of the district, canal/rail interchange basins were built and canal improvements continued apace: notably the 3,027-yd long Netherton tunnel, with dual towpaths and, originally, lit by gas. It was completed in 1858; the north portal is at OS grid reference SO 967908. From the 1870s onwards, however, the BCN was railway-dominated.

The Shropshire Union Railways & Canal Co. promoted canal traffic and visual evidence of this survives. This is the canalside warehouse at Ellesmere, Shropshire. OS grid ref. SJ 398346.

Canal/Railway Companies

Continued development of the Birmingham canals was almost nullified by proposals of 1845 to convert the line of the Birmingham & Liverpool Junction and adjoining canals into a railway. The B & LJ, after its opening, had had only three years free from railway competition before the opening for freight traffic of the Grand Junction Railway. It never paid a dividend: in 1845 it was absorbed by the Ellesmere & Chester Canal Co. Then, later the same year, at the height of the railway mania, this company obtained powers to change its name to Shropshire Union Railways & Canal Company, to convert many of its canals into railways, and to build others from scratch. It started by building a railway from Stafford to Wellington.

Within a year, circumstances had greatly changed. The railway mania bubble had burst, euphoria had given way to re-action. Furthermore, the amalgamation which formed the London & North Western Railway had taken place. To the LNWR, the Shropshire Union's railway schemes meant dangerous competition. It offered to take the Shropshire Union on lease, and was accepted. The

Shropshire Union company ceased building railways; but its canal and railway system continued to be administered as a distinct entity for many years, managed jointly by the two companies. The canal side was developed, and particularly the company's installations at Ellesmere Port where it joined the Mersey. More recently its warehouses and basins there have provided an appropriate home for the Boat Museum and its unique collection of inland waterways boats and barges.

There were other notable instances of railway-and-canal companies. The town of Huddersfield found itself bypassed by early trunk railway schemes; in 1845 a local company was formed to put it on the railway map, and this styled itself the Huddersfield & Manchester Railway & Canal Company. It bought out the Huddersfield Narrow Canal, and in due course provided Huddersfield with its superb neoclassical station building, one of the finest surviving pieces of railway architecture of its period. The local company was soon swallowed up by the London & North Western, but its name and crest still appear carved in stone on the façade.

The Huddersfield & Manchester Railway & Canal Co.'s crest still appears carved in stone on the façade of Huddersfield station, even though the company was amalgamated with the L.N.W.R. in 1847.

The practice at many early stations was to have one long platform, and Huddersfield's classical frontage, illustrated on page 150, originally backed on to such a single platform, with short bay platforms at each end. Additional platforms were added in the 1880s, but even now the station has a distinctly one-sided appearance.

In the South-East the Thames & Medway Canal Co. employed J. U. Rastrick to lay out a railway beside its canal from Gravesend to Strood, and converted itself into the Gravesend & Rochester Railway & Canal Co. The remarkable feature here was that railway and canal shared the Strood tunnels (one long tunnel had become two shorter ones since a passing place for boats had been excavated in the middle). Through the tunnels the towpath was widened by a continuous timber staging and towpath and staging together carried the track. The railway was opened, for passengers, early in 1845. There were as yet no other railways in the vicinity: at Gravesend trains connected with Thames steam boats, and at Strood with another steam boat which ran on the Medway to Chatham.

Dual use of the tunnels by canal and railway did not last long. The company was bought by the South Eastern Railway Company, the canal through the tunnels filled in, and a double railway track laid. This was opened in 1847; it is still in frequent use by trains between Charing Cross and Gillingham, and is illustrated on page 151.

Canals in the Railway Era

Important canals which were able to remain independent of railways were the Regent's Canal, the Grand Junction Canal and the smaller canals which continued the line to Birmingham and to the Derbyshire/Nottinghamshire Coalfield; the Coventry, Oxford, and Staffs & Worcs Canals; the Aire & Calder Navigation; and (after periods of being leased to railways and subsequently regaining their independence) the Leeds & Liverpool and Rochdale Canals.

During the steam railway era, a very large part of the canal network was therefore composed of canals which were either owned by or associated with railway companies. Whether traffic on them was obstructed or encouraged depended almost entirely on what suited the appropriate railway companies, and the interests of adjoining independent canals were left out of consideration. Since there were sufficient of these railway-owned or associated canals to split apart those canals which remained independent, the canal network, as a national alternative to a railway network, ceased to exist. The overall effect of railways on canals therefore was not one of annihilation, but of stagnation. There were occasional upturns – a revival of interest in water transport reached its zenith with construction of the Manchester Ship Canal late in the nine-

In 1845 and 1846, Strood tunnel (above), built for the Thames & Medway Canal, was shared by canal and railway. This watercolour survives to show the improbable scene. See also page 151.

After the Huddersfield & Manchester Railway & Canal Co. was taken over by the London & North Western Railway, its railway prospered but its canal declined. The latter was navigable until the 1940s but today, in Huddersfield (right), is derelict. Restoration is proposed.

The Rochdale Canal and the Manchester & Leeds Railway at Gauxholme (OS grid ref. SD 932233) in c. 1844 and in 1982. The canal, after a period of railway lease, regained its independence, but eventually closed to navigation in 1952. Here too, reopening is planned.

teenth century, and narrow boats were eventually successfully mechanised by diesel engines early in the twentieth, but when public interest in canals awoke again in the late 1940s it was found they had changed remarkably little over a century.

As for those horse tramroads which had once been such a valuable adjunct to canals, many were upgraded into steam railways, and those that were not eventually closed, unaltered. Traces of them have been mentioned in chapter three.

Railways and Steam Boats

By 1844 there were 75 steamers sailing from the port of Glasgow, of which 47 were small steam boats serving the Firth of Clyde and the remainder were larger vessels going as far afield as Inverness, Sligo, Dublin and Liverpool. At the same period London was served by some 85 steamers, of which 26 were employed about the Thames tideway and estuary, 15 served East Coast ports, 32 crossed to the Continent and about 12 went on distant voyages.

The relationship between steam boats and railways became a complex one. Where a railway was built to carry passengers and parcels between places already served by steam boats, the railway generally prevailed. After the 1830s there was a steady diminution of steam boat services on rivers, up and down estuaries, and along the coast. Some went quickly, some survived a remarkably long time (London–Leith, for instance, into the 1930s), others again survived in the guise of pleasure steamers. Ferry crossings – across estuaries, to islands, between Britain and Ireland, and Britain and the Continent – were a different matter and with these, railways ran in connection to their mutual benefit. Trains started to connect with English Channel steamers in 1843 when the South Eastern Railway reached Folkestone.

There were also many instances where railways, although competing with steam boats between places they served directly, also connected with steam boats to serve places not accessible by rail. For instance, the railways between London and Blackwall, and Glasgow and Greenock, competed with steam boats between their termini, but connected with steam boats serving places further down the Thames and the Clyde. On the Clyde, travel by rail between Glasgow and down-river piers, and by steamer beyond, became a permanent feature. In some cases, however, steamer/rail co-operation was temporary, lasting until a rail route was completed. From 1840, steamers between Liverpool (later Fleetwood) and Ardrossan formed part of a rail-steamer-rail route between London and Glasgow, pending completion of the West Coast all-rail route to Glasgow in 1848.

Screw Propulsion and the S.S. *Great Britain*

The companies set up in the 1830s to operate transatlantic paddle steamer services did not, in the end, have long lives, consequent on, among other things, various disasters to their vessels. In 1840, however, a steamship company which did prove long-lasting was formed, the British & North American Royal Mail Steam Packet Co., forerunner of Cunard Steamship Co. With four steamers it operated a service between Liverpool and Halifax and Boston: the secret of its success was the mail contract from the British Post Office and the subsidy this brought.

Meanwhile, Brunel's *Great Britain* was under construction in Bristol. Brunel and his associates were so impressed by the SS *Archimedes*, the arrival of which in Bristol was mentioned on page 179, that they arranged to have the use of her for several months to carry out a series of trials with screw propellers of various types. From the results of these, and from comparisons made with the PS *Great Western*, Brunel came down firmly in favour of using screw propulsion in his new ship. The hull, compared with a hull for paddle-wheel propulsion, would weigh less, have improved structural stiffness and offer less resistance to head winds and seas. Screw propulsion would be unaffected by the vessel's trim, or by rolling, and it allowed free use of sails. The engine would enjoy regular motion and freedom from shocks, and the steering would be improved. So construction of the paddle engines ceased, and the design of the ship was modified for screw propulsion.

Brunel's report on screw propulsion attracted the attention of the Admiralty and he was asked in 1841 to supervise further trials of screw propellers compared with paddle wheels. There was at this period a strong anti-screw lobby within the Admiralty – Ericsson had already fallen foul of it, and this may have influenced his decision to leave for America – but despite obstruction Brunel eventually carried out the trails: they included the famous tug-of-war in which the screw-driven *Rattler* successfully towed the paddle-wheel driven *Alecto* astern at 2.8 knots when both vessels were steaming full ahead.

While Isambard Brunel had been busy with great rail-ways and great ships, his father Marc Brunel had been steadfastly pursuing the project, against immense difficulty and danger, of boring the tunnel beneath the Thames. A driftway to drain the main tunnel, approaching from the south bank, was eventually cut through into the north bank shaft in 1841; Marc Brunel received a knighthood from the queen. The tunnel was completed in 1843. Later it was adapted for railway use and now forms part of the East London section of London Transport's Metropolitan Line.

As early as 1822 Marc Brunel had patented what he called a triangle engine for paddle steamers. The two cylinders were positioned in line above the keel, at 45 degrees to the horizontal and 90 degrees to one another, so that the connecting rods drove a common crank on the paddle shaft above. Such engines, built by Maudslay, were used to drain the Thames tunnel when under construction; and it was this type of engine, well-tried and familiar to him, that Brunel adapted for screw propulsion to power the *Great Britain*. For so large a vessel, two two-cylinder engines were needed, positioned across the hull with the cylinders of each at an angle of 60 degrees to one another. The cylinders had a diameter of 88 in. and a stroke of 72 in. Drive from crankshaft to propeller shaft was by chains. The main chain drive wheel on the crankshaft was 18 ft 3 in. overall diameter and the driven drum on the propeller shaft 6 ft diameter, an arrangement which increased the crankshaft speed of 18 rpm to a propeller shaft speed of 54 rpm. The Science Museum has a contemporary model of the engines. The original propeller fitted to SS *Great Britain* had six blades of 15 ft 6 in. diameter and 25 ft pitch.

SS *Great Britain* in Service

The *Great Britain* was named by the Prince Consort and launched, by letting water into the dry dock in which she was built, on 19 July 1843. Her iron hull was 322 ft long and 51 ft beam; she had when completed accommodation for 252 passengers, 130 crew and 1,200 tons of cargo. Six masts could carry some 16,000 sq. ft of sails.

Locks had been widened to enable the *Great Britain* to leave the floating harbour at Bristol but, even so, additional masonry had to be removed at the last minute to enable her to get out and pass down the Avon to the sea. So it was not from Bristol, but from the rival port of Liverpool, that on 26 August 1845 she eventually left for New York on her maiden voyage. Her subsequent career equally was

The SS Great Britain *as she appeared during her transatlantic crossings of 1846 (above) – after being re-rigged for the first time, but before she went aground in Dundrum Bay. The hulk of SS* Great Britain *arrives back at the mouth of the Avon in 1970 (above right). She is being restored* *from a derelict hulk to as-new condition in the Bristol dry dock in which she was originally built in the 1840s. This is the stage she had reached by 1981.*

not what her builders had intended, but her hull survivied to become as famous now as when she was built for, back in Bristol, SS *Great Britain* is by far the largest surviving artefact from transport of her period.

She made a promising start, even though the propeller broke up during the second return trip which was finished under sail. A more robust propeller was fitted during the winter, one of her masts removed and her rigging modified. Like this she made two successful return voyages to New York during 1846; and she was starting what should have been a third when faulty navigation put her badly aground in Dundrum Bay on the Irish coast.

The *Great Britain* was salvaged, eventually, but it was the end of the Great Western Steamship Company. Under new owners Gibbs, Bright & Co. (whose senior partner had been associated with the Great Western Railway since its construction) she had a long and successful career working between Liverpool and Melbourne. Then in the early 1880s she was sold and converted to sail only. In this form she made a few voyages between Liverpool and San Francisco until in 1886 she was damaged by gales while attempting to round Cape Horn, and set back to Port Stanley, Falkland Islands. There for many years she was used as a hulk until in 1937 she was scuttled in shallow water.

So robust was that iron hull that it was nevertheless possible for the SS *Great Britain* Project to recover what was left of the ship in 1970 and bring her back to Bristol. This was no mean feat and the story of the project is related in detail by its originator, E. C. B. Corlett, in *The Iron Ship*. On 19 July 1970 the *Great Britain* was returned to the dry dock in which she had been built: the date, dictated by the tides, was to the day the 127th anniversary of her launch, and the consort of the present queen was there to see her re-enter it.

There the SS *Great Britain* is open to the public while the SS *Great Britain* Project makes steady progress towards its aim: to restore the wreck of a ship to her as new 1843 appearance so far as possible. The exterior of the hull has, largely, been restored; a funnel and masts have appeared; and eventually, it is hoped, full-size replica engines will be fitted.

Decline of Sail

With her iron hull and screw propulsion, the *Great Britain* has been described as the forefather of all modern ships*. Brunel, of course, went on to build even bigger with the *Great Eastern* in the 1850s, strictly outside our period, and about the same time steel began to replace iron as a shipbuilding material. But the replacement of sail by steam at sea was a far more gradual process than the replacement of horse by steam on land. In the 1860s fast sailing clippers were still competitive with steam for long-distance carriage of cargo. The total tonnage of British steamships did not equal that of sailing ships until the 1880s; by then the economies resulting from the introduction of compound marine steam engines, and, later on, triple expansion engines, were giving steamships the edge. Sailing ships, however, continued to trade over long distances until the Second World War; on a smaller scale, the last Thames barge to trade under sail did so until 1971. This was the *Cambria*, which is now preserved by the Maritime Trust.

SL *Dolly*

A vessel of earlier date survives to provide a working example of a small screw steamer built as early as the year 1850 or thereabouts. She is steam launch *Dolly*, 41 ft long with elegant clipper bow and counter stern, which was used on Windermere until 1894 when she was moved to Ullswater. There, on 25 February 1895, she sank at her moorings, probably because she filled with water but was inaccessible from the shore because ice was not bearing. Sixty-five years later, in 1960, she was rediscovered on the bed of Ullswater by amateur divers.

She was salvaged during 1962 by members of the Furness Sub-Aqua Club. Oil drums and flexible buoyancy bags were sunk, attached to the wreck, and filled with compressed air to lift her, a task simpler to describe than to carry out. *Dolly* was then taken to Windermere to be restored by G. H. Pattinson. Her wooden hull was treated with oils and preservatives over a period of six months and regained its strength; and, remarkably, it proved possible to reuse, after overhaul, not only the single-cylinder engine but also the boiler. The boat steamed again for the first time in August 1965. The boiler had eventually to be replaced but *Dolly* is still afloat at the Windermere Steamboat Museum, where she supplies a direct link with that period, so long ago and yet so recent, when steam first provided mechanical power for transport by land and water.

*E. C. B. Corlett in the letter to the editor of *The Times* in 1967 from which the recovery project originated.

ACKNOWLEDGEMENTS

I am most grateful for assistance rendered in preparation of this book by the following:
H. Adam (loan of *Steam Boat Companion*); F. E. Alflatt (Science Museum); George Batey (National Mining Museum); D. Blagrove; J. R. Blake (SS *Great Britain* Project); Mrs V. Boa (McLean Museum & Art Gallery, Greenock); A. J. Byrne (Brunel Engineering Centre Trust); J. C. Clayson (Glasgow Museum of Transport); Tony Conder (Waterways Museum, Stoke Bruerne); Mrs C. Constantinides (Post Office Archives); Derek Cross; D. Dyson (Silkstone J. & I. School); M. Ewans; J. Farrugia (Post Office Archives); David De Haan (Ironbridge Gorge Museum Trust); S. G. Dyke (Darlington Railway Museum); T. J. Edgington (National Railway Museum); Ron Fitzgerald (Leeds Industrial Museum); A. R. Griffin (National Mining Museum); A. Jones (Welsh Industrial & Maritime Museum); P. I. King (Northants County Council Archives); D. W. N. Landale; A. P. McGowan (National Maritime Museum); Mrs D. R. Matthews (Windermere Nautical Trust); R. Moore (Silkstone J. & I. School); J. Moxon (Brunel Engineering Centre Trust); E. S. Owen-Jones (Welsh Industrial & Maritime Museum); Mrs E. A. Ransom (for references in *Our Village*, *Lark Rise to Candleford* and *David Copperfield*); John Richards; S. M. Riley (National Maritime Museum); P. Robinson (Birmingham Museum of Science & Industry); S. Sartin (Harris Museum & Art Gallery, Preston); P. W. B. Semmens (National Railway Museum); D. R. Shearer (Paisley Museum & Art Gallery); John Slater (*Railway Magazine*); J. D. Storer (Royal Scottish Museum); Michael Vanns (Ironbridge Gorge Museum Trust); D. J. Wicks (Bath Carriage Museum); the Marquess of Zetland; and officials of: Cynon Valley Borough Council; Dodington Carriage Museum; National Library of Scotland; North Yorkshire County Archives; South Yorkshire County Council; Stamford Town Hall.

I am also most grateful to D. Rendell for excellent photographic processing, and to my family for patient support of an author of whom they have seen less and less as the date for completion of the manuscript drew closer and closer.

APPENDIX Addresses of Principal Museums, etc., mentioned in the Text

Bath Carriage Museum
Circus Mews, Bath, Avon

Beamish North of England Open Air Museum
Stanley, Co. Durham

Birmingham Museum of Science & Industry
Newhall Street, Birmingham, B3 1RZ

Blist's Hill Open Air Museum
(part of Ironbridge Gorge Museum, which see)

The Boat Museum, Dockyard Road,
Ellesmere Port, South Wirral, L65 4EF

Bowes Railway
Tyne & Wear Industrial Monuments Trust
Sandyford House, Archbold Terrace,
Newcastle upon Tyne, NE2 1ED

Brunel Engineering Centre Trust
c/o Hon. Secretary A. J. Byrne
Dartington & Co. Ltd, Bush House
72 Prince Street, Bristol, BS1 4HU

Coalbrookdale Museum of Iron
(part of Ironbridge Gorge Museum, which see)

Darlington Railway Museum
North Road Station
Station Road, Darlington, DL3 6ST

Didcot Railway Centre
Great Western Society
Didcot, Oxfordshire, OX11 7NJ

Exeter Maritime Museum
The Quay, Exeter, EX2 4AN

Glasgow Museum of Transport
25 Albert Drive, Glasgow, G41 2PE

Grangemouth Museum
Victoria Library, Bo'ness Road,
Grangemouth, Stirlingshire

Great Western Railway Museum
Swindon, Wiltshire

Greater Manchester Museum of Science &
Industry
Liverpool Road, Castlefield, Manchester
M3 4JP

Ironbridge Gorge Museum Trust
Ironbridge, Telford, Salop, TF8 7AW

Leeds Industrial Museum
Armley Mills, Canal Road,
Leeds, LS12 2QF

McLean Museum & Art Gallery
9 Union Street, Greenock, PA16 8JH

National Maritime Museum
London, SE10 9NF

National Mining Museum, Lound Hall,
Retford, Nottinghamshire

National Railway Museum
Leeman Road, York, YO2 4XJ

Royal Scottish Museum
Chambers Street, Edinburgh, EH1 1JF

Science Museum
South Kensington, London, SW7 2DD

SS *Great Britain* Project
Gas Ferry Road, Bristol, BS1 6TY

Timothy Hackworth Museum
Shildon, Co. Durham

Waterways Museum
Stoke Bruerne, Nr. Towcester
Northants, NN12 7SE

Welsh Industrial & Maritime Museum
Bute Street, Cardiff, CF1 6AN

Windermere Steamboat Museum
Rayrigg Road, Windermere
Cumbria, LA23 1BN

BIBLIOGRAPHY

The following have been the principal works consulted.

Eighteenth and Nineteenth Century Works
(contemporary or near-contemporary with their contents)

Bell, H., *Observations on the Utility of Applying Steam Engines to Vessels etc.* Glasgow, 1813

Brees, S. C., *Railway Practice* second series 1840, third and fourth series 1847

De Quincey, T., *The English Mail Coach* MacDonald, London, 1956 (1854 version re-issued)

Dodd, G., *An Historical and Technical Dissertation on Steam Engines and Steam Packets . . .* London, 1818

Fulton, R., *A Treatise on the Improvement of Canal Navigation* I & J Taylor, London, 1796

McAdam, J. L., *Remarks on the Present System of Road Making* Seventh edition, 1823

Malet, H. E., *Annals of the Road* Longmans Green & Co. London, 1876

Mechanics' Magazine, various issues

Mitchell, J., *Reminiscences of My Life in the Highlands* Volumes I and II, David & Charles, Newton Abbot, 1971 (re-issue)

Mitford, M. R., *Our Village* Cassell & Co. London 1909

Nimrod (Apperley, C. J.), *The Chace, The Turf and The Road* John Murray, London, 1843

Rees, A., *Cyclopaedia* 1819

Reports of Select Committees of the House of Commons:
    Highways and Turnpike Roads 1811
    Holyhead Roads 1811
    Explosion on Steam Boats 1817
    Holyhead Roads 1822
    Railroad Communications and Transport of Letters 1838
    Turnpike Trusts 1839
    Guards of Mails 1841
    Railway and Canal Amalgamations 1846

Simms, F. W., *Public Works of Great Britain*, 1838

Symington, W., *A Brief History of Steam Navigation* Edinburgh, 1863 (re-issue of 1829 publication)

Steam-Boat Companion J. Lumsden & Sons, Glasgow, 1831

Telford, T., (edited by Rickman, J.) *Life of Thomas Telford*, 1838

Woodcroft, B., *A Sketch of the Origin and Progress of Steam Navigation* Taylor & Walton, London, 1848

Biographies

Bell, D. and Napier, D., *David Napier Engineer* J. Maclehose & Sons, Glasgow, 1912

Brooks, P. R. B., *William Hedley Locomotive Pioneer* Tyne & Wear Industrial Monuments Trust, Newcastle upon Tyne, 1980

Carswell, C., *The Life of Robert Burns* Chatto & Windus, London, 1936

Church, W. C., *The Life of John Ericsson* London, 1890

Dickinson, H. W., *Robert Fulton* John Lane, London, 1913

Dickinson, H. W. and Jenkins, R., *James Watt and the Steam Engine* Moorland Publishing, Ashbourne, 1981

Dickinson, H. W. and Titley, A., *Richard Trevithick* Cambridge University Press, Cambridge, 1934

Dictionary of National Biography

Gilbert, K. R., *Henry Maudslay* HMSO, London, 1971

Hadfield, C., and Skempton, A. W., *William Jessop, Engineer* David & Charles, Newton Abbot, 1979

Harvey, W. S. and Downs Rose, G., *William Symington* Northgate Publishing Co. 1980

Harris, T. R., *Sir Goldsworthy Gurney* Trevithick Society, 1975

Malet, H., *Bridgewater The Canal Duke* Manchester University Press, Manchester, 1977

Morris, E., *The Life of Henry Bell* Glasgow, 1844

Rankine, J. and Rankine, W. H., *Biography of William Symington* A. Johnston, Falkirk, 1862

Reader, W. J., *Macadam The McAdam Family and the Turnpike Roads 1798–1861* Heinemann, London, 1980

Rolt, L. T. C., *George and Robert Stephenson* Longmans Green & Co., London, 1960

Rolt, L. T. C., *Isambard Kingdom Brunel* Longmans Green & Co., London, 1957

Rolt, L. T. C., *Thomas Telford* Longmans Green & Co., London, 1958

Scott, E. K., (editor) *Matthew Murray Pioneer Engineer* 1928

Smiles, S., *The Lives of George and Robert Stephenson* Folio Society, London 1975 (re-issue of 1874 edition)

Trevithick, F. E., *Life of Richard Trevithick* E. F. & N. Spon, London, 1872

Young, R., *Timothy Hackworth and the Locomotive* Shildon 'Stockton & Darlington Railway' Jubilee Committee, Shildon, 1975

Recent Works except Biographies

Albert, W., *The Turnpike Road System in England 1663–1840* Cambridge University Press, Cambridge, 1972.

Anderson, R. C. and Anderson, J. M., *Quicksilver* David & Charles, Newton Abbot, 1973

Baxter, B., *Stone Blocks and Iron Rails* David & Charles, Newton Abbot, 1966

Bird, A., *Roads and Vehicles* Arrow Books Ltd, London, 1973

Body, G., *British Paddle Steamers* David & Charles, Newton Abbot, 1971

Boyes, J., and Russell, R., *The Canals of Eastern England* David & Charles, Newton Abbot, 1977

Carlson, R. E., *The Liverpool & Manchester Railway Project 1821–1831* David & Charles, Newton Abbot, 1969

Clinker, C. R., *The Leicester & Swannington Railway* Avon-Anglia, Bristol, 1977

Clinker, C. R. and Hadfield, C., *The Ashby de la Zouch Canal and its Railways* Avon Anglia, Bristol, 1978

Clowes, G. S. L., *Sailing Ships Their History and Development* HMSO, London, 1930

Corlett, E., *The Iron Ship* Moonraker Press, Bradford-on-Avon, 1980

Cossons, N., *The BP Book of Industrial Archaeology* David & Charles, Newton Abbot, 1975

Delany, D. R., *The Grand Canal of Ireland* David & Charles, Newton Abbot, 1973

Delany, V. T. H. and Delany, D. R., *The Canals of the South of Ireland* David & Charles, Newton Abbot, 1966

Davison, C. St C. B., *History of Steam Road Vehicles* HMSO, 1953

De Maré, E., *The Bridges of Britain* Batsford, London, 1954

Ellis, H., *British Railway History* G. Allen & Unwin Ltd, London, Vol I 1954, Vol II 1959

Ellis, H., *Four Main Lines* G. Allen & Unwin Ltd, London, 1950

Fitzgerald, R. S., *Liverpool Road Station, Manchester* Manchester University Press, Manchester, 1980

Gard, R. M. and Hartley, J. R., *Railways in the Making* (Archive Teaching Unit) University of Newcastle upon Tyne School of Education, Newcastle upon Tyne, 1969

Gregory, J. W., *The Story of the Road* A & C. Black, London, 1938

Griffin, A. R., *Coalmining* Longman, London, 1971

Hadfield, C., *The Canals of the East Midlands* David & Charles, Newton Abbot, 1970

Hadfield, C., *The Canals of the West Midlands*, David & Charles, Newton Abbot, 1969

Hadfield, C., *The Canals of South and South East England* David & Charles, Newton Abbot, 1969

Hadfield, C., *The Canals of South Wales and the Border* David & Charles, Newton Abbot, 1967

Hadfield, C., *The Canals of Yorkshire and North East England* David & Charles, Newton Abbot, Vol I 1972, Vol II 1973

Hadfield, C. and Biddle, G., *The Canals of North West England* David & Charles, Newton Abbot, 1970

Hadfield, C., and Norris, J., *Waterways to Stratford* David & Charles, Newton Abbot, 1968

Haldane, A. R. B., *New Ways through the Glens* T. Nelson & Sons Ltd, London, 1962

Hine, R. L., *The History of Hitchin* G. Allen & Unwin, London, 1927

Jackman, W. T., *The Development of Transportation in Modern England* Cambridge University Press, Cambridge, 1916

Jarvis, A. and Morris, L., *Lion*, Merseyside County Museums, Liverpool, 1980

Lead, P., *The Caldon Canal and Tramroads* Oakwood Press, Blandford, 1979

Lee, C. E., *The First Passenger Railway* Railway Publishing Co., London, 1942

Lewis, M. J. T., *Early Wooden Railways* Routledge & Kegan Paul, London, 1970

Lindsay, J., *The Canals of Scotland* David & Charles, Newton Abbot, 1968

McCutcheon, W. A., *The Canals of the North of Ireland* David & Charles, Newton Abbot, 1965

McGowan, A., *The Ship The Century before Steam* HMSO, 1980

Makepeace, C. E., *Oldest in the World* Liverpool Road Station Society, Manchester, 1980

Marshall, C. F. D., *A History of British Railways down to the Year 1830* Oxford University Press, Oxford, 1938

Marshall, C. F. D., *A History of Railway Locomotives down to the End of the Year 1831* Locomotive Publishing Co., London, 1953

Morgan, B., *Railway Relics* Ian Allan Ltd, London, 1969

Owen-Jones, E. S., *The Penydarren Locomotive* National Museum of Wales, Cardiff, 1980

Paar, M. W., *An Industrial Tour of the Wye Valley and the Forest of Dean* West London Industrial Archaeology Society, London, 1980

Paxton, R., and Ruddock, E., *A Heritage of Bridges* Institution of Civil Engineers, Edinburgh, 1982

Ratcliffe, R. L., *The Canterbury & Whitstable Railway* Locomotive Club of Great Britain, London, 1980

Rimmer, A., *The Cromford & High Peak Railway* Oakwood Press, Lingfield, 1971

Ripley, D., *The Peak Forest Tramway* Oakwood Press, Lingfield, 1972

Roberts, R. A., *The Clarkes of Silkstone and their Colliers* Workers' Educational Association, Barnsley, 1981

Rogers, H. C. B., *Turnpike to Iron Road* Seeley, Service & Co., 1961

Rowland, K. T., *Steam at Sea* David & Charles, Newton Abbot, 1970

Salvage of Steam Launch Dolly Windermere Nautical Trust, Windermere, 1979

Semmens, P. W. B., *Exploring the Stockton & Darlington Railway* Frank Graham, Newcastle upon Tyne, 1975

Simmons, J., *The Railways of Britain* Routledge & Kegan Paul, London, 1962

Spratt, H. P., *The Birth of the Steamboat* C. Griffin & Co., London, 1958

Spratt, H. P., *Marine Engineering* HMSO, London

Spratt, H. P., *Merchant Steamers and Motor Ships* HMSO, London

Sullivan, R., *Old Ships, Boats and Maritime Museums* Coracle Books, London, 1978

Taylor, W., *The Military Roads in Scotland* David & Charles, Newton Abbot, 1976

Tomlinson, W. W., *The North Eastern Railway* A. Reid & Co., Newcastle upon Tyne, 1914

Vale, E., *The Mail Coach Men of the late Eighteenth Century* David & Charles, Newton Abbot, 1967

Van Riemsdijk, J. T., and Brown, K., *The Pictorial History of Steam Power* Octopus Books Ltd, London, 1980

Warn, C. R., *Waggonways and Early Railways of Northumberland* F. Graham, Newcastle upon Tyne, 1976

Watney, M., *The Elegant Carriage* J. A. Allen, London, 1961

Webster, N. W., *Britain's First Trunk Line* Adams & Dart, Bath, 1977

Wright, L., *Historical Sources for Central Scotland* Central Regional Council, Stirling, 1980

Periodicals

Bulletin of the Association for Industrial Archaeology

Horse & Driving

Industrial Archaeology

Industrial Archaeology Review

Industrial Past

Railway & Canal Historical Society *Journal*

Railway Magazine

Railway World

Transactions of the Newcomen Society

Waterways News

Waterways World

Index

Bold page numbers refer to illustrations